Lectures on Psychopathology

Dr. Thomas E. Smith

Books by the Financial Therapy Center

More than Numbers: Everyday Financial Therapy Facilitator Guide
More than Numbers: Everyday Financial Therapy Participant Workbook

Journal Publications

Shelton, V. M., Smith, T. E., & Panisch, L. S. (2018). Financial therapy with groups: a case of the Five Step model. *Journal of Financial Counseling and Planning.*

Smith, T. E., Richards, K. V., Panisch, L. S., & Wilson, T. (2017). Financial therapy with families. *Families in Society 98*(4) 235-242. https://10.1606/1044-3894.2017.98.38

Smith, T. E., Williams, J. M., Richards, K. V., & Panisch, L. S. (2017). Online financial therapy. *Journal of Family Psychotherapy.* https://doi.org/10.1080/08975353.2017.1368812

Smith, T. E., Malespin, T., Richards, K. V., & Shelton, V. M. (2017). Financial therapy in foster care. *Journal of Human Behavior in the Social Environment, 27*(3),165-170. http://dx.doi.org/10.1080/10911359.2016.1268553

Smith, T. E., Richards, K. V., Panisch, L. S., & Shelton, V. M. (2017). Teaching financial problem solving: A curriculum model from a pilot BSW course. *Journal of Baccalaureate Social Work.*

Smith, T. E., Richards, K. V., & Shelton, V. M. (2016). Solution-focused financial therapy with couples. *Journal of Human Behavior in the Social Environment, 26(5),* 452-460. http://dx.doi.org/10.1080/10911359.2015.1087921

Smith, T. E., Malespin, T. S., Pereira, M. G., & Richards, K. V. (2016). Factors relating to the use of family therapy with adolescent marijuana abusers. *Children and Adolescent Social Work Journal. 33*(3), 237-243. http://dx.doi.org/10.1007/s10560-015-0417-1

Smith, T. E., Richards, K. V., & Shelton, V. M. (2016). Mindfulness in financial literacy. *Journal of Human Behavior in the Social Environment, 26(2), 154–161.* http://dx.doi.org/10.1080/10911359.2015.1052914

Smith, T. E., Richards, K. V., & Shelton, V. M. (2016). The language of money. *Journal of Human Behavior in the Social Environment,* 26(2), 202-209. http://dx.doi.org/10.1080/10911359.2015.1083503

© 2015 Financial Therapy Center

All rights reserved. No portion of this book may be reproduced, stored in a retrieval system or transmitted in any form or by any means—electronic, mechanical, photocopy, recording, scanning, or other—except for brief quotations in critical reviews or articles, without the prior written permission of the publisher.

Published by Southeastern Professional Books, Seattle, WA 98116.

www.financialtherapycenter.com

ISBN:9780988392946

Printed in the United States of America

Library of Congress Control Number

Preface

The following materials were taken from my lectures on psychopathology. It includes a letter from a previous student, diagrams that were used to illustrate different psychiatric phenomena, actual lectures, case examples, and examples of exam questions. It includes types of interview assessments that can be made. The book is broken into "sessions" that roughly correspond to different chapters in the DSM-5. The case examples and exam questions are presented as a form of self-exam. The actual course includes other case examples and exam questions.

TS

Letter from a Student Who Finished the Course

Dear Student of Psychopathology,

I have recently taken the Psychopathology in Clinical Practice course and I have some advice to offer you. Things you probably already know. Things not to do…Don't let things pile up. Procrastination is a normal part of some people's lives. You tell yourself you'll be able to get those Study Questions whipped out in 30 minutes, so you wait until late Sunday evening and realize you had to watch a movie in order to answer the question, and now you don't have time. Use a mental pie chart for your life: work, school, home, leisure. They are all important; don't borrow from one to overdo the other.

Things to definitely do…Create a system of organization for your assignments. A simple list with dates works for me rather than juggling syllabi. Reminders in your phone, an agenda book, whatever. But use it. What I have learned from my experience…. and the best idea I have to offer you…Lots of reading; you need a plan. I'm a hopper-back-and-forther. I can't possibly sit and read the DSM-5 straight through. Not sure how anyone could. But I can print out the lectures, print out the presentation questions, and go back and forth between them and a particular section in the DSM.

The thing worthiest of spending extra effort to understand in this course is…differential diagnoses, because if you understand why one diagnosis may look like another and what differentiates the two, then you've got a good handle on that diagnosis.
The most valuable things I took from this course were from the extra discussion board assignments which ask you to think more in depth or reflect about particular topics which is always a good idea.

The most valuable ideas to apply to one's life from this course are…just the idea that you never know what other people are dealing with, whether in their own life or a friend or family member. Even clients with the most destructive conditions -- either self-destructive or detrimental to relationships – especially those clients, are deserving of our empathy. Somewhere I read that those in need of love the most show that to you in the least loving ways. Every client is someone's son, daughter, mother, father, loved one. Try to remember that.

It's a fascinating class. Take the time to learn and enjoy.

Sincerely,

Paige

A Student Who Has Gone Before You

SESSION #1
Theme: Introduction; measurement, cultural and gender implications

Congratulations! You're entering the world of psychopathology with me. I've given this course a lot of thought and believe that you can learn a lot about what is needed for you to master the concepts of psychopathology. Stick with me and you'll pass the course. It may not always be easy, but you'll more than you think that you can. But to do so, we'll have to be partners in this learning enterprise.

I will always be available via email, office hours, and by appointment if you're just plain stuck. That's my job. Your peers are a second source of information. Feel free to share information, questions, complain about me, and so on. The key words here are "active learning." The more that you participate, the more that you'll learn in this course. The worst part of this course is that you'll have to learn a lot of the material yourself. I've assigned readings in your textbooks and augmented the mini-lectures with some other lecturettes. Mostly, however, you'll have to spend time at your computer and read and read and read and read and read. There is a lot of reading and memorizing in this course.

People have asked me for 20 years why I stress that you should memorize the DSM. It's an excellent question. Albert Einstein always insisted that it was pointless to memorize anything that was already published in a book. Let me explain. First, we're not Albert Einstein and clinicians need a basic amount of knowledge to be able to know where to begin to start their diagnostic process. In short, much of the difficulty in making a diagnosis is in knowing what to exclude. This requires an integration of knowledge. If you start each client with a tabula rasa, it will take you much longer to make a diagnosis (thus fatiguing your clients), your chances of error will go up (because you have to relearn what's not right with each new client) and most important of all, you'll look silly to coworkers in different disciplines. Other disciplines like medicine and law are notable because they master a body of knowledge and use it in their clinical practice. If we insist that we are above learning the materials, then we won't have the basic tools in a daily clinical practice. And besides, even Albert had to memorize multiplication tables!

Art of Making Scientific Decisions

What is your first thought when you think about psychopathology? For some people, its part of an assessment process; for others, it's part of a labeling process that is necessary for receiving insurance payments. And for others, it's a political process that is used to oppress people who are in lower socioeconomic classes. Psychopathology is many things to many people. My personal take on psychopathology is that it is the art of making scientific decisions.

Why art? Why science? Like most things in life, you need both art and science to make psychopathology complete. There just isn't enough science to make the decision making completely standardized. And art by itself may be too subjective and without much, if any, standardization. In short, the subjectivity fills in what the objectivity leaves out. So, how does psychopathology assist in the art of making scientific decisions?

First, psychopathology relies on a reference book, "Diagnostic and Statistical Manual," that is in its 5th edition). This massive book, the required text for this course, is used by all mental health clinicians in making psychiatric diagnoses. It purports to be highly scientific although its critics claim that the DSM falls far short of its lofty goal. Whether people like it or not, it is universally used by insurance companies, hospitals, clinicians, and so on in making decisions about assessment and treatment. Because of its universal acceptance, it has become a de facto standard of what people must know to demonstrate their competence regarding psychiatric disorders. That's why psychopathology is a key part of most licensure exams. In addition, its universal acceptance has made diagnoses part of the legal process. Your ability to give "correct" diagnoses is critical to keep you away from malpractice suits! Used correctly, the DSM can protect clients and workers alike.

Are diagnoses labels? Well, since just about everything is a label of one sort or another, yes, diagnoses are labels. The more important question is whether they are absolutely necessary. A second question is whether they can be used to benefit clients. And yet a third question is trying to find ways to prevent clients from being harmed by diagnostic labels. Finally, it should be asked in passing whether the diagnoses are reliable and valid. These are questions that you should ask yourself every time you give a client a diagnosis.

Let's start with the first question on whether diagnoses are absolutely necessary. I suppose in a perfect world; they would not be necessary. Hmm, well, you could communicate using some form of Charades. Or simply sing songs or cite poems or do something to communicate with your colleagues. Without diagnoses, how can you communicate your assessment of your clients? Well, there is the option of giving some form of index or measure, but let's hold off on that discussion just for a minute.

I remember talking to another professor about my dissatisfaction with the course on Evaluating Practice. I gave a great criticism of it. He waited patiently and then said that I was expecting too much from the course. His point is that anything can be criticized but the difficult part is finding a good substitute. I remember listening to another professor say that psychiatric diagnoses were all bad and people should be allowed to live in supportive environments where they can be allowed to thrive. Nice sentiment, but it's a zero-sum game. If all the resources go into creating "supportive environments," then some other social need will get shortchanged. So . . . what does all this mean?

The world of psychiatry is a complex system. It's easy to take potshots but eventually reality strikes and you've got to cope with crazy clients and even crazier colleagues. Your primary goal is to help your client and at least "First of all, do no harm." Your role as a guide is to help your clients navigate through the treacherous and uncaring societal shoals. It is possible to provide a great sermon or philosophical talk, but at the end of the day, you're left wondering what to tell your clients, their families and your colleagues. If you can make diagnostic discussions part of your advocacy, then you have truly made a beneficial impact. Leave philosophy for philosophers

The second question was on how to use diagnoses to benefit clients. There is a lot of subjectivity in making diagnoses. In fact, you can probably get away with diagnosing a client with just about any diagnosis. That makes the DSM a lame document. Fair enough. The plus side of this subjectivity is that you can legitimately over diagnose and underdiagnose clients. Basically, you can use the DSM subjectivity to your advantage. Given a choice, you can make the diagnosis as "gentle" as possible. I only think of gentleness in terms of the intrusiveness of the consequences.

Consequences can have three meanings here. One consequence is your clients' self-esteem. A second consequence is the relief or dread experienced by their friends and families. A third consequence that is probably the most important is the intrusiveness of the treatment. Let's take the first consequence of your clients' self-esteem. Diagnosing a client with something like a "Borderline Schizophrenic with Delusional Depression" with Badass personality traits doesn't do anyone much good at all. At some level, it's just name calling. You remember the old "Sticks and stones can break my bones but words will never hurt me." Ah, yes, that was from a gentler era. Words especially diagnoses can damage a person's sense of self. It may even result in a person developing a sense of helpless/hopeless attitude toward their life. If possible, my goal is to always seek a way of giving no diagnosis.

A second consequence is to manage the relief or dread experienced by friends and families. You too can terrorize people by saying that there are few cures and only a heroic treatment can make life livable for a psychiatrically ill person. Sounds like Stage Four cancer to me. Few psychiatric disorders are progressive in nature. Progressive means that there are no upsides on the diagnoses. The person will die because of the disorder and not because of old age. Only dementia has that dire prospect.

Diagnoses can give friends and families relief. It may well provide an explanation for the weird behavior that a client is showing. Remember, if it's a close friend or family member, an explanation of any sort gives some way of reducing uncertainty especially if there is a predictable course the disorder. Prognosis with a predictable course can mean a lot to people and give them hope. Uncertainty is the enemy and hope is always the goal.

The third consequence is the most important: how toxic is the treatment? For better or worse, most psychiatric treatment will consist of form of medication. I actually don't trust most people when they talk about drugs. I always wonder about their angle. Most people will either praise them or damn them. People who praise them probably make money from selling them. People who damn them want to feel important and self-righteous. Drugs are like words. It's possible to give them an absolute right or wrong. But how about trying to balance their benefits and weaknesses?

Some drugs are pretty benign. Aspirin, anyone? If fact, just about any substance can be seen as one drug or another. Some clients will drink large quantities of water as part of their craziness. The major issue is to balance the positives and negatives. Most people will say that aspirin in moderation is a good thing without many downsides. By the same token, antipsychotic medication is a toxic, brain-altering chemical. Its upside? It lessens hallucinations and delusions. Downsides? It is toxic. There is no panacea here. Me, my heart goes out to families who are faced with Sophie's Choice in living with their troubled members.

The last question is whether the DSM is reliable and valid. Well, that's always a funny question. Very few things in life are reliable and valid. Myself, I think of myself as being reliable and valid but my friends tell me that I'm delusional. Well, at least, they are reliable in their assessment of me as being delusional but I don't think that their assessment is valid. Reliable means that given the same stimulus, you will always make the same assessment. Valid means that the assessment is correct according to some accepted standard.

It's not rocket science to say that the DSM is a pathetic measure of psychiatric behavior. After all, the psychiatric diagnoses themselves have changed greatly over time. They are a moving target. You've probably heard a lot of terms thrown around: assessment, measuring, diagnosis, syndrome and even nosology. So, I thought that I'd go over some of these terms. Symptoms are indicators or behaviors that give you a clue on the diagnosis that give you a syndrome that may be a diagnostic category. And the classification of mental disorders is called a nosology. Therefore, the DSM is an example of a nosology. The different diagnoses are different categories of the nosology. And criteria represent indicators of the diagnoses. Now, as you might guess, the criteria include symptoms of a disorder although some of the criteria are not symptoms. For example, one of the criteria of a disorder is that someone be in their twenties. Surely, this is not a symptom of a disorder? But usually criteria do represent symptoms.

A collection of symptoms is called a syndrome. Thus, you can say that phobia is a syndrome. Generally, however you call something a syndrome only when the symptoms are tightly "grouped." Some disorders have a weird combination of symptoms because that's what people have found empirically. Or put another way, diagnosticians have used the same group of criteria to diagnose a disorder whether they make sense or not. Plus, there are syndromes that are not in the DSM. For example, there are other ways of classifying schizophrenia than what is presented in the DSM. Or of Borderline Personality Disorders. And that brings us to the issue of a nosology.

Generally speaking, a nosology can consist of empirical or theoretical classifications. The DSM is an example of the first type of classifications. It's pretty straightforward. You get a bunch of people agreeing on what constitutes a disorder and you have an "empirically determined nosology." Hey, stick with me; I have a million of these one-liners. Another type of nosology is determined by theoretical concerns or even of treatment oriented concerns. For example, with Borderline Personality Disorders, a lot of theorists have considered it to be an indicator of "poor ego development and identification." Cool, huh? Others have called it a "lack of differentiation." Bowen, be still my heart. As you might guess, the latter two types of BPD syndromes are determined by the theorists who came up with a specific treatment approach.

Thus far, we have talked about nosology, symptoms, syndromes, diagnostic indicators, and mental disorders. We have not however talked about measurement tools or the process of assessment in general. Let's start with assessment. Assessment represents the overall attempt to determine what's wrong (or right) with a client. So, assessment might consider how family members are reacting to the client's syndrome. Or it might consider the impact of poverty. And so on. Thus, assessment is a much larger effort that takes into consideration all aspects of context that are ignored by a diagnosis.

Finally, we get into the issue of measurement tools. A measurement tool can assess any part of a syndrome, a diagnostic classification, treatment readiness or whatever. Thus, a measurement tool is not synonymous with mental disorders, syndromes, or assessment. It just measures one part of any aspect of a mental disorder or a syndrome, or even of an assessment effort. The Beck Depression Inventory (BDI) measures the existence of a bunch of symptoms found in depression. And that's depression with a small "d." The BDI is definitely not a measure of a Major Depression Disorder, Depressive Episode or even Dysthymia. It may include parts of one or even all three. You've got to be very careful when you use a measurement that you examine it to make sure that it measures "depression" in the same way that DSM classifies "Major Depression Disorder" or even the way that various theorists have conceptualized depression.

You probably have to choose between what is called "sensitivity" and "specificity" in public health jargon. Basically, these terms refer to different kinds of error. With "sensitivity," your intention is to be sure that everyone with a particular disorder is identified as such. With "specificity," your intention is to be sure that no one except people with the disorder is diagnosed. Part of what you have to decide is what kind of balance you wish to strike between these two kinds of "diagnostic error." In the former, you may include people who do not have the disorder; in the latter, you may not include other individuals who in fact do have the disorder.

If you don't like talking about error, let's go to a traditional social work focus in examining the whole diagnostic enterprise by balancing a focus on strengths (i.e., health) versus deficits (i.e., psychiatric disorders). Fourth, you may have noticed that I kept referring to a "diagnostic process." It really is a process. But what kind of process? In making decisions about what a person is or is not, you can use two separate kinds of processes: a process of elimination and a process of selection. Both are present within the DSM and both play a role in making diagnoses. First, the process of elimination. In a process of elimination, you eliminate all "incorrect" diagnoses until only one "correct" one is left. Think of it as a Darwinian process: survival of the fittest diagnoses, or the strongest idea, or even the diagnosis most likely to be reimbursed by insurance companies! The assumptions being made here is that you have a comprehensive map of the disorders so that eliminating all the incorrect diagnoses will inevitably leave you with the "correct" one. What would happen if there were a couple diagnoses that were somehow not in DSM? It would mean that the process of elimination was seriously flawed. To make matters more confusing, there is the business of a process of selection.

The process of selection means that you decide on some set of criteria and make a selection from a predetermined list of choices. Your choice of diagnoses is based on how closely your client's attributes resemble the profile of the given number of choices. As you might guess, the problem here is that your clients won't always resemble the choices that are available. For example, what will be your choice when your client only has half the attributes of a given profile? In comparing the two approaches, a process of elimination may result in a more thorough assessment of your client. By forcing you to eliminate all but one diagnosis, you're forced to consider all the options. In a process of selection, you may be tempted to make a diagnosis based on partial information of what a client is presenting to you. In short, you may select a diagnosis based on an incomplete assessment. Lest it sound like I'm favoring a process of elimination, keep in mind that you may make errors if you don't have enough information to eliminate all but one diagnosis or if the diagnostic schema (DSM) is incomplete. (By the way, did you know that DSM doesn't allow for a diagnosis of "healthy" to be given? The only possible diagnosis there is that the person is not diagnosable!)

In general, a process of elimination is ego-dystonic. Ego-dystonic diagnoses simply mean that the individual experiences discomfort from the disorder. Personality disorders use a process of selection and are ego-syntonic. Ego-syntonic disorders generally imply that the client does not experience discomfort from the disorder and because they don't experience discomfort, family and friends probably do experience discomfort and are the ones who bring clients into treatment. Now, I wish that I could say that all disorders that use a process of elimination have a lot of options for treatment, but it just wouldn't be true. For example, it's really hard to ask a person in the process of having a psychotic break whether they're having a hallucination! So . . . the whole thing about a process of elimination is that it's a general guide with plenty of exceptions. And of course, you'll find that the whole DSM is filled with exceptions. Aren't you glad that you're taking this course?

The history and course of your client's symptoms and disorders must be considered when making a diagnosis. There is only so much that you can actually discern from talking to a person who is experiencing an acute psychotic break! By gathering the course and history of symptoms and prior disorders, you can assemble a pattern. From that pattern, you'll have a better idea of how to diagnose your client.

You should also consider the client's affect, behavior and cognition in making a diagnosis. Affect or an emotional state is probably the key to many of the most severe diagnostic categories. Cognition is the second most important aspect of a client's functioning. However, what is most apparent will usually be behavior. Remember to consider all three in making a diagnosis. As we go through specific diagnostic categories, I'll highlight what to look for in affect, cognition, and behavior (i.e., ABC). Because diagnoses may not always be easy to discern, it's important to be very observant. Being able to differentiate diagnoses that resemble each other is called making a "differential diagnosis."

It's an unfortunate truism that people who are different from the diagnostician will be more likely to be given a diagnosis that is incorrect, more restrictive, or just plain flat out morally wrong. The reason is because when we are confronted by people we don't know; their culture and speech may be unknown to us. From there, it's not much of a jump to say that because a person is "strange," they may also be crazy. On the other hand, we may give much more latitude to a person down the street whom you know. The person down the street may be "eccentric" but the impoverished person from a different ethnic group may be "crazy."

Let's get into the pragmatics of mental disorders. All mental disorders have a code attached to it. The codes are all defined in something called the DSM-5 published by the American Psychiatric Association. When someone tells you that they have a diagnosis, they are referring to a coded diagnosis from the DSM-5. If the diagnosis is not in the DSM, it can't be given as a legitimate diagnosis. But why is that important? It's because people are stuck with the diagnoses that are in the DSM. And sometimes they just don't fit.

Thoughts about Culture and Ethnicity

Well, let's talk about culture and gender as considerations in psychopathology. These topics can be somewhat sensitive so a lot of caution goes a long way. It's really tough to know exactly what behavioral manifestations or speech patterns mean in any one person. That's because people can differ in how they look, speak, and act depending on just about anything including geographical location, socio-economic class, gender, culture, and ethnicity. In the past, there was a lot of concern about being gender and culture sensitive. These are important considerations and should not be ignored. But when you stop and think about it, how do you know how to be sensitive with the myriad of factors that make up a single person? Because each person is comprised of a mosaic of factors to consider when making a diagnosis, the need to remain vigilant is heightened for clinicians.

What are the dangers? Well, consider first that it is easy to stereotype anyone by any aspect of their life. Let's take the most obvious example: are all people diagnosed as borderline personality disorders alike? My guess is that most clinicians would say that there are similarities but there are also a lot of differences among patients with that diagnosis. In short, differences among people can far outweigh their similarities. Let's take another example. Is the English language monolithic? Here, monolithic means something is the same, immovable, and long lasting. My guess is that you would probably say that English has changed over the years; it is always in flux as new words and phrases get introduced in people's speech. Further, there are always regional differences in speech. Are there any differences in accent between people in the Deep South and in the Northeastern states? How about the use of jargon? The purpose is to communicate but it's an imperfect method of doing so.

In fact, my guess is that there is a continuum on just about any variable that distinguishes one person from another. Are people the same or different? Tough to say, let's just leave it that there is a continuum on the similarities among people. What makes it even more difficult is the question of "cultural sensitivity." You've all heard about the need to demonstrate cultural sensitivity. Fair enough. But let's take it a step further. For example, I imagine some of you have heard about the need to not make eye contact with Asian-Americans because of cultural mores around the meaning of eye contact (i.e., considered rude). Yet, I assure you that such statements can be a stereotype of Asian-Americans. The problem here may be "how Asian is Asian?" Another problem is that not all Asians are alike. Another problem is that the caveat may have been true thirty years ago but is no longer true. In short, "cultural sensitivity" is a good enough idea but like most things, it has some real limitations in its use. Should you be culturally sensitive? Sounds good. But don't beat it to death. Just be sensitive to all clients. They have their unique set of attributes and you need to consider and reconsider them in all their weirdness. I like the discussion from DSM-5

Diagnostic certainty or diagnostic folly? How certain can anyone ever be about a diagnosis? Remember that the DSM is an empirical document, not a theoretical one. Empirical documents reflect the knowledge available at the time that the document was compiled. It was compiled by a group and has the strengths and weaknesses of a group consensus. The DSM in 50 years will undoubtedly be very different from the one that we have now. Notwithstanding that certainty, the DSM represents the de facto diagnostic schema that is used and you have to use it to the best of your ability.

Finally, idiopathic or nomothetic conclusions? Idiopathic means that you're making highly individual decisions; nomothetic means that you're making group decisions. How do you diagnose a person based on an empirically derived document? Is it a wise thing to do? The dilemma is that you're diagnosing an individual with a group schema. The dangers are obvious: the disenfranchised will be yet again subjected to damaging label. However, what are the dangers of relying completely on an idiopathic diagnostic system or is that an oxymoron?

So...this is a long way of saying that making diagnoses is not easy or simple. It takes a lot of judgment. But here is the most important part to remember: this course only gets you started in knowing how to diagnose people. It's not the final word or will be enough for you to feel comfortable in making diagnoses. In fact, it may be more confusing than enlightening. But let's get confused together; it's not as lonely when we're wondering why on Earth that we are trying to learn this stuff.

In another section, I had students give advice as "From Those Who Went Before You" Doesn't that sound ominous? Well, it boiled down to saying that you shouldn't procrastinate, do the assignments and practice, practice, and more practice. It's not bad advice. So... it's an interesting course but it's not easy but it'll be fun in some weird ways.

You didn't think that the lecture was finished, did you? Here's a talk that I gave on culture:

Psst. I don't normally try to put my name on everything and I probably shouldn't this time. But the fact is that I'm not culturally sensitive. Now, before you think ill of me (well at least not more ill than you already do), let me explain. My mother is (or was, anyway, since she's been dead a good long while) Japanese. You now, her parents were Japanese, born in Japan, her relatives were Japanese, wore Japanese clothes and even ate sushi. I mean, really, really Japanese. Then, there's me. Japanese mother (a really, really Japanese one), Arkansas chicken farmer as a dad (well, I don't know whether he was really a chicken farmer, but it makes a good story), and lots of other unimportant details. I spent a lot of formative years in Japan, spoke Japanese (not so much now), had Japanese friends, lived in a Japanese part of town, and I even look the part. That means that I am more or less Japanese, right? But that's not important, what is important is that you should treat me like a Japanese person since I have all the qualifications. That seems right, doesn't it? I mean I could be more Japanese, but I mean, what does a person have to do to be Japanese? So, I looked up my social work cultural sensitivity book, it told me that I was more or less Japanese and that you shouldn't give me any eye contact, you should bow all the time and a lot of other stuff when you come across a Japanese person like me.

Nonsense. I'll say again, nonsense. We have to be careful lest cultural sensitivity become a social work way of stereotyping people. I mean I'm a professor, I speak and write a lot of English, married a Mississippian, have a US passport, look people in the eye when they're trying to sell me a used car, and I eat pizza. That makes me a complete white person, right? Well, am I or not?

So there you have it. Most social work writings on cultural sensitivity run afoul in trying to distinguish individual people from categories. If a person looked sad for two weeks and had problems sleeping and eating, would you say that they are "Depressed" and nothing else? (not if you're in my class, you shouldn't) So, now would you act toward a Depressed like you act toward any other Depressed? Probably not. In fact, you might even say that I am stereotyping or labeling depressed persons if you do so.

On the other hand, there are lots and lots of times when you can't start from square one in knowing how what to do when someone doesn't look like, act like, talk like or eat pizza. You could say that I am from another culture and so I want you to know that I won't stereotype you. The kid will probably say, "Thanks, dude, now would you get out of the way? I've got things to do right now." But what should you say? Pretty much what you would with anyone who is strange (i.e., doesn't eat pizza). Explain in a normal business tone who you are and what you are trying to do. Let them take the first step. If they look puzzled, repeat yourself using different words. If they are still puzzled, do the universal sign of peace: give them a slice of pizza (or pizza with sushi toppings if you're like me).

By now, you're probably wondering why I'm writing something about culture, ethnicity, and race. I'm working at a disadvantage here; I'm probably offended all those people teaching cultural sensitivity. To keep me honest, let's go and see what the DSM has to say about it.

Cultural concepts of distress refer to ways that cultural groups experience, understand, and communicate suffering, behavioral problems, or troubling thoughts and emotions. Three main types of cultural concepts may be distinguished. *Cultural syndromes* are clusters of symptoms and attributions that tend to co-occur among individuals in specific cultural groups, communities, or contexts and that are recognized locally as coherent patterns of experience. *Cultural idioms of distress* are ways of expressing distress that may not involve specific symptoms or syndromes, but that provide collective, shared ways of experiencing and talking about personal or social concerns. For example, everyday talk about "nerves" or "depression" may refer to widely varying forms of suffering without mapping onto a discrete set of symptoms, syndrome, or disorder. *Cultural explanations* or *perceived causes* are labels, attributions, or features of an explanatory model that indicate culturally recognized meaning or etiology for symptoms, illness, or distress.

But having given you all these caveats, let's continue with DSM stuff. Let's go through some examples. Dementia is a great example of the need for extreme care in conducting a mental status exam. Tests of a general fund of knowledge may not have much meaning for someone who is a recent immigrant. The DSM has documented examples of some cultures in which birthdays are not celebrated, thus making such questions meaningless. Yet other cultures have a different sense of time and place, making orientation questions problematic. Prevalence of dementia varies from culture to culture. This is important because you're more likely to see some disorders in some cultures more so than others. Thus, you're statistically more likely to be "correct" in your diagnosis where the diagnosis is more prevalent.

Substance use and abuse is censured in some cultures more so than others. This is important because substance abuse may not be considered a disorder. It definitely would not be considered a disease. Marked differences characterize the quantity, frequency, and pattern of alcohol consumption in different countries. Further, consider the functional purpose of alcohol abuse/dependency. What is the meaning of alcohol abuse/dependency? What role does it play in different cultures, different people? Since alcohol abuse/dependency varies, it is critical that you ask the clients whether the alcohol abuse/dependency is a problem for them.

In making a diagnosis of Schizophrenia, care must be taken to ensure that the behaviors and speech that would be considered as delusional are not part of sanctioned, accepted behaviors in other cultures. The same thing is true about most aspects of anxiety disorders. And there are some cultures in which talking about sexual disorders would be a real mistake—as in getting your client, his/her relatives, the government and so on irritated at your lack of sensitivity to local mores. Look in the back of the DSM for some definitions of how certain cultures exhibit behaviors that in a Eurocentric (isn't this a great word?) culture would not be considered as evidence of mental disorders.

My advice to you? Be a learner. Don't assume that you know more than you do. Let your clients guide you to let you understand them. I give some more thoughts on cultural sensitivity on the lecture on culture.

So, I will retreat into talking about the three terms in research definitions and move away from all those cultural sensitivity books. I warn you, it's going to be a lot trying to make clear distinctions between addiction, substance abuse disorders, disease models, and so on.

So, I tried something easy. I went to Ask.com and they gave me the following definition. "Culture, ethnicity, and race are concepts that are often confused. Culture refers to a shared system of learned and shared values, beliefs and rules of conduct. This includes language, religion, cuisine, music, arts, and more. Ethnicity is applied to a group of people whose members identify with each other, on the basis of genealogy or ancestry. Commonly recognized ethnic groups include American Indians, Latinos, and, African Americans. A race is a dividing of people based on physical characteristics. Races are usually assumed by skin color.
Reference:
www.harmony.gov.au"

OK, what's the problem? Well, I'm still Japanese according to Ask.com, but I still like pizza. I know (or used to know) Japanese, music (well, but each to own taste), arts, and other variables. I have a lot of values that my cousin tells me are Japanese-like. Most importantly, the federal government tells me that I am Asian (I guess that I'm not Japanese after all, I've been morphed into an Asian). I guess that I'm Japanese but I just don't know it. I will now have to go to Japanese culture schools where I am trained to say and believe that I am Japanese. So, I'm not satisfied with Ask.com

I went into research articles and found one that was interesting. It said that culture could be defined as "variable systems of meaning." Don't you feel good, now? The authors said that culture was defined by things that learned and shared by an identifiable segment of the population. So, the take away was that culture is learned and shared. Things like social norms, roles, beliefs, and values are what are used to define culture. When you've got roles and values, you've got measurement. So, one down and two left to go. Basically, it said that you've got to be able to measure things for it to be real. Onto "race" as a discussion point. Well, here again I've got a gripe. The federal government and a lot of other researchers tell me that I have to be an Asian, not even Japanese. Now, I have to go to Asian school to learn to believe that I am Asian? Do they eat sushi? Like is hard. But I persevered and went onto read that race is defined in terms of physical characteristics. Others say that this is an arbitrary distinction because there are more within race characteristics than there are between race characteristics. OK, finally, I don't have to be just Japanese because we don't all look and talk alike. However, there was a stinger in which the authors said that there were a lot of physical characteristics that members of race share in common. So, I'm kinda Japanese in my race, but I wasn't sure. The same researcher said that culture was a better predictor than race, but that the latter was useful in public health studies of hypertension and so on. Still, there was no mention of biology in culture but there was in race.

I was almost out of energy, but I had to finish by looking up "ethnicity." Here, the literature did not help me. The authors just said that the differences between culture and ethnicity were not always clear. Duh. They said that you had to use cultural variables in studying ethnicity. But there was a nugget of usefulness. It has to do with identification. With ethnicity, there are elements of shared identity. C'mon, give me a break. OK, where does that leave us? I liked the discussion on culture. You know, the one on learned and shared meanings? No biology, just what is learned and shared. Race has some aspects of biological that are useful in public health research but not so much in terms of anthropological or psychological research. But ethnicity and culture share a lot in common. I've attached the article for those of you who might suspect that I've taken liberties in my read of the article. OK, I'm more white in my in my culture, I'm Japanese in my race, and I'm kinda both white and Japanese in my ethnicity. Well, at least for today. But, I'll always like pizza but hold the sushi.

All this talk about sushi got me hungry. I mean, hungry to eat and not for evidence-based sensitivity, critical culturalism and strength-focused thinking. You may be thinking why anyone would hunger for such strange words. Well, they seem to be buzzwords about which many people get excited and excitable. I thought that people just wanted to get some kind of recognition and awards for their buzzwords. After all, there are awards given to cultural competence, cultural sensitivity, and cultural collaboration and just about anything cultural. And it led me to wonder about buzzword mania in social work. I realized that I was behind the eight ball. I really didn't like buzzwords, was not excited by them, and definitely didn't want to become excitable about them. I'm a moderate kind of guy.

Well, imagine my surprise when a diversity report came out that had a Righteous Revolt by students who enrolled in a MSW program. A sizable number of people who were devout in their faith had been systematically told that they were "out of touch" and that they should not be so judgmental and narrow in their worldview. I had always thought that they were no narrower or judgmental than anyone who had strong beliefs. Well, it appears that these poor souls complained that faculty and students alike were both critical of them and they had learned to be discreet. They learned to never, ever profess their faith.

I reflected that it's always the same. There will always be a minority of some sort who are bullied by other minorities. Further, there will always be minorities who have no voice because they fear the power of flunk. For these folks, no one else will even know that they are being bullied. And the beat goes on. . . Power dynamics are the same although the voices change over time. Who are victims now will become bullies later. I guess in the end; everyone competes to see whether they can belong to a minority who can be the biggest bully. But, remember, bullies are mostly known by buzzwords. That's why I think that a lot of people get excited and excitable when they differ on the choice of buzzwords.

There are many, many buzzwords. I think that people who use one type of buzzword don't always use another set of buzzwords. So... that means that "culturally sensitive" people may not be "evidence-based." Lo and behold, the people who advocate cultural sensitivity may not advocate evidence-based buzzwords. And that can lead to an argument in which buzzwords are used as formidable weapons of much destruction. I sought some help from something called "critical thinking" since I was told that it went beyond the use of buzzwords. After talking to some advocates of critical thinking, I found that, alas, I was wrong; it too was no more than a holy mantra. In desperation, I examined the time-honored mantra of being "strength-focused." But I also realized that it too was nothing more than a couple of buzzwords. Then, I realized the error of my thinking.

I should tell students that it is important for them to use a cafeteria of buzzwords. In the table below, students should take one item from Column A and another one from Column B. Voila, they would have a new buzzword on which to chew and digest.

A La Carte Method of Buzzword Superiority

Column A	Column B
Evidence-Based	Thinking
Critical	Competency
Strength-Focused	Practice

This is called the a la carte method of conceptual formulation. But, sadly, I realized that my table should be improved by adding more cafeteria items. Whoops, more and more buzzwords have to be put into the table

Column A	Column B
Evidence-Based	Thinking
Critical	Competency
Strength-Focused	Practice
Conceptual	Formulation
Cultural	Sensitivity

If a person continues to take one word from Column A and match it with any word from Column B, then it can be asserted that a person or thing has an important attribute. Personally, I think that I have Critical Sensitivity as an attribute. But based on the first part of this report, people may think that my key attribute is in Cultural Thinking.

To do things up right, I should volunteer to teach a course from my a la carte attribute. After all, it is important to have skills in that area. I'm always been told that I have to consult with an Instructional Designer and come up with Objective, Evidence, and Assignments. Wow, that now begins to be a Herculean task. I mean what are the objectives of "Strength-Focused Thinking?" What would be evidence that a person had achieved such a feat? Finally, what assignments would provide the evidence that would meet the objectives? I think that the true goal of a la carte approach is to defeat the allies of jargon who encroach on innocent students.

Whether it's cultural anarchy or evidence-based bullying, jargon shouldn't replace civility and curiosity about differences among people. The product of victory should not always be bitterness or self-righteousness. Doesn't really matter who wins, because the a la carte method of deciding valor and virtue will still be around. My goal is to get as many buzzwords as possible so I can be all that I can be.

Thoughts about Mental Illness and Mental Health

Is it the difference between sanity and craziness? It all depends. Sanity is difference to different people. Some people who grew up in crazy families think that craziness is okay. Let's go to why I'm going to use the word, "crazy" or "brat" or anything that's not jargon. The friend of stigma is jargon. Jargon sounds official and can make people think that it's permanent. *Think of jargon as a foreign language.* Most people can figure out nuance in English; jargon however takes away the ability to hear nuance. I really don't like for people to think that they have a mental disorder when they only have a bad case of jargon. I'll use the word "crazy" any day to prevent someone from being stigmatized into a mental disorder. So, forgive my casual use of slang. I prefer it to jargon.

Why on earth would having a mental disorder cause someone to be stigmatized? It's probably because it all has to do with "unknown" and "different." *It's easy to be frightened "unknown different people."* So, with fear comes wariness comes becoming upset. Voila, a person becomes stigmatized. One purpose of the class is to reduce the unknown. The differences may still be there, but I think that you'll find that a lot of people that you think of as being pretty much normal probably have a couple mental disorders. On the other hand, you may find someone to be crazy but actually is just strange but mentally disordered. If the course is successful, you'll probably think just about everyone is somewhat crazy but actually is a close approximation of "sane enough."

The most important thing to remember about mental disorders is that there is a lot of pain to go around. The pain is relational. That's what makes a basic disorder excruciating. The main difference among disorders is how much pain that they cause. Other people think that mental disorders are about the powerful people subjugating poor people by the use of labels. Other people are quick to see everyone as fitting into one diagnosis or another. And of course, there are the "boutique disorders" or the disorder of the month. Some things that you've got to avoid are situations where the practitioners are trying to do two things. For example, when you go to hospitals, you may be invited to be part of "clinical trial." All that means is that you may or may not actually get some sort of treatment. That is, you may be getting Diet Coke when you wanted the real thing. Buyer beware.

Let's go back to the idea of mental health. *Mental health is also one of those terms that sound great but actually means that the mentally healthy person doesn't look or act in a strange way.* Mental health just means that you know the person and their behavior and his or her speech is predictable and nonthreatening. *All this is to say that there is a really important social aspect of mental health and mental illness.* It's like the "rubber ruler" effect. That said, what are mental disorders? *They are the original "nature/nurture" phenomena.* So, that's like saying that people with mental disorders have both genetic and social/upbringing/parental influence on what they show. It's not purely anything. Think of it as being half genetics and half upbringing. And there you have it: mental disorders are a murky business.

A List of "Gotta Know Those Triage Questions"

Yup, gotta have some cutting questions. I know that it sounds rude, but trust me, these are good ones. A pretty important question is to ask "What brings you here today?" or something like that. Clinically, it's useful to know why on earth anyone would ever want to be in a situation in which they are receiving psychiatric care.

1. Presenting Problem ("What brings you here today?")

2. Client Statement of Presenting Problem (what are the clients' words minus jargon)

3. Orientation x 3 (person, place, time/date) ("Do you know your name?" "Do you know where you are?" and "Do you know what day that it is?" "Do you know what time that it is?")

4. Under care of physician ("Have you seen a doctor recently? What did he or she say about your health?"

5. Medication/Illicit Drugs ("Are you using any prescription drugs?" "Are you using any illegal drugs?")

6. Depression ("Have you ever felt so sad that it was hard to get out of bed?")

7. Hallucinations ("Have you ever seen or heard things that no one can see or hear?")

8. Delusions ("Have people told you that you believe things that no one else does?)

9. Eating ("How's your appetite?")

10. Sleeping ("How's your sleeping?")

11. Suicide ("Have you ever thought of harming yourself?")

12. Homicide ("Have you ever thought of harming somebody?")

Thoughts on Analyzing Psychiatric Diagnoses

Here are some ideas on how to analyze a diagnosis. There are five things to consider.

1. Criteria: This is your basic listing of symptoms. Generally speaking, the symptoms found in A & B cover most of them BUT there are plenty of disorders in which that's not true. What seems to be the case is that the last couple symptoms are more generic and fit in many disorders (i.e., disorders cause socioemotional difficulties).

2. Features: This is the section usually at the beginning of the disorder or chapter that describes the disorders. They are found in a narrative versus in a listing of symptoms. The section is good for getting a "feel" of a disorder.

3. Onset/Prevalence: These ideas are good for distinguishing different disorders. For example, what is the onset of schizophrenia or depression? It basically asks the clinicians to pinpoint when the disorder first started.

4. Course: This is the beginning, middle and end of a disorder. Sometimes, called prodromal, active, and residual phases of a disorder. "Beginning" is the onset, "active" is when the symptoms are most evident, "residual" in when the symptoms are in remission or are no longer present.

5. Gender/Culture: These variables distinguish disorders by who is most likely to exhibit the symptoms of a disorder. For gender, I call it:

    a. Is it a "boy" disorder? Or a "girl" disorder?
    b. Culture depends on the race and ethnicity of a client.

Thoughts on Differential Diagnosis, Anyone?

So, why are differential diagnoses important to consider? Well, it's like this. Remember, I already told you that diagnoses are based on a process of elimination? Well, you eliminate possibly diagnostic conclusions based on a consideration of differential diagnoses. They are no more than deciding on which of the three or four choices are the best in describing your client. So, choose a couple of possible diagnoses that could possibly be the right one and find one that fits the best. It helps when there is a section in the DSM called "Differential Diagnoses." You can look at the list and it tells you that a bunch of diagnoses are close but no cigar. So, that's why it's a process of elimination. It's the best one left standing. All the others got voted off the island.

SESSION 2: Neurocognitive Disorders
Theme: Neurocognitive Disorders, Delirium, Mental Status Exam

There is simply no way to adequately discuss the topic of neurocognitive disorders in one lecture. It is a vast topic that involves an intimate understanding of the biopsychosocial functioning of your client. Before we jump into the topic, let's remember however that neurocognitive disorders must be differentiated from the normal signs of aging. What I hope to do during this session is to give you assistance in making that differential diagnosis.

A key part of making any diagnosis, including those in neurocognitive disorders is to rule out a bunch of pre-existing conditions that might contribute to the copycat symptoms. You've got to rule out medical conditions that would be a better diagnosis. They would be a "better" diagnosis because the treatment would be more straightforward and hopefully less stressful. There is no "cure" for neurocognitive disorders whereas there may be for a medical condition that mimics neurocognitive disorders. In short, get a physician to rule out any medical condition that might be contributing to the symptomology that you're seeing. In line with that recommendation, make sure that your client is not using any legal or illegal drugs. Remember, most drugs will affect your clients' functioning and in some instances the drugs, their dosages, and their interactions are all critical in your ability to make a good differential diagnosis. To summarize: first, get a physician to rule any pre-existing medical condition that might better account for the psychiatric symptomology that you're witnessing and second, make sure that your client is not using any legal or illegal drug that might better account for their symptoms.

The diagnosis of cognitive disorders is more complex in older patients because physical problems interact with emotional and social troubles in a significant way. As neurocognitive disorders worsen, behavioral problems emerge. Problem behavior often because staff may not understand patients' needs. It is important to identify the cause of the neurocognitive disorders before rushing into pharmacologic treatment. Patients can exhibit problems because they are hungry, thirsty, bored, constipated, tired, sexually aroused, or in pain. Patients with neurocognitive disorders need to feel loved. They benefit from opportunities to develop self-esteem. An initial psychosocial approach to these problematic patients should assess whether these needs are being met. This interaction is rendered more complicated because normal aging also brings about distinct cognitive change.

Another feature of DSM is that disorders like neurocognitive disorders are usually grouped into a cluster of disorders. The difference between the disorders in the cluster is generally their etiology or cause. For example, in neurocognitive disorders, there are a bunch of disorders that are commonly called "dementia;" the difference: the stated cause of how the neurocognitive disorders developed. Some neurocognitive disorders are caused by viral invasions and others by a history of substance abuse. Because the cause of the neurocognitive disorders may have some implications for treatment, it's important to be able to make a correct differential diagnosis.

Now, I'll present four core concepts in neurocognitive disorders (NCD). First, *agnosia* is the inability to recognize objects despite intact sensory function. Here, a person can see, touch, hear, taste, and smell, but can't correctly recognize objects. It's a good indicator that some crucial cognitive processing capacity is not functioning. Second, *aphasia* is a disturbance in language. Generally, this means that your client has difficulty in speaking. Problems with syntax, vocabulary, and grammar are all good indicators that there are some critical cognitive processing capacities that are impaired. Third, *apraxia* is the inability to carry out motor activities previously produced without impairment of motor function. Here, your client is demonstrating an inability to do something that he or she was previously able to do. Whether it's something complex like driving to a known location or relatively simple, like cooking breakfast, apraxia means that your client shows an impairment to do what was previously doable. The last category, *executive functioning*, is the ability to plan, organize, and use inductive reasoning or abstraction. As suggested by the label, this category is the "brains" of the core concepts. Executive functioning allows a person to plan and organize their life activities. Some might conceptualize executive functioning as "problem solving." In the cognitive disorders, symptoms will be defined by one or more of these concepts.

Delirium

Unfortunately, DSM-5 has made some changes in how to approach the diagnosis of NCD. Let's start with *Diagnostic Criteria* of delirium. Just think when you've been watching an old movie with a person, gently moaning, not cognizant of where they are, who they are, and unable to attend to the events around them. Delirium is generally caused by some organic process (i.e., disorder or disease). Here is the ol' DSM with its statement of criteria (APA, 2013):

   A. A disturbance in attention (i.e., reduced ability to direct, focus, sustain, and shift attention) and awareness (reduced orientation to the environment).

   B. The disturbance develops over a short period of time (usually hours to a few days), represents a change from baseline attention and awareness, and tends to fluctuate in severity during the course of a day.

   C. An additional disturbance in cognition (e.g., memory deficit, disorientation, language, visuospatial ability, or perception).

   D. The disturbances in Criteria A and C are not better explained by another pre-existing, established, or evolving neurocognitive disorder and do not occur in the context of a severely reduced level of arousal, such as coma.

   E. There is evidence from the history, physical examination, or laboratory findings that the disturbance is a direct physiological consequence of another medical condition, substance intoxication or withdrawal (i.e., due to a drug of abuse or to a medication), or exposure to a toxin, or is due to multiple etiologies.

Specify whether:

- Substance intoxication delirium: This diagnosis should be made instead of substance intoxication when the symptoms in Criteria A and C predominate in the clinical picture and when they are sufficiently severe to warrant clinical attention.

- Substance withdrawal delirium: This diagnosis should be made instead of substance withdrawal when the symptoms in Criteria A and C predominate in the clinical picture and when they are sufficiently severe to warrant clinical attention.

- Medication-induced delirium: This diagnosis applies when the symptoms in Criteria A and C arise as a side effect of a medication taken as prescribed.

- Delirium due to another medical condition: There is evidence from the history, physical examination, or laboratory findings that the disturbance is attributable to the physiological consequences of another medical condition.

- Delirium due to multiple etiologies: There is evidence from the history, physical examination, or laboratory findings that the delirium has more than one etiology (e.g., more than one etiological medical condition; another medical condition plus substance intoxication or medication side effect).

Specify if:

- Acute: Lasting a few hours or days.
- Persistent: Lasting weeks or months.

Specify if:

- Hyperactive: The individual has a hyperactive level of psychomotor activity that may be accompanied by mood lability, agitation, and/or refusal to cooperate with medical care.

- Hypoactive: The individual has a hypoactive level of psychomotor activity that may be accompanied by sluggishness and lethargy that approaches stupor.

- Mixed level of activity: The individual has a normal level of psychomotor activity even though attention and awareness are disturbed. Also includes individuals whose activity level rapidly fluctuates.

- The essential feature of delirium is a disturbance of attention or awareness that is accompanied by a change in baseline cognition that cannot be better explained by a preexisting or evolving neurocognitive disorder (NCD). The disturbance in attention (Criterion A) is manifested by reduced ability to direct, focus, sustain, and shift attention. Questions must be repeated because the individual's attention wanders, or the individual may perseverate with an answer to a previous question rather than appropriately shift attention. The individual is easily distracted by irrelevant stimuli. The disturbance in awareness is manifested by a reduced orientation to the environment or at times even to oneself.

- The disturbance develops over a short period of time, usually hours to a few days, and tends to fluctuate during the course of the day, often with worsening in the evening and night when external orienting stimuli decrease (Criterion B). There is evidence from the history, physical examination, or laboratory findings that the disturbance is a physiological consequence of an underlying medical condition, substance intoxication or withdrawal, use of a medication, or a toxin exposure, or a combination of these factors

(Criterion E). The etiology should be coded according to the etiologically appropriate subtype (i.e., substance or medication intoxication, substance withdrawal, another medical condition, or multiple etiologies). Delirium often occurs in the context of an underlying NCD.

Criteria A: Disturbance of attention that is accompanied by a change in baseline cognition. Easy for them to say. The key is to read the next sentence. "…reduced ability to direct, focus, sustain and shift attention." The person with NCD can't follow conversations very well and will resort to saying or responding to one stimulus over and over again. The "sundown" effect is always a consideration (i.e., gets worse in evenings). One key consideration is that delirium is comorbid with some other NCD. It doesn't usually happen by itself. Delirium is a disorder that makes good practice for a Mental Status Exam.

Delirium is usually part of a Sleep-Wake Disorder whether it's insomnia, hypersomnia or their ilk. It's not uncommon for a person with NCD to be restless at night and be anxious, fearful, depression and irritable. Labile mood shifts are common. Yelling is common. Prevalence progresses with age and can reach 30% after age 85. Delirium rises up to 83% at end of life. OK, had enough? Sounds scary to me.

One problem is making a diagnosis of any cognitive disorder is differentiating it from others that may be similar to it. Four areas that are present in many cognitive disorders or may be indicative of a disorder with multiple features are disturbance of consciousness, change in cognition or a perceptual disturbance (not better accounted for solely by neurocognitive disorders), rapid onset with a fluctuating or short-term course, and finally cognitive impairment that is the direct physiological consequence of a substance or medical condition (often a disease process outside of the central nervous system). What these four areas suggest is that if one of these four is present, something other than a purely cognitive disorder is present. Before we go further, please review what we said about the triage questions. Remember, you gotta rule out some disease process or substance abuse or some other condition that would better explain the presenting NCD symptomology.

Speaking of jargon, you may be wondering why the DSM gets so loaded with "specify if" statements. Well, the DSM is trying to make clinicians be careful in their thinking. Think of it as asking whether the disorder is specialized or is the routine stuff. The question of course is whether this level of precision is always justified. In my opinion, the DSM is nowhere near as "precise" as some people would have us believe. But the upside is that "specify if" statements make clinicians think longer about the correct diagnosis. Sounds good to me.

Major and Mild Neurocognitive Disorders

Next, let's differentiate Major and Mild Neurocognitive Disorders. First are the criteria (APA, 2013) Major NCD.

    A. Evidence of significant cognitive decline from a previous level of performance in one or more cognitive domains (complex attention, executive function, learning and memory, language, perceptual-motor, or social cognition) based on:

1. Concern of the individual, a knowledgeable informant, or the clinician that there has been a significant decline in cognitive function; and
2. A substantial impairment in cognitive performance, preferably documented by standardized neuropsychological testing or, in its absence, another quantified clinical assessment.

B. The cognitive deficits interfere with independence in everyday activities (i.e., at a minimum, requiring assistance with complex instrumental activities of daily living such as paying bills or managing medications).

C. The cognitive deficits do not occur exclusively in the context of a delirium.

D. The cognitive deficits are not better explained by another mental disorder (e.g., major depressive disorder, schizophrenia)

Second are the criteria (APA, 2013) for Mild NCD

The only difference is that Mild NCD is less major than Major NCD. Really. There's only one word different: "significant" versus "mild." That's the difference. So, I'll only go through Major NCD. The specifiers are really important in NCD. They provide the etiology (i.e., cause) of the NCD. DSM lists Alzheimer's disease, Frontotemporal lobar degeneration, Lewy body disease, Vascular disease, Traumatic brain injury, Substance/medication use, HIV infection, Prion disease, Parkinson's disease, Huntington's disease, Another medical condition, Multiple etiologies, Unspecified. First, the bad news. NCD are progressive (i.e., gets worse over time; can't get past Go; no exceptions). Second, psychotic features are common in Major NCD. Third, mood disorders can also be present. Fourth, agitation, fifth, apathy. Hmmm, doesn't sound good. Basically, NCD can have medical causes that show up as apathetic and agitated psychotics.

OK, let's go with subtypes of NCD: *Alzheimer's Disorder*

A. There is insidious onset and gradual progression of impairment in one or more cognitive domains (for major neurocognitive disorder, at least two domains must be impaired).
 1. complex attention: sustained/selective attention, processing speed
 2. executive ability: planning, decision-making, error correction, mental flexibility, overriding habits
 3. learning and memory: recent and immediate
 4. language: expressive and receptive
 5. visuoconstruction-perceptual ability: construction, visual perception
 6. social cognition: behavioral regulation

The prevalence is completely by age. Only 7% of people between 65 and 74 and 53% of people between 65 and 74, but only 40% of people over 75. Why the drop-off? Yes, you guessed, at those ages, people die before they get neurocognitive disorders.

For major neurocognitive disorder:

Probable Alzheimer's disease is diagnosed if either of the following is present; otherwise, possible Alzheimer's disease should be diagnosed.
   7. Evidence of a causative Alzheimer's disease genetic mutation from family history or genetic testing.
   8. All three of the following are present:
      a. Clear evidence of decline in memory and learning and at least one other cognitive domain (based on detailed history or serial neuropsychological testing).
      b. Steadily progressive, gradual decline in cognition, without extended plateaus.
      c. No evidence of mixed etiology (i.e., absence of other neurodegenerative or cerebrovascular disease, or another neurological, mental, or systemic disease or condition likely contributing to cognitive decline).

The criteria (APA, 2013) for NCD states that someone close to the patient must have noticed a significant cognitive decline from a previous level of performance in one or more cognitive domains (complex attention, executive function, learning and memory, language, perceptual-motor, or social cognition). As you might guess, it's always better to augment subject report with some sort of assessment tool. Confabulation (i.e., ability to be charmingly deceptive) may make it difficult for you to make a confident assessment.

Evidence of modest cognitive decline from a previous level of performance in one or more cognitive domains (complex attention, executive function, learning and memory, language, perceptual-motor, or social cognition) based on:

1. Concern of the individual, a knowledgeable informant, or the clinician that there has been a mild decline in cognitive function; and

2. A modest impairment in cognitive performance, preferably documented by standardized neuropsychological testing or, in its absence, another quantified clinical assessment.

   B. The cognitive deficits do not interfere with capacity for independence in everyday activities (i.e., complex instrumental activities of daily living such as paying bills or managing medications are preserved, but greater effort, compensatory strategies, or accommodation may be required).

   C. The cognitive deficits do not occur exclusively in the context of a delirium.

   D. The cognitive deficits are not better explained by another mental disorder (e.g., major depressive disorder, schizophrenia).

Frontotemporal lobar degeneration

These individuals meet the criteria for NCD and the disorder has insidious onset and gradual progression. There are two varieties of which only one needs to be present for a diagnosis to be made. Behavioral variant includes three or more of the following behavioral symptoms and a decline in social cognition and executive functioning. Here are the behavioral symptoms:

i. Behavioral disinhibition.
ii. Apathy or inertia.
iii. Loss of sympathy or empathy.
iv. Perseverative, stereotyped or compulsive/ritualistic behavior.
v. Hyperorality and dietary changes.

The other variant is that of language that includes prominent decline in language ability, in the form of speech production, word finding and object naming, grammar, or word comprehension.

There is early decline in social interpersonal conduct. Emotional blunting and apathy also occur early without insight. There's a marked decline in personal hygiene and significant distractibility and motor impersistence (i.e., failure to maintain a motor activity). In the types associated with aphasia, language is affected more significantly than personality.

During early stages of frontal lobe NCD, there can be personality change, lack of insight, and poor judgment. When different parts of the brain begin to malfunction, patients may become apathetic or disinhibited. Prodromal symptoms such social withdrawal and behavioral disinhibition may precede the onset of neurocognitive disorders by several years. Memory is usually the first thing to go but attention, language, and visuospatial skills can be unaffected.

In patients whose frontal lobe neurocognitive disorders primarily affect frontal language, loss of spontaneity of speech is often the first noticeable symptom. What is spontaneity of speech? Think of slowed thinking in terms of knowing what to say. As a social gathering, I was being introduced by an elderly gentleman who has known me for years. He forgot my name. I covered for him but it took him a couple minutes to recover his memory. For people with selective language defects, there may not be an overall cognitive decline but something like a progressive aphasia occurs. Onset is considerably earlier than Alzheimer's, starting in a person's 60's. After onset of symptoms, a person generally lives between 5 and 10 years. 40% of FLD have a family history (as in genetic contribution). As might be expected, the early onset heavily affects home and work life. The functional impairment of hyperorality, impulsive wandering and other disinhibited behaviors cause more problems than simple cognitive impairment. This is a good example in which these symptoms require vigilance and results in institutionalization. The liability or oppressive worry of having patients or family members wanders outside precipitate placements that may not foster a more positive quality of life.

Lewy Bodies NCD

Alright, this is a serious topic and it must be because I'm getting brain dead. I say Lewy Bodies and I thought "Lewd Bodies" Sigh. Must be an indicator of my neurocognitive deficits. But back to Lewy Bodies. Here are the criteria (APA, 2013).

Diagnostic Criteria

A. The criteria are met for major or mild neurocognitive disorder.

B. The disorder has an insidious onset and gradual progression.

C. The disorder meets a combination of core *Diagnostic Features* and suggestive *Diagnostic Features* for either probable or possible neurocognitive disorder with Lewy bodies.

- Core *Diagnostic Features*:
    1. Fluctuating cognition with pronounced variations in attention and alertness.
    2. Recurrent visual hallucinations that are well formed and detailed.
    3. Spontaneous features of Parkinsonism, with onset subsequent to the development of cognitive decline.
    4. Suggestive *Diagnostic Features*:
        a. Meets criteria for rapid eye movement sleep behavior disorder.
        b. Severe neuroleptic sensitivity.

D. The disturbance is not better explained by cerebrovascular disease, another neurodegenerative disease, the effects of a substance, or another mental, neurological, or systemic disorder.

So, what about Lewy Bodies? Some dementias are really more medical than psychiatric and this is one of them. It is insidious and has a gradual progression. The client may show initial confusion and problems with executive functioning more so learning and memory. Probably problems with sleep and can have symptoms of delirium. So, learn about it and let it go.

Vascular Neurocognitive Disorder

OK, the first couple criteria (APA, 2013) are pretty much the same as with all the neurocognitive disorders. Criteria A is going to be part of all the neurocognitive disorders. Here are the rest of them.

Diagnostic Criteria

A. The criteria are met for major or mild neurocognitive disorder.

B. The clinical features are consistent with a vascular etiology, as suggested by either of the following:
    1. Onset of the cognitive deficits is temporally related to one or more cerebrovascular events.
    2. Evidence for decline is prominent in complex attention (including processing speed) and frontal-executive function.

C. There is evidence of the presence of cerebrovascular disease from history, physical examination, and/or neuroimaging considered sufficient to account for the neurocognitive deficits.

D. The symptoms are not better explained by another brain disease or systemic disorder.

Some dementias are better left to cardiologists and neurologists. This is one of them. Basically, it comes down to cognitive deficits caused by high blood pressure and strokes. So, in your history taking, it's important to ask about high blood pressure and strokes as way to moving toward NCD due to cerebrovascular events. One observation may be helpful. When people have suffered a serious stroke, they may also have a personality change. For example, they may go from being an executive to an immature adolescent in their behaviors. They may also become emotionally labile and depressed.

Traumatic Brain Injury (TBI) NCD

This is one of those increasingly relevant disorders. You've heard of pro football players retiring at 30, going nuts, and dying at 50? Have you also heard why any concussion is treated seriously at the college level; players may be forced to sit out a season. I read the other day that 40% of retired professional football may have some level of TBI. That's quite a price to pay for playing in a game that they love and at a level about which they have dreamed. When someone goes down and is unconscious, the criteria (APA, 2013) below are what they first examine.

A. The criteria are met for major or mild neurocognitive disorder.

B. There is evidence of a traumatic brain injury—that is, an impact to the head or other mechanisms of rapid movement or displacement of the brain within the skull, with one or more of the following:

1. Loss of consciousness.

2. Posttraumatic amnesia.

3. Disorientation and confusion.

4. Neurological signs (e.g., neuroimaging demonstrating injury; a new onset of seizures; a marked worsening of a preexisting seizure disorder; visual field cuts; anosmia; hemiparesis).

C. The neurocognitive disorder presents immediately after the occurrence of the traumatic brain injury or immediately after recovery of consciousness and persists past the acute post-injury period.

Some features of TBI related neurocognitive disorders are emotional turmoil, personality change, apathy, and suspiciousness. There may also be headaches, seizures, fatigue, sleep problems and vertigo. The DSM has other associated features as well. This is pretty serious stuff; football teams at every level are now taking TBI seriously. The features differ widely by age and gender. The course is also variable. As with the cerebrovascular related CND, there is a pattern of recovery from TBI that may foreshadow Alzheimer's. Generally, there is rapid recovery followed by a plateau and then by a gradual deterioration (assuming that the NCD continues its course). The optimism in the recovery may create despondency when there is a plateau.

Substance/Medication-Induced Major or Mild Neurocognitive Disorder

This is straightforward. Some substance causes NCD. That's about it. Clinically, this is something that is most likely with alcohol dependency over a long period of time. If the person is alcohol-dependent and has nutritional deficits, there is a much higher risk of some form of NCD. NCD induced by alcohol shows up as problems in executive-function and memory and learning domains (i.e., almost sounds like Alzheimer's, doesn't it?). Other substances like opioid dependency are much less associated with NCD. When it does occur, the NCD will take on the features of the drug itself.

Major or Mild Neurocognitive Disorder Due to HIV Infection

HIV infection is obviously a medical disorder with a lot of medical treatment strategies. Way beyond what we have to worry about. We should be grateful.

Diagnostic Criteria

A. The criteria are met for major or mild neurocognitive disorder.

B. There is documented infection with human immunodeficiency virus (HIV).

C. The neurocognitive disorder is not better explained by non-HIV conditions, including secondary brain diseases such as progressive multifocal leukoencephalopathy or cryptococcal meningitis.

D. The neurocognitive disorder is not attributable to another medical condition and is not better explained by a mental disorder.

HIV is an autoimmune disorder with all its complications and complexities. HIV-related NCD is variable in its course. The DSM notes that it is unlikely that there would be significant NCD programs because of the HIV by itself. Thus, serious mental status problems mean that someone else is going on. Here is a paradox related to HIV-related NCD: the prevalence is not really going down despite the increasing use of antiretroviral drugs. Lots of other disorders and problems are comorbid with HIV. That's generally why the NCD rate doesn't go down. The HIV gets better but nothing else.

Major or Mild Neurocognitive Disorder Due to Prion Disease

Another really, really medical disorder but with a kicker. Read on.

Diagnostic Criteria

What is a Prion disease? I have to admit that I was getting irritated by all these medical disorders that were creeping into an innocent course on psychopathology. I mean, give me a break. But I read on and it started getting interesting. Basically, this group of diseases is related to subacute spongiform encephalopathies. Wow, isn't that better? You can go about your day knowing that subacute spongiform encephalopathies have something to do with the Prion disease. But it may be relevant because it is related to diseases like Creutzfeldt-Jakob disease (CJD) otherwise known as the "mad-cow disease." Yup, you got it. Eating bad burgers can cause NCD. There's a long story behind mad-cow disease that has to do with federal carelessness and mindless profit seeking ranchers, but that's for another day.

A. The criteria are met for major or mild neurocognitive disorder.

B. There is insidious onset, and rapid progression of impairment is common.

C. There are motor features of prion disease, such as myoclonus (i.e., involuntary muscle twitching) or ataxia, or biomarker evidence.

D. The neurocognitive disorder is not attributable to another medical condition and is not better explained by another mental disorder.

CJD, once symptoms become emerging, goes to major NCD within 6 months. That's pretty scary. TBI can go backwards and forwards and maybe reaching NCD after 10-20 years. CJD, 6 months. Depression is the disorder most commonly associated with CJD. Be suspicious anytime that anyone really, really wants you to eat a burger. . .

Major or Mild Neurocognitive Disorder Due to Parkinson's disease

Diagnostic Criteria

A. The criteria are met for major or mild neurocognitive disorder.

B. The disturbance occurs in the setting of established Parkinson's disease.

C. There is insidious onset and gradual progression of impairment.

D. The neurocognitive disorder is not attributable to another medical condition and is not better explained by another mental disorder.

Major or mild neurocognitive disorder probably due to Parkinson's disease should be diagnosed if 1 and 2 are both met. Major or mild neurocognitive disorder possibly due to Parkinson's disease should be diagnosed if 1 or 2 is met:

1. There is no evidence of mixed etiology (i.e., absence of other neurodegenerative or cerebrovascular disease or another neurological, mental, or systemic disease or condition likely contributing to cognitive decline).

2. The Parkinson's disease clearly precedes the onset of the neurocognitive disorder.

OK, first, what is Parkinson's disease? Well, I'm not a MD so I won't try to answer it. However, it does take the initial form of movement-related symptoms including rigidity, shaking, and difficulty with walking. And thinking and behavioral problems come later followed by diagnoses of NCD. No, it's not quite that dire but it is pretty bad. Only a couple percent of the population will have Parkinson's. However, 75% of those who do have Parkinson's will develop a major NCD. Onset is in early sixties with mild NCD while major NCD is closer to when a person is 90 or older.

Major or Mild Neurocognitive Disorder Due to Huntington's Disease

Huntington's disease is a terrible disorder. It's insidious and progressive. It causes muscle, behavioral, and psychiatric impairment. It is incurable. It's genetically based so people will know the likelihood that they will die from Huntington's disease. This disease is characterized by muscle writhing and involuntary contractions.

Diagnostic Criteria

A. The criteria are met for major or mild neurocognitive disorder.

B. There is insidious onset and gradual progression.

C. There is clinically established Huntington's disease, or risk for Huntington's disease based on family history or genetic testing.

D. The neurocognitive disorder is not attributable to another medical condition and is not better explained by another mental disorder.

Onset is generally between 35 and 44 years of age. Cognitive and psychiatric symptoms show up before motoric behavioral problems. The psychiatric problems consist of moodiness and anxiety. Apathy, impulsivity, and impaired insight are common early on and only get worse.

The other disorders are not otherwise specified or multiple etiologies or anything where there is no really well-known cause. It just is.

Some notes on interviewing for NCD

There are some common questions that are used in ascertaining whether a client has a cognitive impairment. The two-step process consists of first establishing that symptoms are consistent with one of the syndromes of cognitive impairment and second identifying the underlying physiological cause (often based on temporal correlation rather than established cause-effect). Key diagnostic questions include: Is there a disturbance of consciousness? Is there any impairment in cognition? What is the temporal course of the impairment? Is there an identifiable medical condition or substance etiologically related to the disturbance? In other words, is the person conscious, does he/she have cognitive deficits (as defined above), what happened before and after the impairment, and can the impairment be attributed to a medical condition or substance abuse?

Aging brains don't work as well as those that are younger. That's just a fact. An older brain however doesn't mean NCD. Here's the deal: smart older people can mask their deficits a long time. They are better at faking it than the rest of us. Cognitive decline related to aging produces impaired memory, diminished capacity for complex ideas, mental rigidity, cautious responses, and behavioral slowing. Slowing of responses is the most consistent cognitive change. There are many different ways of discussing it. It can be considered a syndrome that has multiple reversible and irreversible causes. A **Mental Status Exam** is helpful because it helps organize your assessment of your client's possible neurocognitive disorders. Because mental status exams focus on areas like language, memory, motoric behavior, and executive function, they are an ideal method of performing an initial non-medical, non-intrusive examination. One outline of a Mental Status Exam is given at the end of this session.

Depression in elderly persons can mimic the effects of neurocognitive disorders in part because psychomotor retardation and decreased motivation can result in nondemented persons appearing to have cognitive disorders resulting from disease processes. In addition, depression can also cause a nondemented person to over-report the severity of a cognitive disturbance. Consequently, it is important to carefully assess for the presence of depression when evaluating whether to diagnose a client with neurocognitive disorders and age-related cognitive declines. And finally it is entirely possible for depression and neurocognitive disorders to be co-morbid. As a result, it takes longer to provide professional services to older people

The removal of drugs that cause confusion corrects cognitive deficits in these patients. Although psychotropics can be used to reduce agitation or hallucinations, it may also worsen patients' functioning. In addition, there may be multiple drug interactions. Psychopharmacology has real risks and benefits. Case management becomes an essential feature of any competent care for older people. Lots of medication taken as part of a daily regimen can resemble a witch's brew. On the plus side, they don't make people into toads as far as I know. Rivet, rivet, rivet.

Patients and their families should be educated about the nature of the specific illness and the rationale for treatment. Disease processes that cause cognitive deficits may be very complex. Families are often exceedingly anxious because they expect to be forced to accept change in a meaningful relationship. They demand answers. Serious social and financial hardships add to a sense of dread about the future. Most families benefit from a thorough explanation of the patient's condition. Ultimately, social workers should work with physicians to explain the contribution made by various disease processes. You must know how to deliver bad news so that family members can take proper steps to prepare for the future. In the process, families have a reasonable expectation that you will respect the dignity of the patient who experiences cognitive deficits. Whenever possible, clinicians must try to help the family salvage hope and meaning.

Patients with depressive neurocognitive disorders often exhibit early morning awakening, anxiety, weight loss, psychomotor retardation, and decreased libido. Patients with neurocognitive disorders present with disorientation and their daily activities are more seriously impaired. Despite these differences, there is no definitive diagnostic tool. Cognitive decline in depressed older people commonly has a multifactorial etiology. In fact, depression may be the presenting symptom of a degenerative disorder.

A subjective sense of memory loss appears first, followed by loss of memory detail and temporal relationships. All areas of memory function deteriorate including encoding, retrieval, and consolidation. Patients forget landmarks in their lives less often than other events. Agnosia (failure to recognize or identify objects), aphasia (language disturbance), and apraxia occur later; however, a mild amnestic aphasia may be an early finding.

In the early stages of Alzheimer's Disease, a subjective memory deficit is difficult to distinguish from benign forgetfulness. Deficits in memory, language, concept formation, and visual spatial praxis evolve slowly. Later, patients with Alzheimer's Disease become passive, coarse, and less spontaneous. Some become depressed.

More than half of Alzheimer's patients with mild cognitive impairment present with at least one psychiatric symptom and one third present with two or more symptoms. After the initial stage of the disease, patients enter a stage of global cognitive impairment. Denial replaces anxiety, and cognitive deficits are noticeable to family and friends. In the final stages, patients become aimless, abulic (i.e., unable to make decisions), aphasic, and restless. Memory loss is common in nondemented seniors. Many of these patients become terrified that they have Alzheimer's disease and seek medical help. Physicians have difficulty distinguishing normal age-associated memory loss, benign forgetfulness, and early Alzheimer's disease. Benign senile forgetfulness is a condition that occurs when effects of aging on memory are greater than expected. Elderly patients with benign forgetfulness forget unimportant details. This contrasts with Alzheimer's patients, who forget events randomly. Seniors who experience benign senile forgetfulness have trouble remembering recent information; typically, Alzheimer's patients have difficulty with recent and remote memory. Benign senile forgetfulness usually qualifies as a mild cognitive impairment in accordance with DSM-5. The most important aspect of the treatment of benign senile forgetfulness is reassurance, but cognitive retraining can sometimes be helpful. Some of these patients later develop more serious disorders,

Mental Status Exams

So, what is a Mental Status Examination? Well, it's basically a longer set of triage questions that you got in Session #1. It's in this session because it can be used with clients who are exhibited symptoms of dementia. Unfortunately, it is also used when examining clients for psychotic disorder. Weird? Well, yes and no. Yes, because clients with NCD are not crazy. No, because clients with NCD exhibit many thoughts and behaviors that are consistent with people with psychotic disorders. It's really important to keep them separate.

Although its precise organization may vary, it typically contains the following elements:

Appearance and general behavior. In describing the patient's appearance, factors such as approximate age, body habitus, dress, grooming, hygiene, and distinguishing features (e.g., scars, tattoos) may be noted. The patient's general behavior, level of distress, degree of eye contact, and attitude toward the interviewer are also considered.

Motor activity. The patient's level of psychomotor activity is noted, as is the presence of any gait abnormalities or purposeless, repetitive, or unusual postures or movements (e.g., tremors, dyskinesia, akathisia, mannerisms, tics, stereotypies, catatonic posturing, echopraxia, apparent responses to hallucinations).

Speech. Characteristics of the patient's speech are described and may include consideration of rate, rhythm, volume, amount, accent, inflection, fluency, and articulation.

Mood and affect. The patient's expressions of mood and affect are noted. Although the use and definitions of the terms mood and affect vary, mood is typically viewed as referring to the patient's internal, subjective, and more sustained emotional state, whereas affect relates to the patient's externally observable and more changeable emotional state. Affect is often described in terms of its range, intensity, stability, appropriateness, and congruence with the topic being discussed in the interview.

Thought processes. Features of the patient's associations and flow of ideas are described, such as vagueness, incoherence, circumstantiality, tangentiality, neologisms, perseveration, flight of ideas, loose or idiosyncratic associations, and self-contradictory statements.

Thought content. The patient's current thought content is assessed by noting the patient's spontaneously expressed worries, concerns, thoughts, and impulses, as well as through specific questioning about commonly observed symptoms of specific mental disorders. These symptoms include delusions (e.g., erotomania or delusions of persecution, passivity, grandeur, infidelity, infestation, poverty, somatic illness, guilt, worthlessness, thought insertion, thought withdrawal, or thought broadcasting), ideas of reference, overvalued ideas, ruminations, obsessions, compulsions, and phobias. Assessment of suicidal, homicidal, aggressive, or self-injurious thoughts, feelings, or impulses is essential for determining the patient's level of risk to self or others as part of the clinical formulation. If such features are present, details are elicited regarding their intensity and specificity, when they occur, and what prevents the patient from acting on them.

Perceptual disturbances. Hallucinations (i.e., a perception in the absence of a stimulus) and illusions (i.e., an erroneous perception in the presence of a stimulus) may occur in any sensory modality (e.g., auditory, visual, tactile, olfactory, gustatory). Other perceptual disturbances that patients may experience include depersonalization and derealization.

Sensorium and cognition. Systematic assessment of cognitive functions is an essential part of the general psychiatric evaluation, although the level of detail necessary and the appropriateness of particular formal tests will depend on the purpose of the evaluation and the psychiatrist's clinical judgment. Evaluation of the patient's sensorium includes a description of the level of consciousness and its stability. Elements of the patient's cognitive status that may be assessed include orientation (e.g., person, place, time, and situation), attention and concentration, and memory (e.g., registration, short-term, long-term). Arithmetic calculations may be used to assess concentration or knowledge; other aspects of the patient's fund of knowledge may also be assessed as appropriate to sociocultural and educational background. Additional aspects of the cognitive examination may include assessment of level of intelligence, language functions (e.g., naming, comprehension, repetition, reading, writing), drawing (e.g., copying a figure or drawing a clock face), abstract reasoning (e.g., explaining similarities or interpreting proverbs), and executive functions (e.g., list making, inhibiting impulsive answers, resisting distraction, recognizing contradictions).

Insight. The patient's insight into his or her current situation is typically assessed by inquiring about the patient's awareness of any problems and their implications. Patients may or may not recognize that psychosis or other symptoms may reflect an underlying illness or that their behavior affects their relationships with other individuals. They also may or may not recognize the potential benefits of treatment.

Another element of insight involves the patient's motivation to change his or her health risk behaviors. Such motivation often fluctuates over time from denial and resistance to ambivalence to commitment, a sequence that has been referred to as "stages of change". The stages, which are not necessarily discrete, have been labeled precontemplation (denial, minimization); contemplation (musing or thinking about doing something); preparation (actually getting ready to do something); action (implementing concrete actions to deal with the problem); and maintenance (acting to ensure that the changes are maintained). Patients who are not quite ready to change may vacillate about modifying their behaviors before actually committing to change and acting on it. Assessing stages of change as part of the evaluative process leads to stage-appropriate educational and therapeutic interventions that attempt to help patients move to more adaptive stages in a patient-centered manner.

Judgment. The quality of the patient's judgment has sometimes been assessed by asking for the patient's responses to hypothetical situations (e.g., smelling smoke in a theater). However, in assessing judgment, it is generally more helpful to learn about the patient's responses and decision making in terms of his or her own self-care, interactions, and other aspects of his or her recent or current situation and behavior. If poor judgment is present, a more detailed explication of the patient's decision-making processes may help differentiate the potential causes of this impairment.

SESSION #3
Theme: Neurodevelopmental Disorder

There are 20 disorders listed in the chapter on neurodevelopment. It spans a large number of topics from learning disabilities to mental retardation (i.e., intellectual disability) to autism to motoric coordination. That's simply too broad a range of topics to cover in a week. Thus, I'll be limiting the discussion to Social (Pragmatic) Communication Disorder, Autism Spectrum Disorder, Attention-Deficit/Hyperactivity Disorder, and Tic Disorders. Aren't you glad that I've eliminated 16 disorders from this discussion? There still is a lot of ground to cover. So, let's get started.

Social Communication Disorder

First, here are some criteria (APA, 2013).

Diagnostic Criteria

Persistent difficulties in the social use of verbal and nonverbal communication as manifested by all of the following:
1. Deficits in using communication for social purposes, such as greeting and sharing information, in a manner that is appropriate for the social context.
2. Impairment of the ability to change communication to match context or the needs of the listener, such as speaking differently in a classroom than on a playground, talking differently to a child than to an adult, and avoiding use of overly formal language.
3. Difficulties following rules for conversation and storytelling, such as taking turns in conversation, rephrasing when misunderstood, and knowing how to use verbal and nonverbal signals to regulate interaction.
4. Difficulties understanding what is not explicitly stated (e.g., making inferences) and nonliteral or ambiguous meanings of language (e.g., idioms, humor, metaphors, multiple meanings that depend on the context for interpretation).

B. The deficits result in functional limitations in effective communication, social participation, social relationships, academic achievement, or occupational performance, individually or in combination.
C. The onset of the symptoms is in the early developmental period (but deficits may not become fully manifest until social communication demands exceed limited capacities).
D. The symptoms are not attributable to another medical or neurological condition or to low abilities in the domains of word structure and grammar, and are not better explained by autism spectrum disorder, intellectual disability (intellectual developmental disorder), global developmental delay, or another mental disorder.

Hmmm, how best to describe this disorder? Imagine a child who doesn't read social cues but still can talk. Some signs of social communication (but I'm still trying to learn them!) are greeting, sharing information, talking in context ("inside talk" versus "outside talk"), or talking differentially to people (e.g., adult versus child). Another area is to follow rules of conversation (i.e., taking turns, rephrasing when not understood, use of verbal and nonverbal signs to regulate social interaction, and understanding ambiguous statements made by other (i.e., not being to infer nonconcrete statements). As you might, social communication is the oil that makes the car run. Without the oil, the vehicle of social intercourse comes to a screeching halt. Don't you just love metaphors? Without effective social communication, it's difficult to be part of social groups, succeed in social relationships and academics in school, and any job possibilities.

Social Communication Disorder is the logical outcome of a child not meeting communication developmental milestones. Such delays adversely affect the essential socialization that allows success in school and community settings.

Autism Spectrum Disorder

Diagnostic Criteria
Persistent deficits in social communication and social interaction across multiple contexts, as manifested by the following, currently or by history (examples are illustrative, not exhaustive; see text):
  1. Deficits in social-emotional reciprocity, ranging, for example, from abnormal social approach and failure of normal back-and-forth conversation; to reduced sharing of interests, emotions, or affect; to failure to initiate or respond to social interactions.
  2. Deficits in nonverbal communicative behaviors used for social interaction, ranging, for example, from poorly integrated verbal and nonverbal communication; to abnormalities in eye contact and body language or deficits in understanding and use of gestures; to a total lack of facial expressions and nonverbal communication.
  3. Deficits in developing, maintaining, and understanding relationships, ranging, for example, from difficulties adjusting behavior to suit various social contexts; to difficulties in sharing imaginative play or in making friends; to absence of interest in peers.

Specify current severity:
  - Severity is based on social communication impairments and restricted, repetitive patterns of behavior.
  B. Restricted, repetitive patterns of behavior, interests, or activities, as manifested by at least two of the following, currently or by history (examples are illustrative, not exhaustive; see text):
  1. Stereotyped or repetitive motor movements, use of objects, or speech (e.g., simple motor stereotypies, lining up toys or flipping objects, echolalia, idiosyncratic phrases).
  2. Insistence on sameness, inflexible adherence to routines, or ritualized patterns of verbal or nonverbal behavior (e.g., extreme distress at small changes, difficulties

with transitions, rigid thinking patterns, greeting rituals, need to take same route or eat same food every day).
3. Highly restricted, fixated interests that are abnormal in intensity or focus (e.g., strong attachment to or preoccupation with unusual objects, excessively circumscribed or perseverative interests).
4. Hyper- or hyporeactivity to sensory input or unusual interest in sensory aspects of the environment (e.g., apparent indifference to pain/temperature, adverse response to specific sounds or textures, excessive smelling or touching of objects, visual fascination with lights or movement).

Specify current severity:
C. Severity is based on social communication impairments and restricted, repetitive patterns of behavior
D. Symptoms must be present in the early developmental period (but may not become fully manifest until social demands exceed limited capacities, or may be masked by learned strategies in later life).
E. Symptoms cause clinically significant impairment in social, occupational, or other important areas of current functioning.
F. These disturbances are not better explained by intellectual disability (intellectual developmental disorder) or global developmental delay. Intellectual disability and autism spectrum disorder frequently co-occur; to make comorbid diagnoses of autism spectrum disorder and intellectual disability, social communication should be below that expected for general developmental level.

Specify if:
- With or without accompanying intellectual impairment
- With or without accompanying language impairment
- Associated with a known medical or genetic condition or environmental factor
- Associated with another neurodevelopmental, mental, or behavioral disorder.
- With catatonia

OK, let's get started with the discussion of Autism Spectrum Disorder (ASD). In DSM-IV TR, there were a bunch of disorders all which were called Pervasive Developmental Disorders (PDD). Fair enough. The problem was that kids were too variable and didn't fit neatly into the PDD. But there did appear to be a spectrum of different disorders in terms of functionality. So, DSM-5 did away with specific disorder and came up with ASD instead. The good part is that the artificial distinctions were no longer necessary. However, some old favorites such as Asperger's Disorder or Childhood Disintegrative Disorder were jettisoned. So, it's good in some ways, but it also did away with other helpful distinctions.

The first area basically is around social interactions and communication. The term that is used is "social reciprocity." Social reciprocity refers to the give-and-take or back-and-forth of any conversation. What is said by one person is considered when making a reply. The failure to reciprocate can make an autistic child seem cold or superior. Nonverbal communications are also a problem. Eye contact, gestures, and body language are generally used to convey a lot of social information. When they are absent or used oddly, the net effect is to have hampered communication. The final area can be phrased as "play." Autistic kids have limited imaginative play because of their inability to read and respond to social cues. Thus, friendships are not formed and the ability to adjust to different social contexts is not developed.

The second grouping of areas revolves around restricted and repetitive patterns of behavior, interests, and activities. Basically, two restricted and repetitive patterns must be shown for the diagnosis to be made. The DSM has four patterns listed above. Classic examples of autistic behavior are

Lining up objects, echolalia
Inflexible adherence to routines, rigid adherence to ritualized behavior
Preoccupation with unusual objects or topics
Hypersensitivity to sensory aspects of the environment (e.g., visual fascination of lights or movement, adverse response to sounds and textures)

Another characteristic of children with ASD is self-injurious behavior. As you might guess, this characteristic requires careful attention. For more information, here is a helpful site.
http://www.autism.com/symptoms_self-injury

The 3rd criteria area can be a heartbreaker. A toddler's developmental capacities may be able to handle the social demands of someone that age. However, at a later age, the demands may exceed those same capacities. So, a toddler may look normal until the social demands get too much for the developmental disability. Autistic children vary in their intellectual impairment; many will show language impairment. However, even those individuals with average or high intelligence will be uneven in their skills and capacities. There is a gap between the intelligence and what they can do with it (i.e., discontent between what they should be able to do and what they end up doing). Autism is comorbid with anxiety and depression but may even be with catatonia as well.

Onset is between 12 and 24 months but the disorder is not progressive (i.e., doesn't get worse with time). The first indications may show up as a lack of or interest in social interactions. As usual, early onset has a worse prognosis than a late onset. There is a large genetic component with estimates going as high as 90%. However, it is not at all certain that there are gene markers for autism. Autism is still polygenic with hundreds of genetic loci making small contributions. In short, the genetic makeup of people is too complex to make a one on one relationship.

Males are 4 times more likely than females to be autistic. When females are diagnosed as autistic, they are more likely to have intellectual impairments. This suggests that females more so than males have social skills that mask the presence of autism.

Attention-Deficit/Hyperactivity Disorder

Well, we had to eventually get to one of those controversial topics: ADHD. I think that just about everyone has either treated or knows of someone who has been treated for ADHD. Looking through the DSM, the descriptors are words like "inattentive," "careless," "restless," "fidgety," and so on. This sounds like me when I'm at a long, long faculty meeting. So, we immediately have a problem: when is ADHD not a problem?

Alright, that was good rhetoric, but it's time to get serious. Lots of kids (and increasingly adults) are diagnosed with ADHD each year. Lots of parents swear by the use of stimulants for their kids . . . and other parents swear at the people who prescribe them. It's not an easy disorder about which to provide an even-handed discussion. With no further ado, here are the criteria (APA, 2013)

Criterion A states that there must be persistent pattern of inattention that is more severe than other people at a comparable stage of development. What a weasel way of saying about nothing! OK, let me see, kids with ADHD have to be more inattentive than other kids about the same age. I feel smart, don't you? But the DSM goes the next step and states that the symptoms must have caused problems should have been seen before age 12. In the previous edition, the criterion was six months before age 7. This was widely accepted by most researchers. This change was puzzling to most clinicians, but what the hey? This is the DSM. However, the age limit still is helpful because it gives us an idea of the course of the disorder. The writers of the DSM also have provided the a la carte approach of diagnosing ADHD: patients must demonstrate six of the nine in the menu.

At first, I was irritated by this a la carte method of diagnosing ADHD. But as usual, I was proven wrong. It does make sense in an odd way. By showing a bunch of symptoms (as in six of nine of them), patients probably look more severe than say, others with just four or five of them. Basically, it implies severity. And that makes sense to me. A patient should be showing a lot of symptoms before he/she should be diagnosed with ADHD. Bottom line is that the patient should have lots of symptoms happening a lot to be diagnosable. The symptoms are pretty much those that you'd guess:

a. often fails to give close attention to details or makes careless mistakes in schoolwork, work, or other activities

b. often has difficulty sustaining attention in tasks or play activities

c. often does not seem to listen when spoken to directly

d. often does not follow through on instructions and fails to finish schoolwork, chores, or duties in the workplace (not due to oppositional behavior or failure to understand instructions)

e. often has difficulty organizing tasks and activities

f. often avoids, dislikes, or is reluctant to engage in tasks that require sustained mental effort (such as schoolwork or homework)

g. often loses things necessary for tasks or activities (e.g., toys, school assignments, pencils, books, or tools)

h. is often easily distracted by extraneous stimuli

i. is often forgetful in daily activities (American Psychiatric Association)

OK, let's try to get a picture of what all this looks like. Here are some symptoms: makes careless errors on boring stuff like schoolwork, doesn't seem to pay attention to people, not much follow through, poor organizational skills, easily bored (that accounts for not liking activities that require sustained mental effort and easily distracted), loses stuff, and is forgetful.

Any one of those items or even a couple of them probably doesn't mean much. But taken together, it becomes a lot more serious. There's term that is frequently used, "executive functioning." Basically, it means being able to go from point A to point B. If a person is easily distracted, poorly organized, loses items, and forgets important items, he/she won't be able to accomplish much in life. But wait, there's more. Not a lot of follow-through and that's the rub. When a person shows all these items, he/she has a lot going against him/her. And that's what makes the first part of Criterion A ("Inattention) a disorder. Here is the first part of ADHD.

The second part of Criterion A, "Hyperactivity/Impulsivity" is similar to the first part; symptoms must have been present 6 months or more and must be severe enough to cause impairment. However, unlike the first part, the second part has two entrees: "Hyperactivity" and "Impulsivity." The former has six items:

a. often fidgets with hands or feet or squirms in seat
b. often leaves seat in classroom or in other situations in which remaining seated is expected
c. often runs about or climbs excessively in situations in which it is inappropriate (in adolescents or adults, may be limited to subjective feelings of restlessness)
d. often has difficulty playing or engaging in leisure activities quietly
e. is often "on the go" or often acts as if "driven by a motor"
f. often talks excessively

The latter has 3 items:

g. often blurts out answers before questions have been completed
h. often has difficulty awaiting turn
i. often interrupts or intrudes on others (e.g., butts into conversations or games)

So, to be described as "Hyperactive," a patient must be described with any six of the nine items. My guess is that "Hyperactive" and "Impulsive" are close enough alike to make it reasonable to collapse the two types into one type. Let's go back and try to describe hyperactivity: think the Ever-Ready Bunny. We're talking about anything repetitive (i.e., movement, talking). Yup, can't relax, can't sit still, impulsively getting into situations, can't wait, and is just rude. That's someone who is hyperactive-impulsive.

But enough about Criterion A. Let's go over the remainder of the criteria. Criterion B is about course (i.e., symptoms were present before age 12); Criterion C is about pervasiveness (i.e., symptoms must cause impairment in two or more settings; Criterion D is about severity (i.e., must be significant impairment); Criterion E is about exclusion (i.e., can't be anything else). Got it? Basically, it's Criterion A with all the menu items that must have started before age 12, must be seen in a couple areas, must have caused significant impairment and must not be due to anything else. The first two are important because they speak to course and pervasiveness. The last two are pretty much seen in all disorders so they're easy to remember.

There are three subtypes:

1. Combined Type (i.e., combining Attention-Deficit and Hyperactive/Impulsive)
2. Predominantly Inattentive Type (i.e., second part (Criterion A2 hasn't been seen in 6 months)
3. Predominantly Hyperactive/Impulsive Type (i.e., Criterion A1 hasn't been seen in last 6 months)

Prevalence is about 5% of the population (wow! That is really a high prevalence rate). Developmentally, many children with ADHD remain impaired as adults. In terms of temperament, kids with ADHD are more likely to excessively disinhibited and lack self-regulation. They show negative emotionality which is a type of unhappiness with the world and manifest anger, contempt, disgust and fear. ADHD is associated with various social ills (i.e., child abuse and neglect, multiple foster placements, neurotoxins (i.e., lead poisoning) and fetal alcohol. Kids with ADHD are more likely to have a conduct disorder and not do well in school. Overall, ADHD affects social, familial and academic/occupational success. The most common comorbid disorders are conduct disorder, learning disabilities, OCD, and tic disorders.

Tic Disorders

Hmmm, let's start with the diagnostic disorders as a jump-off point for discussion. First, a definition: A tic is a sudden, rapid, recurrent, nonrhythmic motor movement or vocalization. Now, onto the criteria (APA, 2013)

Tourette's Disorder
A. Both multiple motor and one or more vocal tics have been present at some time during the illness, although not necessarily concurrently.
B. The tics may wax and wane in frequency but have persisted for more than 1 year since first tic onset.

C. Onset is before age 18 years.
D. The disturbance is not attributable to the physiological effects of a substance (e.g., cocaine) or another medical condition (e.g., Huntington's disease, postviral encephalitis).

Persistent (Chronic) Motor or Vocal Tic Disorder
A. Single or multiple motor or vocal tics have been present during the illness, but not both motor and vocal.
B. The tics may wax and wane in frequency but have persisted for more than 1 year since first tic onset.
C. Onset is before age 18 years.
D. The disturbance is not attributable to the physiological effects of a substance (e.g., cocaine) or another medical condition (e.g., Huntington's disease, postviral encephalitis).
E. Criteria have never been met for Tourette's disorder.

The DSM states that tic disorders are hierarchical in order (i.e., Tourette's disorder, followed by persistent [chronic] motor or vocal tic disorder, followed by provisional tic disorder, followed by the other specified and unspecified tic disorders), such that once a tic disorder at one level of the hierarchy is diagnosed, a lower hierarchy diagnosis cannot be made (Criterion E). Basically, the diagnoses are mutually exclusive and Tourette's should always be considered first. The most common tics are involuntary eye blinking and throat clearing that can however be suppressed for varying lengths of time. Higher order tics have both motor and vocal tics.

Onset is between 4 and 6 years; onset in adulthood is rare. Peak severity is between ages 10 and 12; adolescents and adults decline in their severity. Basically, it's worse for latency and prepubescent kids; it's not frequent for teens and adults. Tics are preceded by an "urge" to "do it right." Tics will continue until they have been done "right." Once urges are identified, they can be controlled because they are seen as not being inevitable.

Tics are the least evident when there is a calm and focused environment (e.g., school) and worst with unfocused (e.g., home) or anxious/stressful arenas (i.e., social interactions). More males than females have tics. OK, that's it for today's lecture. Please congratulate me for NOT saying that "that's tic" for today's lecture.

SESSION #4
Theme: Disruptive, Impulse Control, and Conduct Disorders

This lecture focuses on Oppositional Defiant Disorder, Intermittent Explosive Disorder, Conduct Disorder, Antisocial Personality Disorder, Pyromania, Kleptomania, Disruptive, Impulse Control, and Conduct Disorders NOS. These disorders are characterized by the recurrence of excited tension, followed acting on the impulse, experiencing pleasure, and followed by remorse and guilt. In a sentence: these disorders relate to self-regulation of emotions and behaviors. In short, it's all about impulsive people. It also is linked to a couple personality dimensions in the externalizing spectrum: *disinhibition* and *constraint*. The externalizing spectrum complements the internalizing spectrum. Externalizing is what shows on the outside; internalizing is what is going on internally. That's why aggression is an externalized behavior while depression is an internalized behavior. DSM-5 has made a significant change from the DSM-IV TR chapter on Impulse Control Disorders. It now includes a couple kid disorders, takes out a couple disorders, and even inserts a personality disorder. Wow! It changes the flavor of this chapter altogether. It really is all about a spectrum of disorders that span childhood through adulthood. The distinction between kid and adult disorders is erased in this edition of the DSM. As you might guess, to diagnose these disorders, the pattern of behaviors must not already exist in other disorders. For example, if clients with Antisocial Personality Disorders engage in a pattern of physical assault and destructive acts, then the diagnosis should not be Intermittent Explosive Disorders. As we will see, the distinction may be faint between Disruptive, Impulse Control, and Conduct Disorders and their brethren.

Oppositional Defiant Disorders (ODD)

I always paired ODD with Conduct Disorders only because it was more severe (in part because of age) than ODD. Here are the criteria (APA, 2013) for *Oppositional Defiant Disorder*:

A. A pattern of angry/irritable mood, argumentative/defiant behavior, or vindictiveness lasting at least 6 months as evidenced by at least four symptoms from any of the following categories, and exhibited during interaction with at least one individual who is not a sibling.
- *Angry/Irritable Mood*
2. Often loses temper.
3. Is often touchy or easily annoyed.
4. Is often angry and resentful.
- *Argumentative/Defiant Behavior*
5. Often argues with authority figures or, for children and adolescents, with adults.
6. Often actively defies or refuses to comply with requests from authority figures or with rules.
7. Often deliberately annoys others.
8. Often blames others for his or her mistakes or misbehavior.
- *Vindictiveness*
9. Has been spiteful or vindictive at least twice within the past 6 months.

- Note: The persistence and frequency of these behaviors should be used to distinguish a behavior that is within normal limits from a behavior that is symptomatic. For children younger than 5 years, the behavior should occur on most days for a period of at least 6 months unless otherwise noted (Criterion A8). For individuals 5 years or older, the behavior should occur at least once per week for at least 6 months, unless otherwise noted (Criterion A8). While these frequency criteria provide guidance on a minimal level of frequency to define symptoms, other factors should also be considered, such as whether the frequency and intensity of the behaviors are outside a range that is normative for the individual's developmental level, gender, and culture.
B. The disturbance in behavior is associated with distress in the individual or others in his or her immediate social context (e.g., family, peer group, work colleagues), or it impacts negatively on social, educational, occupational, or other important areas of functioning.
C. The behaviors do not occur exclusively during the course of a psychotic, substance use, depressive, or bipolar disorder. Also, the criteria are not met for disruptive mood dysregulation disorder.

ODD (Oppositional Defiant Disorders) represent grist for family therapists. Their parents call these kids "disrespectful" and "disobedient." Further, ODD kids may only show these behaviors at home. Lucky parents, huh? Basically, think of ODD kids are being rotten brats and you've got it. Moody, angry, vindictive. Yeah, like I said, rotten kids. But, kids can be moody and still be a good kid. That's why there must be four or more symptoms to be diagnosed as ODD. One problem is that the ODD kids think that they are simply reacting to unfair demands or attributions of other people. In short, they see themselves as being more or less innocent. Well, actually, a lot of these kids don't see themselves as innocent. They do regard themselves as trapped in a hostile environment in which their family members play a part. In terms of course, ODD starts during preschool and rarely goes beyond early teenhood. They are also prodromal for conduct and anxiety disorders.

Now comes the family systems understanding of ODD. It is easy to see that ODD behaviors are in reaction to a punishing and harsh family environment. It is also possible that family members lack empathy because the kid has a aggressive and combative temperament. It becomes a chicken or egg problem. One side note: Rates of ODD are higher in samples of patients with ADHD.

Intermittent Explosive Disorders

For Intermittent Explosive Disorders, the *Diagnostic Features* include anger toward people and things. The anger typically results in purposeful and serious physical assault or destruction. The assault or destruction should be significant and not preceded by provocation out of proportion to the assaultive or destructive behaviors. Although the assaultive behaviors are purposeful when they are committed, clients may express remorse afterwards. But remember the overall pattern is one of impulsive. If it there is a buildup some period of time (DSM says something about 30 minutes although that seems like an artificial number to me). The pattern is an increasing tension culminating in explosive rage followed by calmness and finally remorse. The calmness may almost be seen as relief or pleasure. Here are the DSM-5 criteria (APA, 2013):

A. Recurrent behavioral outbursts representing a failure to control aggressive impulses as manifested by either of the following:
   1. Verbal aggression (e.g., temper tantrums, tirades, verbal arguments or fights) or physical aggression toward property, animals, or other individuals, occurring twice weekly, on average, for a period of 3 months. The physical aggression does not result in damage or destruction of property and does not result in physical injury to animals or other individuals.
   2. Three behavioral outbursts involving damage or destruction of property and/or physical assault involving physical injury against animals or other individuals occurring within a 12-month period.
B. The magnitude of aggressiveness expressed during the recurrent outbursts is grossly out of proportion to the provocation or to any precipitating psychosocial stressors.
C. The recurrent aggressive outbursts are not premeditated (i.e., they are impulsive and/or anger-based) and are not committed to achieve some tangible objective (e.g., money, power, intimidation).
D. The recurrent aggressive outbursts cause either marked distress in the individual or impairment in occupational or interpersonal functioning, or are associated with financial or legal consequences.
E. Chronological age is at least 6 years (or equivalent developmental level).
F. The recurrent aggressive outbursts are not better explained by another mental disorder (e.g., major depressive disorder, bipolar disorder, disruptive mood dysregulation disorder, a psychotic disorder, antisocial personality disorder, borderline personality disorder) and are not attributable to another medical condition (e.g., head trauma, Alzheimer's disease) or to the physiological effects of a substance (e.g., a drug of abuse, a medication). For children ages 6–18 years, aggressive behavior that occurs as part of an adjustment disorder should not be considered for this diagnosis.

Probably the least intuitive aspect of this disorder is the relief/pleasure that clients may express or exhibit. One explanation is that the clients are "out of control" during a "spell or anger attack," and that once over, the clients are relieved that they are no longer out of control. Note that such a "spell" may be used to defend the client. For example, friends may describe the person with the disorder as a "nice person" who is given to "spells," but that he/she is basically good. I suppose that among friends, people may joke that the "devil made him do it" as way of minimizing the assault or destruction. Is there a moral element here? "Nice people" should not hurt people or destroy things but the impulse was just out of control and that the rage will not happen again. The next statement was that there was provocation. Yet another statement might be that there is some type of developmental disorder that gives rise to the "anger attacks." And you know, there might even be some truth to all these considerations. The distinction may be the diagnosis versus the etiology. In DSM, the distinction may not be important. A syndrome of heightened tension, explosive actions, calmness/pleasure, and ending in remorse is all that is necessary to make the diagnosis. At times, clients will be able to control their impulses and not Treatment and/or criminal sentences may well take into consideration the etiology of the intermittent rage. The treatment or judicial intervention may well consider the etiology of the rage.

I would be remiss if I did not discuss the obvious social implications of intermittent explosive disorders: domestic violence. The *Diagnostic Criteria* for intermittent explosive disorders are identical to those that are described for batterers. Domestic violence is typically described as increasing tension (with or without provocation), explosive rage, calmness, and finally remorse. In addition to the remorse, there are usually the repetitive reassurances that the incident would not occur again. However, the term "intermittent" is the key here. The rage will happen again (assuming that the incident cannot be explained by drugs or a somatic condition) and the consequences may be worse. Whether there will be escalation is not addressed in DSM-5. It may well be that any escalation will depend on the individual patient.

Who is associated with intermittent explosive disorders? Virtually anyone. If you read the Big Purple Book carefully, you'll note that these raging outbursts can be seen as part of a manic episode, a psychotic break, social pressures, personality disorders to name just a few disorders. Everyone gets angry occasionally (and some, lamentably more than others; you should have seen my "anger attack" when I saw my utility bill), but the difference is the level of rage. I repeat, the important part in this diagnosis is the interpersonal and social problems caused by this disorder. Think of it as substance abuse; everyone drinks, but not everyone's alcohol use and abuse result in socioeconomic consequences. As you might guess, Intermittent Explosive Disorders are associated more with men than with women. Judging by the increasing number of women who are incarcerated for serious crimes, this pattern may also change. The DSM states that Intermittent Explosive Disorders are fairly rare? Yeah, right.

The DSM describes "running amok" as a single episode of explosive anger as opposed to Intermittent Explosive Disorders. Further, the patient presents with a claim of dissociative features (i.e., "I can't remember anything after I started feeling really tense"). The DSM states that "running amok" is commonly associated with Southeastern countries. Come to think of it, I did explain to everyone that I couldn't remember running amok after I got that utility bill. In terms of relevance and course, the DSM says that the disorder could be abrupt or have a prodromal phase, could start in childhood or later in adulthood, course could end in adulthood or continue further into late life. This is a nice way of saying that existing data don't tell us much of any use on the prevalence and course of this disorder. It probably doesn't surprise you that people who have this kind of rage have family members who also exhibit the same behaviors.

Finally, there is the problem of whether the disorder is purposeful. If it is not purposeful, then a diagnosis of Intermittent Explosive Disorder is possible. If the rage is purposeful, then a careful examination of some type personality disorder is necessary. If fact, the rage may not be so much out of control as it is a method of intimidating someone.

Just a quick note: The DSM-IV TR had an interesting observation that is still good today about "echoes"

"Many people with this disorder report the following sensations just before or during an episode:

Tingling sensations.
Tremors.
Pounding heart.
Chest tightness.
Head pressure.
Hearing an echo.
These episodes may not always be directed at others. Sometimes these episodes result in self-inflicted injuries and suicide attempts. The greatest risk of self-inflicted injury occurs in those who are also addicted to drugs or have a serious mental disorder, such as depression."

How's that for crazy symptoms?

Conduct Disorders

Onto clients with Conduct Disorders. Easy way to remember it is as a kid version of an *Antisocial Personality Disorder*. Hmmm, that sounds pretty grim. Well, it's useful in setting a high bar before labeling a kid as having a Conduct Disorder. That said; let's look at the criteria (APA, 2013) in DSM-5.

A. A repetitive and persistent pattern of behavior in which the basic rights of others or major age-appropriate societal norms or rules are violated, as manifested by the presence of at least three of the following 15 criteria in the past 12 months from any of the categories below, with at least one criterion present in the past 6 months:
  - *Aggression to People and Animals*
    - Often bullies, threatens, or intimidates others.
    - Often initiates physical fights.
    - Has used a weapon that can cause serious physical harm to others (e.g., a bat, brick, broken bottle, knife, gun).
    - Has been physically cruel to people.
    - Has been physically cruel to animals.
    - Has stolen while confronting a victim (e.g., mugging, purse snatching, extortion, armed robbery).
    - Has forced someone into sexual activity.
      - *Destruction of Property*
    - Has deliberately engaged in fire setting with the intention of causing serious damage.
    - Has deliberately destroyed others' property (other than by fire setting).
      - *Deceitfulness or Theft*
    - Has broken into someone else's house, building, or car.
    - Often lies to obtain goods or favors or to avoid obligations (i.e., "cons" others).
    - Has stolen items of nontrivial value without confronting a victim (e.g., shoplifting, but without breaking and entering; forgery).
      - *Serious Violations of Rules*

- Often stays out at night despite parental prohibitions, beginning before age 13 years.
- Has run away from home overnight at least twice while living in the parental or parental surrogate home, or once without returning for a lengthy period.
- Is often truant from school, beginning before age 13 years.

B. The disturbance in behavior causes clinically significant impairment in social, academic, or occupational functioning.

C. If the individual is age 18 years or older, criteria are not met for antisocial personality disorder.

Specify whether:
- Childhood-onset type: Individuals show at least one symptom characteristic of conduct disorder prior to age 10 years.
- Adolescent-onset type: Individuals show no symptom characteristic of conduct disorder prior to age 10 years.
- Unspecified onset: Criteria for a diagnosis of conduct disorder are met, but there is not enough information available to determine whether the onset of the first symptom was before or after age 10 years.

Specify if:
- With limited prosocial emotions: To qualify for this specifier, an individual must have displayed at least two of the following characteristics persistently over at least 12 months and in multiple relationships and settings. These characteristics reflect the individual's typical pattern of interpersonal and emotional functioning over this period and not just occasional occurrences in some situations. Thus, to assess the criteria for the specifier, multiple information sources are necessary. In addition to the individual's self-report, it is necessary to consider reports by others who have known the individual for extended periods of time (e.g., parents, teachers, co-workers, extended family members, peers).
    - *Lack of remorse or guilt*: Does not feel bad or guilty when he or she does something wrong (exclude remorse when expressed only when caught and/or facing punishment). The individual shows a general lack of concern about the negative consequences of his or her actions. For example, the individual is not remorseful after hurting someone or does not care about the consequences of breaking rules.
    - *Callous – lack of empathy*: Disregards and is unconcerned about the feelings of others. The individual is described as cold and uncaring. The person appears more concerned about the effects of his or her actions on himself or herself, rather than their effects on others, even when they result in substantial harm to others.
    - *Unconcerned about performance*: Does not show concern about poor/problematic performance at school, at work, or in other important activities. The individual does not put forth the effort necessary to perform well, even when expectations are clear, and typically blames others for his or her poor performance.
    - *Shallow or deficient affect*: Does not express feelings or show emotions to others, except in ways that seem shallow, insincere, or superficial (e.g., actions contradict the emotion displayed; can turn emotions "on" or "off" quickly) or when emotional expressions are used for gain (e.g., emotions displayed to manipulate or intimidate others).

So, these are the adolescents who are aggressive, cruel, destructive, lack empathy, and a liar. Usually a male who is aged middle to late teens. There is one good thing: the later a kid starts these behaviors, the more hope exists that they won't end up being a sociopath. Make no mistake; a kid with these characteristics is not a nice person. OK, but here's the other side, you've got to assess the severity of the person before you. Just count the symptoms and you'll know how grim the prognosis is for a conduct disordered lad. Most kids grow out of Conduct Disorders. They still may be jerks, but they're not psychiatric jerks.

Antisocial Personality Disorder

Let's start discussing Antisocial Personality Disorder in this lecture but we'll complete it in the session on personality disorders. So, let's just talk about its role in *Disruptive, Impulse Control, and Conduct Disorders*. The DSM puts it in this chapter because it's considered part of the externalizing spectrum: ODD, CD, and finally APD. Don't you just love those acronyms? I don't know whether I talked about the externalizing-internalizing spectrum, but it's an interesting way to look at differences among disorders. Externalizing means outward; internalized means inward. Aggression toward other people and pets (it's hard to tell the difference between them, isn't it. That reminds of the story. . .but not here, this is a serious course). Back to the lecture, depression is an example of an internalizing disorder. Well, you guessed it (I know, I know, I didn't ask you to guess), APD is an example of an externalizing disorder. What else is notable about APD? Boisterous, gregarious, and in their own way, charming. But also impulsive and not terribly interested in rules. We'll talk more about it in the Session on Personality Disorders.

Kleptomania

Kleptomania or compulsive stealing is characterized the familiar tension, action, calmness/relief, and remorse. Unlike other disorders, the diagnostic is more of an addiction versus some desires to control or injury others. In fact, in Kleptomania, the fascination is with activities whose motivation is the "thrill of not getting caught." However, because the entire syndrome is characterized as impulsive behaviors, there is not preplanning or preparation (thus, getting caught is a typical outcome) or assistance from other people. Despite the fascination with theft, it is ego-dystonic to clients. Further, there is acknowledgment that theft is wrong.

Hey, did you know that kleptos start during adolescence? All those sales in department, discount, and high end stores were just too much temptation. I suppose that kleptos can blame wanton sales mongering stores for their disorder. However, kleptos are also depressed and guilty as well. Not surprisingly, there is a neuroprocessing that is part of kleptomania. Its neurochemical pathways can resemble those of addiction pathways. I suppose if you're addicted to Twinkies, you can also be addicted to stealing stuff.

Women are much more likely than men to present with kleptomania. The disorder is relatively rare with variable onset (i.e., it can begin at any time) and there is generally a chronic course. The DSM includes a statement that patients with kleptomania have relatives with Obsessive-Compulsive Disorder.

Kleptomania differs from ordinary acts of theft or shoplifting in its impulsive nature. Only about 4 to 24% of shoplifters are kleptos. Wow, that seems high to me. However, it doesn't surprise me. I think that it's possible for a person to go from being a shoplifter to a kleptos without even knowing that's what's happening. The DSM states that "There is little systematic information on the course of kleptomania, but three typical courses have been described: sporadic with brief episodes and long periods of remission; episodic with protracted periods of stealing and periods of remission; and chronic with some degree of fluctuation. The disorder may continue for years, despite multiple convictions for shoplifting." This suggests that kleptos are a diverse group of people. One of the comorbid disorders is depression. I'd always check out depression and alcohol with kleptos.

Ordinary theft is purposeful and motivated by greed. Other incidents of theft may occur as a result of a dare, typically with adolescents. The DSM-5 criteria (APA, 2013) are listed below.

A. Recurrent failure to resist impulses to steal objects that are not needed for personal use or for their monetary value.
B. Increasing sense of tension immediately before committing the theft.
C. Pleasure, gratification, or relief at the time of committing the theft.
D. The stealing is not committed to express anger or vengeance and is not in response to a delusion or a hallucination.
E. The stealing is not better explained by conduct disorder, a manic episode, or antisocial personality disorder.

Pyromania

I know what you're thinking: you're one of those pyromaniacs . . . relax, if you're like me (a dangerous proposition at best), fires in a fireplace or at a campfire are mesmerizing and a source of relaxation and occasionally mischief when 10 year boys are trying to roast marshmallows. Like most psychiatric disorders, pyromania goes far beyond fireplaces and campfires. People with this disorder are fascinated by, attracted to, and derive pleasure with the consequences of fires. In short, fires are their hobby and I guess in some ways, they stalk fires.

As you might guess, people with this disorder derive no monetary gain but can devote hours and hours in planning an impulsive act. Confusing? Well, sort of. People with pyromania are similar to kleptomania in the tension and pleasure aspects of the disorder but differ in the planning and the lack of remorse. There may be remorse but it's overwhelmed by the sense of pleasure. The lack of remorse is reminiscent of a trait found in sociopathy: the not caring of harm to others or to their property. In short, kleptomania involves the inability to know right (not committing arson) from wrong (injuring others and their property).

So, the mounting tension and pleasure in committing arson is what causes this disorder to be characterized as an Impulse-Control Disorder. The extensive planning and the lack of remorse make it significantly differ from other disorders in this category.

On the one hand, the DSM has notations that this disorder and on the other hand, stays that fire setting is a major problem in children and adolescents with conduct disorder. In fact, over 40% of arsons are committed by children and adolescents. Rare, hmm, that doesn't seem consistent with the argument that arsons are mostly committed by children and adolescents given the incidence of conduct disorders in children and adolescents.

Onset and course are pretty much unknown. It can wax and wane and it can have variable onset. However, it appears that pyromania is much more common among males than females. In terms of differential diagnosis, it's important to differentiate pyromania from garden variety fire setting for profit, acts of terrorism, attention-drawing acts, angry development actions and arsons used to control others. Hmm, I don't know about you but pyromania seems pretty muddled. For me, if it's a significant arson and doesn't seem purposeful, then it's pyromania. In either event, it's more of a crime than a psychiatric disorder.

A. Deliberate and purposeful fire setting on more than one occasion.
B. Tension or affective arousal before the act.
C. Fascination with, interest in, curiosity about, or attraction to fire and its situational contexts (e.g., paraphernalia, uses, consequences).
D. Pleasure, gratification, or relief when setting fires or when witnessing or participating in their aftermath.
E. The fire setting is not done for monetary gain, as an expression of sociopolitical ideology, to conceal criminal activity, to express anger or vengeance, to improve one's living circumstances, in response to a delusion or hallucination, or as a result of impaired judgment (e.g., in major neurocognitive disorder, intellectual disability [intellectual developmental disorder], substance intoxication).
F. The fire setting is not better explained by conduct disorder, a manic episode, or antisocial personality disorder.

You can probably categorize these guys as being impulsive people without a whole lot of skill in regulating their emotions and behavior. They really need to get into Zen or mindfulness or something. Green tea anyone?

SESSION #5
Theme: Personality Disorders

Ever hear about someone being a "borderline" or a "narcissist" or "paranoid?" Well, these might be classified as "character disorders" or more commonly as personality disorders. You've got to really know these disorders; they are pretty central to diagnostic thinking.

Cluster A Personality Disorders: Paranoid, Schizoid and Schizotypal
Cluster B Personality Disorders: Antisocial, Borderline, Histrionic, and Narcissistic
Cluster C Personality Disorders: Dependent, Obsessive-Compulsive and Avoidant

Core concepts for personality disorders include symptoms that begin by early adulthood, symptoms often interfere with normal interpersonal relationships; symptoms produce functional impairment or subjective distress. Some definitions that you'll need in studying personality disorders include entitlement (i.e., an unreasonable expectation, communicated to others, that one is special and deserves special treatment); narcissism (i.e., excessive love or investment in oneself with the corresponding inability to love another or be empathic to their concerns); paranoid (i.e., pervasive suspiciousness with mistrust of others and their motives; constant scanning of the environment to detect injurious behavior from others); flattened affect (i.e., limited emotional range with few highs and lows); ideas of reference (i.e., clients' beliefs that casual incidents or external events have a specific and unusual meaning for themselves)

Criteria that are applicable to most personality disorders include an enduring pattern of inner experience and behavior that deviates markedly from one's cultural expectations that manifest themselves in two or more of the following areas (i.e., cognition, affectivity, interpersonal functioning and impulse control); pattern is inflexible and pervasive across a broad range of personal and social situations; leads to significant impairment in socioeconomic functioning; pattern is stable, of long duration and onset can be traced back to adolescence or early adulthood; symptoms are not better accounted for by another disorder; symptoms are not due to a substance or general medical condition. Differential diagnosis is always going to be difficult for Personality Disorders. Why? They don't normally rely on a process of exclusion; rather it depends on a process of selection (if this doesn't sound familiar, go back to the initial lecture). What makes this discussion more difficult is that DSM-5 really doesn't address this change very well (i.e., process of elimination). Thus, demonstrations of abnormal or maladaptive behavior or modes of thought are necessary. Some behavior may be considered abnormal in any context (i.e., suicidal or exceedingly reckless behavior). Yet, other behaviors are contextually "normal" when limited in intensity or the target of their expression is limited to a few specific situations. Accordingly, the mere presence of abnormal or maladaptive behavior is not sufficient for diagnosis. Three factors must be considered for diagnosis: Pervasiveness is a common and frequent exhibition of the behavior in many different settings; pattern is a set of different behaviors that present a consistent theme; characteristic group of behaviors must appear together and define a syndrome though different clusters of behaviors may express the same core problem (i.e., any combination of the required criteria within a diagnosis); intensity of the behavioral manifestation must be in excess (in terms of strength or duration) to what is normally expressed in society.

Personality disorders were originally thought to represent a state of being during which coping mechanisms were breaking down. "Coping mechanisms breaking down?" What on earth does that mean? Essentially, I suppose that it means that a person has tried to resolve significant problems in ways other than solving them. Because solving them may appear too painful, the thinking was that a person tries other strategies that aren't altogether effective but it reduces the panic-like feelings. If you think that this resembles Obsessive-Compulsive Disorders, you're absolutely right. When compulsive behaviors cause more problems than they cure, then the "coping mechanism has broken down." This idea is pretty much from the 1950s (my generation) and is still used by some clinicians although it is increasingly rare to hear people seriously talking about them.

There are two major steps in making a diagnosis of personality disorder: identify maladaptive or abnormal behaviors; make a clinical judgment of whether the pattern constitutes a recognized syndrome that is sufficiently different from "normal" and sufficiently pervasive and intense to fulfill the criteria. The ten personality disorders are divided into Clusters A, B, and C. Cluster A Personality Disorders are characterized by odd, eccentric, isolative, or suspicious behaviors. There are three personality disorders: Paranoid Personality Disorder, Schizoid Personality Disorder, and Schizotypal Personality Disorder. Paranoid Personality Disorders generally include pervasive distrust and suspiciousness of others; interpret motives as malevolent, requires 4 or more of 7 criteria. The seven criteria include clients suspect that others are exploiting them without sufficient basis for the belief; preoccupied with the loyalty of friends and associates; reluctant to confide in others because of the fear that information will used against them; reads hidden meaning in benign remarks; keeps grudges a long, long time; perceives attacks to self not apparent to others; is suspicious of the fidelity of spouses without justification. Wow! Paranoid Personalities can be a little much. But before we start really saying that they're crazy and so on, let's take a break and think about when such behavior and beliefs might be beneficial. For example, let's say that your client worked as an undercover cop for a long time. Wouldn't you become just a little paranoid? Or let's say that your client is a business that is highly competitive. You don't think that Bill Gates trusted every one of his associates, do you? This is another way of saying that paranoid tendencies are probably normal depending on your context. I'm told that students in the College of Business can be quite paranoid that others are trying to gain advantage at their expense. When there is a lot of competition, then the level of paranoia will increase. Nor am I suggesting that paranoia is always bad. It just makes a person a little more reserved, cold, suspicious, unable to relate, more stubborn than most social workers. On the other hand, paranoia might be a great attribute in soldiers, business people, cops, bureaucrats of all kinds, politicians, movie stars, and so on. Let's put paranoia in perspective: on the far left, we have complete trust and on the far right, we have Paranoid Schizophrenia. Now, what I want you to do is to fill in the Paranoia continuum. We already have complete trust, mild paranoia, paranoid tendencies, and Paranoid Personality Disorders. Later, we'll fill in the remainder of the continuum when we examine some of the delusional and psychotic disorders.

Schizoid Personality Disorder

This doozey (a word from a long time ago) is a pervasive pattern of detachment from others with a restricted range of emotional expression that begins in early adulthood. Four or more of the following seven criteria are apparent in Schizoids: they neither desire nor enjoy close relationships (including being part of their own family although I'm not really sure that this is always such a bad idea?); almost always solitary activities; not much interest, if any, in sex with anyone; anhedonia (i.e., takes pleasure in few, if any, activities); lacks close friends or confidants; appears indifferent to praise or criticism; appears emotionally cold, detached with some flattened affect. A Schizoid just wants to be left alone; that's about it. So, why do people insist on making them into something that they're not? Well, it could be that we're not comfortable in a true loner. After all, a person who is indifferent to praise, criticism, sexual desire, pleasure, relationships, and doesn't appear to care about work probably comes across as abnormal. Maybe they are abnormal to most people, but they could just be a little odd without being truly crazy.

Schizotypal Personality Disorder

Now this one is a pervasive pattern of deficits marked by discomfort with and reduced capacity for close relationships with cognitive or perceptual distortions and eccentricities of behavior that begin by early adulthood and present in many contexts. Clients with this disorder present with five or more of the following symptoms: ideas of reference; odd beliefs or magical thinking that is inconsistent with cultural norms; unusual perceptual experiences; odd thinking and speech; suspiciousness; inappropriate and/or constricted affect; odd, eccentric, or peculiar behavior; lack of close friends; excessive social anxiety that does diminish with familiarity and is associated with paranoid fears. What can I say? Schizotypal Personality is a lot like Schizophrenia Lite. A lot of the criteria will be repeated in Schizophrenia only more so. Sometimes, the only difference will be in their intensity. What is clear is that Schizotypal Personality Disorders will present as odd individuals in their appearance, speech, and beliefs. Chances are that they won't have many friends, either. Interestingly enough, DSM reports that relatively few Schizotypal Personality Disorders go on to develop Schizophrenia. You might also place Schizotypal Personality Disorders on a continuum. DSM-5 mentions Schizotypal Personality Disorders as being on the Schizophrenia spectrum, but not Schizoid. Fair enough, they are the experts. However, I've always thoughts of Schizoid Personality Disorders, then Schizotypal Personality Disorders, and next we go onto the psychotic disorders. The continuum doesn't show course of the disorder as much as it is a guide in making a diagnosis. The underlying dimension of this continuum is the severity of the oddness in appearance, speech, behavior, and beliefs.

Paranoid Personality Disorders

You might be wondering why I placed in the same continuum as the Schizotypals and Schizoids? It is a good question; should I tell you now or later? Alright, I won't tease you any further. Paranoid Personality Disorders are a lot more "organized" than Schizotypal Personality Disorders. Paranoids tend to be more purposeful and able to get more things accomplished

Schizotypals are plagued by their bizarre ideation and so on and it interferes with their ability to organize themselves. But it beats a lot of the other personality disorders because it's "organized." That's a really important idea. When disorders are disorganized, they're all over the place. It's hard to know when they begin and when they end. It's hard to decide how to best understand the symptoms. In part, paranoia is a useful trait in settings when personal or professional dangers are imminent. Personal danger as in a war zone or inner city areas. Professional danger as in business settings where espionage, theft, free market antics and competition are constant threats to survival. I guess that's why CEOs are so strange; their paranoia is both strange and functional. Go figure.

Cluster B is characterized by dramatic, emotional, erratic or impulsive behavior or a reduced capacity for empathy; there are four disorders within this cluster: Antisocial Personality Disorder, Borderline Personality Disorder, Histrionic Personality Disorder, Narcissistic Personality Disorder.

Antisocial Personality Disorder (APD) is characterized by clients who from at least 15 years old demonstrated a pervasive pattern of disregard for and violation of rights of others. This is indicated when clients show three or more of the seven criteria below: breaking the law (should have been arrested even if they got away with the crime); lies a lot, especially for personal gain; impulsive behavior/lack of foresight; lots of fights; reckless disregard for safety of self and/or others; repeated failures to keep a job and pay financial obligations; lack of remorse after having hurt someone. First, we should talk about the similarities and differences between sociopathy and APD. Similarities include that they lack empathy, probably break the law, lie, harm others, and have a high risk threshold. However, sociopaths can be highly organized in their activities so they can hold jobs easily and can appear to be empathic. Remember Ted Bundy? Although sociopaths are willing to fight, they don't necessarily get into fights impulsively. In that sense, APDs are like a sociopath in training. They're also much common in lower socioeconomic groups and in urban setting. If you believe statistics, nearly every inmate in prison is an APD. Prisons also have a disproportionate number of ethnic minority individuals. Do you see the problem here? It's just way too easy to diagnose anyone who's poor, a minority, or lives in the inner city as being an APD. A lot of people who are wealthy, white, and live in the suburbs are also APD. These folks may not appear on police blotters, but they fight using accountants and attorneys, may lie for personal gain, show a lack of remorse after lots of people, refuse to pay financial obligations even if they have lots of money, demonstrate a remarkable lack of foresight and so on. If you think this is far-fetched, think of the executives at Enron and the accountants at Arthur Andersen. Aren't they as much an APD as a common criminal in prison? Personally, I think that they're probably worse because of how many people that they hurt. APDs may also have dysphoric (i.e., depressed) mood and be irritable at times. Now, some last questions to think about: is someone who is a suicide bomber an APD? a sociopath? a religious zealot? or all three? I'm sure that the families of their victims don't care much about the subtle distinctions.

Borderline Personality Disorder (BPD)

Well, this is the big kahuna of personality disorders. It is a pervasive pattern of instability in interpersonal relationships, self-image, affect and control over impulse starting by early

adulthood. Typically, BPD must show 5 or more of the following criteria (APA, 2013): frantic efforts to avoid real or imagined abandonment; pattern of unstable and intense relationships characterized by alternating extremes of idealization and devaluation; identity disturbance (i.e., markedly and persistently unstable self-image);
impulsive behavior in two potentially self-damaging areas (e.g., eating, sex, gambling, substance abuse, reckless driving); recurrent suicidal behavior, gestures, and/or threats, including self-mutilation; affective instability due to reactive mood swings; chronic feelings of emptiness; inappropriate, intense anger or difficulty controlling anger; temporary, stress-related paranoid ideation or severe dissociative symptoms. I've known lots of clinicians who decided to do something easy like skydiving rather than treating BPDs. What makes BPDs so tough to treat? It's the sheer instability of mood and behavior that BPDs have come to represent. One moment a BPD can be your best friend; the next moment, a BPD is threatening your friend. It's that "pattern of unstable and intense relationships" that characterizes the treatment relationship. The reason for the pattern is that BPD fear abandonment more than anything else. Of course, anytime you try to set some boundaries, your BPD client may interpret your behavior as abandonment. And of course if you succeed in setting boundaries, then they may attempt or at least threaten suicide. Between making your life miserable by personal threats to you and your family followed by suicidal threats and gestures, they may also engage in self-destructive behaviors such as those listed above. All in all, these clients burn out clinicians very quickly. Part of the pattern of BPDs is that they will self-destruct just as they're about to succeed. The reason? Their search for someone's concern and caring. Probably, the important thing to remember about BPD besides self-destructive behaviors is the identity disturbances that characterize the clients with this disorder.

Histrionic Personality Disorder

Now this one is a pervasive pattern of excessive emotionality and attention seeking by early adulthood. Clients with this disorder should have five or more of the following symptoms: discomfort when not the center of attention; sexual provocation that is inappropriate (I know, I know, this sounds so fuddy-duddy); rapidly shifting and shallow expression of emotions; consistent use of physical appearance to draw attention self; speech that is excessively impressionistic and lacking in detail; exaggerated display of emotion, theatrics; highly suggestible (i.e., easily influenced by others); considers relationships to be more intimate than they really are. It would be a cheap shot to say that actors all suffer from Histrionic Personality Disorders, but it does give you a sense of the glitz and the sense of what this disorder looks like. Lots of not really believable emotion (think daytime soap opera, not subtle British drama), lots of provocative behavior, especially those of a sexual nature, and use of physical appearance and you've got Histrionic Personality Disorders. Broadway, anyone?

Narcissistic Personality Disorder

It is characterized by a pervasive pattern of grandiosity, need for admiration, and lack of empathy that starts in early adulthood and is seen in multiple contexts. Five or more of the following symptoms must be evident: has a grandiose sense of self-importance; preoccupied with fantasies of unlimited success, power, brilliance, beauty; believes in the specialness of self and that only high-status individuals are able to discern the extent of the specialness; requires lots and lots of admiration; has a sense of entitlement that won't quit (i.e., expectations of privileges and special treatment); takes advantage of others; lacks empathy; envious of others or believes that others are envious of self; demonstrates plenty of arrogance and haughty behavior. Whew! Narcissists have a low threshold for criticism and high sense of entitlement. Kind of like a spoiled kid. Narcissists really want to be part of an "in crowd" but will frequently avoid them for fear of not being accepted. If they are accepted, it's only because others must have begged them frequently to be part of the group. The idealized relationships don't help matters much. Because Narcissists have an unrealistic idea of what actually happens in relationships, they almost consign themselves to be isolates.

Cluster C is characterized by anxious, fearful or perfectionist behavior; there are three disorders within this cluster: *Avoidant Personality Disorder, Dependent Personality Disorder*, and *Obsessive-Compulsive Personality Disorder*.

Avoidant Personality Disorder

These guys (this word is like "dude;" has no real gender implication) have a pervasive pattern of social inhibition, feelings of inadequacy and hypersensitivity to negative evaluation beginning by early adulthood and requires four or more of the seven following criteria. These criteria are an avoidance of occupational activities that require significant interpersonal contact because of a fear of criticism; an unwillingness to get involved with people unless there is a certainty of being liked; restraint within intimate relationships because of a fear of being shamed or criticized; inhibition in new interpersonal situations because of feelings of inadequacy; belief in self as socially inept, personally undesirable, or inferior; reluctant to take personal risks. Hmm, not what you'd call a wild and crazy type of guy. So, what is the difference between this personality disorder and a person who is just shy? It's the severity of the isolation that the person experiences because of the fear of being rejected. These folks don't get involved in many activities, don't have much in the way of relationships and even when they do have relationships, they're "constricted." The sad thing is that these folks look like you and me. Well, maybe more like you than me since you're good looking and socially desirable and I'm not. Wait, maybe I'm suffering from a partial Avoidant Personality Disorder? Just be nice to me.

Dependent Personality Disorder

Now, a person with this diagnosis has a pervasive and excessive need to be taken care of, leading to submissive and clinging behavior and fear of separation that begins by early adulthood and requires five or more of eight criteria (APA, 2013) listed below. They include having difficulty in making decisions with an excessive amount of advice; needs others to assume responsibility for most major life areas; having difficulty in expressing disagreement because of fear of the loss of support; has difficulty in initiating projects because of a lack of self-confidence; goes to excessive length to gain approval to point of doing unpleasant activities; feels discomfort when alone because of unrealistic fears of being unable to care for self; urgently seeks other relationships when close relationship ends; is unrealistically preoccupied with fears of being left to care for self. Think sacrifice for this disorder. Dependent Personalities will go to great lengths to secure approval and to avoid criticism. One corollary is that they may be paralyzed in their socioeconomic functioning because they won't initiate many new projects. One of the difficulties in diagnosing this disorder is differentiating it from people who are nice or from cultural norms that promote cooperation instead of competition. *Dependent Personality Disorder* can only be diagnosed if the fears are unrealistic and if behaviors seem out of keeping with cultural and gender norms. The tough part is separating personal biases from diagnostic decision making.

Obsessive-Compulsive Personality Disorder (OCPD)

Now, we're onto to a personality disorder that describes people who are nice but that really irritate people. They have a pervasive pattern of preoccupation with order, perfection, and control at expense of flexibility, openness, and efficiency beginning by early adulthood and require four or more of eight criteria listed below. The criteria include being so preoccupied with details, rules, lists, order, and organization that their purpose is lost; demonstrates perfectionist behavior at the expense of task completion; is a work-alcoholic; is inflexible and self-righteous about morality, ethics, and values; is a packrat and can't seem to discard even the most worthless items; has difficulty in delegating work unless exacting control over subordinates can be maintained; is a miser and prefers to save money for real or imagined catastrophes; is extraordinarily stubborn and rigid. You might be wondering the difference between this disorder and Obsessive-Compulsive Disorder (OCD)? Great question! This personality disorder is ego-syntonic. Clients generally believe that difficulties that they experience are because of others and not because of their own behaviors. For OCD, the clients know that their difficulties are due to their behavior; they just feel unable to stop them. In addition, OCD requires that clients have true obsessions and compulsions. By comparison, OCPD does not require the presence of true obsessions and compulsions. On a continuum, ornery people start on the far left, followed by OCPD, and then onto OCD. DSM makes a good point that in moderation, OCPD can be highly adaptive to people whose occupations require structure, attention to detail, integrity and so on. Until Enron, accountants were seen as examples of OCPD. The specification about integrity got blurred by the folks at Arthur Andersen.

Remember, one typical method of deciding a personality disorder diagnosis is through prominent symptoms. What is predominant clinical appearance or presentation; can the presentation be identified with one of the three clusters of personality disorders? Within each cluster, identify the most likely diagnosis associated with clinical appearance. For example, within Cluster A, what personality disorder would be most closely associated with odd behavior? social withdrawal? suspicions about everyone? Within Cluster B, what personality disorder would be most closely associated with aggressive, non-conforming behavior? impulsivity and intensity? drama? grandiosity? Within Cluster C, what personality disorders would be most closely associated with fear of criticism? dependency and submission? Rigidity and perfectionism? The most common problems with personality disorder diagnoses are that clients don't quite fulfill the criteria for a specific disorder; criteria are fulfilled but symptoms aren't especially intense or pervasive; or partially fulfills criteria for 2 or more disorders but does not fully satisfy any one disorder. When these situations occur, clinicians must use clinical judgment to decide if the diagnosis is warranted or necessary. Further, no personality disorder takes precedence over another and diagnoses all that are appropriate. I know, I know that's like saying it's a crapshoot.

Diagnostic afterthoughts: a fear of rejection is the key personality trait of Avoidant Personality Disorder; clients with Schizoid Personality Disorder prefer isolation; those with Avoidant Disorder desire close relationships but are fearful of them; schizotypal behavior patterns are generally more bizarre than those found in Schizoid Personality Disorder; sense of entitlement and lack of empathy are hallmarks of Narcissistic Personality Disorder; dependency is common in Borderline, Histrionic, and Dependent Personality Disorders; excessive anger and brief, intense unstable relationships are characteristic of Borderline Personality Disorders.

Now, we'll be discussing treatment issues related to comorbid disorders. Wow, if examining separate disorder wasn't enough, we now look at two (or more) disorders that co-exist. Before I go on any further, let me say that more psychiatric patients have comorbid disorders versus a single disorder. And comorbid disorders pose extraordinary challenges for just about anyone. Interested yet? Well, let's jump in head first; hmm, at least feet first.

Wait, wait, and wait. I just have to talk about co-morbidity before we go on any further. Hmm, as you all know "comorbidity" refers to the presence of two disorders in one person. It's also been called "dual diagnosis." But you've got to call it "comorbid disorder" so you'll sound smart and educated. Back to comorbidity. It's having two disorders at the same time. Typically, comorbid disorders refer to having mental health disorder and a substance abuse disorder simultaneously. The problem is the old chicken and egg (I'll have fried chicken mixed with an egg, ham and bagel breakfast sandwich) problem. Sound unappetizing? It certainly is for clinicians.

Diagnosing comorbid disorders presents a lot of problems in terms of reliability and validity. Remember those terms from your research 101 course? Of course, you do. Reliability is being able to make the same diagnosis twice; validity is making the correct diagnosis. You remember of course all that stuff about making a substance abuse diagnosis; now mix in making a psychiatric disorder as well. As you might guess, the reliability and validity of making a comorbid diagnosis is pretty low. First, the problem is that substance abuse is underreported among psychiatric patients. With some instruments, people have been able to discern the presence of both substance abuse and a psychiatric disorder but haven't been able to make a specific guess as to whether the substance abuse is masking the psychiatric disorder or vice versa.

OK, where do we go from here? Probably the most common comorbid disorder is psychiatric disorders with substance use/abuse. Substance use/abuse can cause psychiatric symptoms and mimic disorders. It doesn't matter whether it's acute or chronic use/abuse; both can cause psychiatric symptoms. As you might guess, the type, duration, and severity of the psychiatric symptoms are related to the type, dose, and chronicity of substance use/abuse. If that weren't bad enough, acute or chronic substance use/abuse can prompt the development, prompt the emergence of the symptoms or make them worse. Hmm, there is the also the problem of self-medication. Patients may use/abuse substances as a means of coping with their symptoms and thus mask the symptoms. It may just look like another bout with substance use/abuse. Of course, trying to go cold turkey after patients are dependent on substances may make also look like a psychiatric disorder. Turn about is fair play: psychiatric symptoms may mimic substance use/abuse.

Even after you've diagnosed the dual diagnoses, one or the other disorder may mask the effectiveness of treatment. For example, if the patient is having a psychotic break, it may look as if they're exhibit bizarre behavior and poor interpersonal skills; this may look as though the clients are simply resisting treatment. Some common examples of comorbid disorders are

    Major Depressive Episode with substances
    Panic Disorders with Alcoholism
    Polydrug use/abuse with Schizophrenia
    Borderline Personality Disorder with episodic polydrug abuse.

And sometimes, your patients can't get a break. I mean, both crazy and depressed?

SESSION #6
Theme: Substance related and addicted disorders

Talking about getting high, stoned, drunk, or whatever you want to call it is about as cultural as it gets. It also is a fascinating area that has attracted clinicians and researchers alike. I've provided links to the National Institute of Health where they have entire books online that you can read about substance use, abuse, and dependency. Make use of them; they're free, and they're for you. So, what do we know about substance use, abuse, and dependency? They mostly inflame people's opinions. They have been the focus of a war (i.e., "war on drugs"--that we've pretty much lost!). They have attracted untold millions of dollars in terms of research and clinical services. Have they affected you or your family? If they have, you can join the ranks of the many, many individuals who have also been adversely affected by legal and illegal substances.

Like most disorders that we'll talk about in this course, it's probably most useful to think substance use, abuse, and dependency as falling on a continuum. DSM-5 has messed up this simple and handy distinction. In DSM-IV TR, there was a continuum, albeit not one that was one-dimensional. If it were one-dimensional, that would make it a "progressive" disorder. In a progressive disorder or disease, death is an inevitable outcome. Thus, in this disorder, it would suggest that dependency would inevitably lead to death. As we'll find later, this is by no means true. There are many commonalities among use, abuse, and dependency and differential diagnoses are by no means an easy task. At the heart of the difficulty is that DSM-IV is primarily oriented toward individual's experiences with substances and the dysfunction that unwise use causes in specific life areas. However, the problem with this definition is that not everyone experiences the same amount or in some cases any dysfunction from their unwise use of substances. Further, because the life areas (i.e., legal, educational, employment, interpersonal, social, medical) are affected by things other than unwise substance use, there is a logical problem in the definition of substance abuse and dependency.

DSM-5 uses a similar but not the same structure with different names and criteria (APA, 2013). It uses substance-induced disorders, substance use disorders, substance-specific intoxication and substance-specific withdrawal disorders. So, generic substance use problem fall on use, abuse, and dependence continuum. *Basically, there are 11 criteria and 11 substances.* There is also the consideration of 11 or 12 disorders that are associated with intoxication and/or withdrawal of the substances. Yowsa! To best use this mishmash of stuff, let's start dumbing it down to make it digestible. OK, DSM-5 breaks up the 11 criteria into four groupings: Impaired control (criteria 1-4), social impairment (5-6), risky use (7-9), and pharmacological criteria (10-11).

Here is the final scoop. There is only substance use disorder but there are intoxication and withdrawal criteria for each substance. Got it? I guess. There is no alcohol use disorder. There is a substance use disorder in which alcohol intoxication and withdrawal are different from caffeine intoxication and withdrawal. There still is only one "use disorder" but the intoxication and withdrawal disorders are presumed to be different for each drug. All intoxication and withdrawal are presumed to be different from a common stem. Got it? It does have some real differences from previous editions of the DSM.

Grouping #1. Impaired control is pretty much an individual thing. A person takes more substances over a longer period of time. Basically, a person needs more and more of the substance. Not rocket science. Second, a person tries to cut down and stop their use ("I can control my use; I can handle) and routinely fails. Third, a person spends an increasing amount of time in getting, using and recovering from the effects of a drug. Finally, a person craves the drug. I mean, really, really wants the stuff to the point where it is the only thing that a person wants . . . and if there was ever a time when they didn't want to use it. DSM-5 also makes the point that there are behavioral patterns that control the use of the drug. All this means is that a person associates drug use with specific times and places. This is the idea that drugs are associated with communities or families. It's hard to stop using when drugs and home are interlinked so tightly.

Grouping #2. Social impairment is straightforward. Think of a social history with all the different areas that need to be assessed. With each category, there is a pattern of failure. First, a person isn't successful at work, home, family and so on. Second, a person uses drugs despite a lot of evidence that it is causing problems in the areas listed above. Finally, a person withdraws from social activities especially those that relate to family and friends. I think that social impairment is measured when a person's entire family and friends has begun to either start or completed in giving up because of drug use.

Grouping #3. Risky behavior is a really important grouping. Basically, a person engages in physically dangerous acts despite knowledge that he or she is endangered. Basically, it means taking dumb risks. It's one thing to take a calculated risk; it's another thing to ignore danger despite knowing about them. I suppose that you can make an argument that kids and teens don't know about the risks of drug use when they use them. On the other hand, they are a lot smarter than you might think. However, there is also the belief that rules and risks apply to other people and not to them. Knowing about risks doesn't mean that kids and teens will actually change their behavior.

Grouping #4. Pharmacological criteria include tolerance and withdrawal. These are the granddaddies of substance use and abuse. As seen above, they are commonly associated with addiction. Further, many people believe that pharmacological criteria are both necessary and sufficient to assess a person as being an addict. As stated earlier (or later) in this lecture, pharmacological criteria are neither necessary nor sufficient to make a DSM-5 diagnosis. That said, always be on the lookout for a person who consistently demonstrate these criteria. Chances are that a diagnosis is lurking around the corner.

Next, intoxication is associated with every psychotic disorder except for sedatives and caffeine in which it is associated with intoxication and withdrawal. Caffeine is not associated with any disorder except for sleep disorder. OCD is not associated with any disorder except with stimulants. Table 1 on p. 482 (APA, 2013) has the remainder of which disorders are associated with which substance. To best remember this stuff, make up rules that reduce the complexity like the three that I created. Now, you create some rules to help you remember this table.

In considering diagnoses, there are six different considerations:

Route of administration, speed of effects, duration, multiple use, lab findings and course.

These are important because they differentiate drugs in terms of the chronicity and danger. Basically, not all drugs are equal: some are much more risky than others. However, that doesn't mean that all substance use and abuse aren't dangerous. I think that all substances are varying degrees of risk. These six considerations will help you understand the degree of risk.

Route of administration and quick onset are associated with the intensity of the "high." Route of administration means how quickly the drug gets into a person's blood stream. DSM-5 lists intravenous, smoking and snorting as three particularly efficient ways that drugs get into a person's blood thus causing a more intense high. So, drugs associated with these routes of administration will result in a steeper decline in effects or withdrawal. There is a hidden danger with slow-acting drugs: a person may use more and more drugs because he or she doesn't experience the high until there is an overdose. This is a common problem with alcohol use and abuse. Duration of effects works the other way. The longer the onset and effects, the longer the time from cessation to withdrawal effects. Marijuana is associated with duration. Although marijuana has a slow onset, its danger is derived from other considerations. I'll provide a teaser and not tell you how or why it's dangerous until we formally talk about it.

Multiple substances and lab findings. Multiple substance use is common and lab findings are needed. Nothing surprising here. The final consideration is course. Drug use can start at any age although mid to late teens are probably when it is expected. Because unwise drug use constitutes risky behavior, it's probably a smart idea to associate drug use with other risky behavior. Basically, when a kid or teen is promiscuous, starting fires, getting into fights and so, drug use is probably lurking around the corner. Don't you like the image of something lurking around the corner? That image is from narrative-based therapy.

Let's talk a little history because what follows is still used a lot in clinical settings.

Talking about narrative-based therapy, addictions (or substance use disorders) is not a terribly useful definition in treatment planning. Further, it is difficult to know how to diagnose couples, families, extended families and so on. The diagnosis of substance use, abuse, and dependency is particularly sensitive to your client's interactions with the people around him/her. Thus, to not systemically include them in the diagnosis presents another logical problem. In short, it pathologizes the identified client and doesn't adequately consider the contributions of the client's collaterals in the difficulties experienced by the identified client.

Before we go any further, let's study some common definitions about drugs. First, there is the common term "addiction." Commonly, it's considered a chronic relapsing condition characterized by compulsive drug-seeking and abuse and by long-lasting chemical changes in the brain. Addiction is the same irrespective of whether the drug is alcohol, amphetamines, cocaine, heroin, marijuana, or nicotine. Every addictive substance induces pleasant states or relieves distress. Continued use of the addictive substance induces adaptive changes in the brain that lead to tolerance, physical dependence, uncontrollable craving and, all too often, relapse. Dependence is at such a point that stopping is very difficult and causes severe physical and mental reactions from withdrawal. The risk of addiction is in part inherited. Genetic factors, for example, account for about 40% of the risk of alcoholism. The genetic factors predisposing to addiction are not yet fully understood.

Let's start with the informal term, "addiction." People, it is slang in these United States. Just slang. Let's see why.

Here are some of the words that were important in addictions.

Chronic
Relapsing
Compulsive
Drug-seeking
Changes in the brain (some temporary, some more permanent)
Causes pleasant states
Relieves stress
Tolerance
Physical Dependency
Uncontrollable craving
Relapse
Severe reactions upon cessation of use
Some genetic contributions

This is also known as the kitchen sink approach. I'll explain some of the implications in a few minutes

With addiction, it includes all the words that are in the other two words. But there isn't much specificity (remember this term from the original lecture?). Without specificity, nearly anything goes. Without sensitivity, nothing fits the description.

Yes, I know that was long ago in the first lecture, but remember this course is supposed to be comprehensive. You've got to remember what was stated (or written) in the first lecture. Addiction has problems with specificity. It's the kitchen sink. It includes everything. But what we don't know is how much of each thing. For example, the definition says that addictions cause pleasant states. Hmm, let's see now, a person is on the street, having been rolled, cold, hungry, and with a couple severely damaged organs. Pleasant state? No, no, no, this is not a normal state; this is not what your in-laws wanted to have done to you. It is really an unpleasant state. So, addictions have unpleasant states as in being cold, hungry and so on. But how much of each type of pleasantness/unpleasantness do you have to have before it is an addiction? And then there's the term "relieves distress." Do you know that many, many studies have disputed that excessive alcohol relieves distress? Maybe, would just say that it's a bad habit that occurs when people are seeking . . . pleasant states. This lack of precision is the same for almost all the other terms. We don't know when, where, how much, who, and even why of each of the difference words as they relate to the word "addiction."

That's why the word addiction is so endemic. There are hundreds of addictions because of its sensitivity (versus specificity); nearly anything can be an addiction. Me, I'm addicted to bad coffee and the DSM. I bet all of you are addicted to all sorts of bad things. No, no, don't tell me all your addictions. Being addicted to sugar doughnuts is not a pleasant thing or is it?

And that's why it's considered slang. There is a kind of imprecision that eventually just makes it a bad name that you call someone when you don't like them. So, it's okay when you're watching Oprah or Dr. Phil but you've got to much more careful when you are seeing clients. Just about all of them will be addicted but that's not saying much. Let's sing the song, "Everyone is addicted in their own way" "How about, Kumbaya, my addiction, kumbaya, o higher power, kumbaya." Addiction is really a serious issue and that's why it deserves something with more oomph to it.

Here's a second term, "disease:" An abnormal condition of the body or mind that causes discomfort or dysfunction; distinct from injury insofar as the latter is usually instantaneously acquired. Alcoholism is a disease that includes the following four symptoms:
- Craving—A strong need, or urge, to drink.
- Loss of control—Not being able to stop drinking once drinking has begun.
- Physical dependence—Withdrawal symptoms, such as nausea, sweating, shakiness, and anxiety after stopping drinking.
- Tolerance—Need to drink greater amounts of alcohol to get "high."

Medical use

Yup, you guessed it: disease, the medical model, everything that is evil in the world; well, maybe not everything, but definitely a medical bad thing.

Here are the terms used in "disease."

Symptoms
Abnormal condition of body or mind
Causes discomfort or dysfunction
Distinct from injury (because injury is acute)
Has four symptoms: Craving, Loss of control, Physical dependence, Tolerance

Well, did you see the differences? According to the different sources (but I didn't really do as thorough a search as I should have), there are subtle differences.

Well, okay, how about the good ol' disease model? Are things like alcoholism a disease? Well, with disease, at least you have the notion that it's an abnormal condition and that it causes dysfunction. You see, there's nothing about those pleasant states in the definition of disease. But most importantly, there are four symptoms that are associated with alcoholism as a disease.

- Craving—A strong need, or urge, to drink.
- Loss of control—Not being able to stop drinking once drinking has begun.
- Physical dependence—Withdrawal symptoms, such as nausea, sweating, shakiness, and anxiety after stopping drinking.
- Tolerance—The need to drink greater amounts of alcohol to get "high."

These are some good ol' terms about which we're comfortable. But let's think some more. Do we need all four for the disease of alcoholism to be present? Okay, maybe, I'm just being picky. How about three of them? Just two, but those two are really, really, really severe. Doesn't that make it a disease? What are the differentials for the alcoholism disease? Are they the same as Alcohol Dependency the psychiatric disorder?

You see, that's why the term, "disease" is problematic. It's a lot like the DSM-IV TR diagnosis of Substance Dependency but is much more relaxed in its definition. But it's probably enough, isn't it? Well, maybe yes, maybe not. With a disease, don't you have a premorbid condition? I mean, the disease just didn't start out when you didn't wash your hands in grade school . . . or did it? The definition leaves the issue of cause somewhat undefined. But at the very end, there's this little stuff about the genetics. Ah, finally, we're at the heart of the disease model. When, you think about it, you've got to have a virus, bacteria, toxins or . . . genetics. In the first three causative agents, something caused the disease. So, presumably, if you washed your hands in grade school, you wouldn't have the disease. On the other hand (maybe you did wash one hand after all), if it's genetic in nature, it's not your fault that you contracted the disease of alcoholism.

And maybe this is the most significant part of disease definition of substance dependency . . . the use of accountability. I mean, the "devil made us drink". . .maybe not the devil, but at least some bad, bad genes. If a person is not responsible for their alcoholism, then it wasn't their fault that they became an alcoholic. So, this definition becomes intriguing because it gets at causal agents or etiology. The other two definitions stay away from this variable.

Well, why would anyone include something about the motivational aspects of alcoholism into the definition? Ah, yes, you guessed correctly. Treatment is formed around that definition. More specifically, a 12-Step program is based on the issue of control of use. If the "disease" is contracted without the volitional control of the client, then there is no fault that can be placed on the alcoholic. The thinking is that alcoholics are guilt-ridden and absolving a person of guilt goes a long way toward alleviating the symptoms. So, the disease concept works with the 12-Steps and with the genetics concept. By the way, I should add that this is a popular concept and is widely advocated by a lot of people, including physicians, psychologists, and social workers.

Here was the DSM-IV TR understanding of being stoned or a lush. Substance dependency: Must have three (or more) of the following, occurring when the alcohol use was at its worst:
1. *Alcohol tolerance*: Either need for markedly increased amounts of alcohol to achieve intoxication, or markedly diminished effect with continued use of the same amount of alcohol.
2. *Alcohol withdrawal symptoms:* Either (a) or (b).

(a) Two (or more) of the following, developing within several hours to a few days of reduction in heavy or prolonged alcohol use:
- sweating or rapid pulse
- increased hand tremor
- insomnia
- nausea or vomiting

- physical agitation
- anxiety
- transient visual, tactile, or auditory hallucinations or illusions
- grand mal seizures

(b) Alcohol is taken to relieve or avoid withdrawal symptoms.
3. Alcohol was often taken in larger amounts or over a longer period than was intended
4. Persistent desire or unsuccessful efforts to cut down or control alcohol use
5. Great deal of time spent in using alcohol, or recovering from hangovers
6. Important social, occupational, or recreational activities given up or reduced because of alcohol use.
7. Alcohol use is continued despite knowledge of having a persistent or recurrent physical or psychological problem that is likely to have been worsened by alcohol (e.g., continued drinking despite knowing that an ulcer was made worse by drinking alcohol)

Yes, all this was from the Big Purple Book in the sky . . . drum roll, please, the DSM.

You know, the old DSM was really an imperfect document. It made all sorts of assumptions and was horribly culture bound. However, it was the best of the bad definitions of alcoholism and other drug users. Why? Let's look at the criteria (APA, 2013). Unlike addictions and disease models, the DSM really tries to find a compromise between competing ideas around drug dependency. Remember, how addictions has a long list of features (i.e., sensitivity) and how disease was narrowly defined by only four symptoms (i.e., specificity)? Drug Dependency in the DSMIV TR was much more colorful. First, there was a very clear continuum: Use, Abuse, and Dependency. This continuum is useful because it includes the possibility that there can be problematic use without it becoming truly serious. The second thing that I like about it, was that it wasn't reductionistic. It provides some definite parameters on what constitutes dependency. It provides criteria that examine the where, when and who of Drug Dependency. This was a welcome relief from the other two definitions. It strikes a balance between being too specific and too sensitive.

The ol' DSM had language around tolerance, withdrawal, and craving. These are hallmark features of drug dependency and are essential. There was language around craving; time spent seeking more drugs, and relapses. By including these features, the DSM really has tried to include the essential parts of the other two definitions. Because the DSM stresses empiricism more so than theoretical development, it avoids the issue of control/motivation/causal agents. It still included some language around genetics, but the focus was much more on objective criteria. That is, in the DSM, alcoholism is a disorder with no effort to examine etiology. And that disorder has a whole lot of criteria.

So, where does that leave us? Well, I think that you can informally talk about addictions, but not apply it to people (i.e., it's okay to apply the term to dogs and infants). The disease model can be applied when being supportive to addicted clients. Finally, the DSM model was the one that you use when you are seeking insurance payment. For research purposes, always use the DSM. Before we go any further, it's important to understand that definitions are always in flux.

Unabridged dictionaries are examined each year to see whether words should be added or deleted. The same thing happens with the DSM or any medical diagnostic system.
The newest wrinkle is that "obesity" is now considered a medical disorder. Wait! Obesity as a disease? Well, there are a couple things to consider. First, medicine gets preoccupied with being able to measure things. Obesity can be measured using all sorts of strategies (e.g., body mass index, waist circumference, waist/hip ratio, skin fold thickness, and various lab measures). Each strategy has pros and cons. On the other hand, the importance may be entirely academic. Whether it is a disease may not matter as much as the health and social consequences of obesity. Does it really matter that it is now a disorder? You decide.

OK, OK, OK, so, what is substance use? It refers to the use of a substance without any apparent indication of discomfort. DSM-5 defines discomfort as lessened social and/or economic functioning. Do you see the problem? In DSM-5, nearly everyone will experience substance use differently and their lessened socioeconomic functioning may be a function of things outside of their substance use. However, it's the definition so let's work with it. Basically, it doesn't matter how much a person is using if there are no diminished socioeconomic functions in the life areas mentioned above (i.e., educational, interpersonal, and so on). That brings up the issue that rich folks can hide substance abuse and dependency more so that poor folks. Rich folks can buy their way out of legal difficulties, can use private rehabilitation facilities (to hide their abuse and dependency) and so on. By contrast, poor folks' problems will show up almost immediately: they'll get arrested, get fired from their jobs (if they have a job), and will be enrolled in public rehabilitation programs and so on. This simply means that you have to be very careful in getting a history when you suspect use, abuse and dependency. The more wealth, the more likely that substance abuse and dependency can be hidden. Perhaps more so than any other psychiatric disorder, the differences between substance use and abuse and dependency are culturally determined. This puts into doubt claims that alcoholics are all alike or follow the same pathway to addiction. Since it's cultural, one would expect that those who are more socially inappropriate will more likely be labeled as addicted. Further, people who are socially skilled will resist the labeling since it classes them with people that are socially repugnant to them.

Fortunately, there are a couple criteria that are useful in differentiating the three subtypes. The most important are our friends: tolerance and withdrawal. Tolerance and Withdrawal effects are notable because they involve a biopsychosocial response to either lessened substance use or increased substance use. From a diagnostic viewpoint, withdrawal and tolerance are crucial indicators; they help differentiate abuse from dependency. The core concept for abuse is that an individual's use results in disruption in their socioeconomic functioning as defined above. Note once again that socioeconomic functioning is the key to whether an individual can be diagnosed with any kind of substance abuse. Perhaps, it is not surprising that a capitalistic society would rely so heavily on socioeconomic disruption as an indicator of psychiatric distress! On the other hand, the poor are once again placed in an unfair position. Current research casts serious doubt on the notion that the mere presence of a drugs results in tolerance or withdrawal. Tolerance means that the bodily reactions become less overt to the same amount of a drug--you can overtly handle more drugs. On the other hand, it means that you need more and more to get the same high. Real bummer in terms of what it can do to your pocketbook, to your body, to your friends, and to your life. Withdrawal means that the body has become accustomed to the presence of a drug and that you feel discomfort when the drug is not present in as high a dosage. Best way to understand this is when someone is having a hangover and asks for a drink to lessen their discomfort. By increasing their blood alcohol level, they are decreasing the withdrawal effects . . . because they have fooled their bodies into thinking that they are not withdrawing from the use of the substance. So, tolerance means that you need more and more and more to get the same effect. Discomfort arises because of the difficulty in getting the substance and your body in adjusting to the sheer quantity of the substance. Withdrawal means that you feel discomfort because there is less of a substance in your body. In either event, your body is trying to accommodate to how much of a substance that you have in your body.

In Dependency, clients also take larger doses than was intended or for longer periods of time. In addition, clients make repeated and unsuccessful efforts to reduce or control their use. As might be expected, a great of effort is expended in securing the increasingly larger amounts of the drug. Socioeconomic disruption and continued use despite the knowledge of the dangers of such use are the final two criteria. So, alright, what's the best way to conceptualize the differences between abuse and dependency? With abuse, you experience distress in your socioeconomic functioning. With dependency, you experience distress in your socioeconomic functioning, possibly experience tolerance, possibly experience withdrawal, and probably experience a pattern of almost involuntary use. I say, "involuntary use" because it's as if you try to stop and can't do so, you try to limit your use and can't do so, and you try to limit how much control the substance has over your life . . . and can't do so. With Substance Dependency, you don't have much control over the substance; it has control over you! Okay, back to the continuum, use means that you use some drug, legal or not. Abuse means that you use some substance and it has adverse effects on your socioeconomic functioning. Dependency means that you don't have effective control over the substance and it has a lot of adverse effects on your socioeconomic functioning.

DSM-5 makes the point that you've got to consider variables like speed of onset and duration of effects in assessing substance use, abuse, and dependency. The reason that these variables are important is because they affect how quickly a person will get "hooked" on a specific drug. Thus, a client may take a lot longer to get "hooked" on marijuana than on cocaine. The speed of onset and the duration of effects make it much likely that a drug like cocaine will adversely affect socioeconomic functioning. Why? Well, mainly because the rush is greater, the descent is greater, and the duration is shorter. The sheer intensity of cocaine will undoubtedly lead people to pursue it. By comparison, marijuana will help a person relax but probably won't give anything close to the same rush and the same descent. So, it's more likely that a person on cocaine will encounter more problems in socioeconomic functioning because their entire focus will be on experiencing the drug effects. It's just that intense. Marijuana however is not necessarily an innocuous drug. Its danger lies in its amotivational effects (e.g., harms academic and employment performance), its adverse effects on motor behaviors (e.g., driving), and interpersonal lethargy. It can well be an insidious drug because it's not as flashy as cocaine but certainly can be harmful.

Think of placing substances on a continuum in terms of their toxicity. For right now, that means biological toxicity. If a person takes enough of any substance, their body won't be able to accommodate it. The body normally acts as a biological detoxification unit. After a person ingests a substance, the body's organs remove vitamins and minerals for use in daily functioning. When body is overloaded with any particular vitamin and mineral, bodily organs begin to experience difficulties in their functioning. The implication is that with increasing levels of toxicity, cultural differences diminish. When the body can no longer metabolize the drug, cultural differences give way to biological consequences. Having stated that toxicity can attenuate the effects of culture, let me finish by saying that problems associated with drug and alcohol use can have different meanings in different groups. In one culture/ethnic/religious group, use of drugs and alcohol are prohibited entirely. Death from such use would be considered a grave issue (note to readers: I didn't see the pun until I was editing this paragraph, but I left it in anyway). In another group, substance use and abuse are daily events and troubles relating to the use may be seen as part of life's miseries. OK, toxicity may kill; may attenuate cultural differences; cultural groups may still define consequences of substance use differently.

Alcoholism

Now, for the specific drugs: the big A of social work. Yes, you guessed it; alcoholism. Or alcohol addiction or alcohol dependency. I'll pretty much use the terms interchangeably although that's really a diagnostic no-no. In the DSM-5, alcohol use disorders is broken up into subcategories. The first subcategory is alcohol intoxication and the second one is alcohol withdrawal. From people who have been around alcoholism a while, this is a strange dichotomy. It sounds like you go from being pleasantly tipsy to having a pharmacological indicator of a lush. It's not as bad as it seem at first blush.

First, it is still a continuum. Withdrawal is worse than Intoxication. Withdrawal has the 11 criteria of which you have to have a couple to be diagnosed as alcohol withdrawal. Remember, intoxication and withdrawal are part of alcohol use disorders. That does imply that intoxication is a disorder. So, the last time that you had one too many glass of wine, you became a walking psychiatric disorder. Even that distinction isn't as idiotic as it might seem. First, it's still a continuum. So, you can look wise and say that "I think that the patient has gone from intoxication to a withdrawal state of an alcohol use disorder." Or has gone from being a chronic drunk to being addicted to alcohol. Alcohol Use Disorders subtype Intoxication is different from intoxication with a small "i." Here are the overall alcohol use disorder criteria (APA, 2013) (as opposed to alcohol intoxication or alcohol withdrawal subcategories) (straight from the DSM-5)

A problematic pattern of alcohol use leading to clinically significant impairment or distress, as manifested by at least two of the following, occurring within a 12-month period:
- Alcohol is often taken in larger amounts or over a longer period than was intended.
- There is a persistent desire or unsuccessful efforts to cut down or control alcohol use.
- A great deal of time is spent in activities necessary to obtain alcohol, use alcohol, or recover from its effects.
- Craving, or a strong desire or urge to use alcohol.
- Recurrent alcohol use resulting in a failure to fulfill major role obligations at work, school, or home.

- Continued alcohol use despite having persistent or recurrent social or interpersonal problems caused or exacerbated by the effects of alcohol.
- Important social, occupational, or recreational activities are given up or reduced because of alcohol use.
- Recurrent alcohol use in situations in which it is physically hazardous.
- Alcohol use is continued despite knowledge of having a persistent or recurrent physical or psychological problem that is likely to have been caused or exacerbated by alcohol.
- Tolerance, as defined by either of the following:
    a. A need for markedly increased amounts of alcohol to achieve intoxication or desired effect.
    b. A markedly diminished effect with continued use of the same amount of alco
    c. to achieve intoxication or desired effect.
    d. A markedly diminished effect with continued use of the same amount of alcohol.
- Withdrawal, as manifested by either of the following:
    a. The characteristic withdrawal syndrome for alcohol (refer to Criteria A and B of the criteria set for alcohol withdrawal).
    b. Alcohol (or a closely related substance, such as a benzodiazepine) is taken to relieve or avoid withdrawal symptoms.

Here is a key in understanding alcohol use disorders: the more criteria that are present in the patient, the more severe the disorder. Remember to break up the 11 criteria into the four subgrouping (i.e., impaired control, social impairment, risky behavior, and pharmacological criteria). The development and course of alcohol use disorders is pretty much what you think. The peak of the alcohol use disorders is in the late teens and early twenties. Withdrawal Disorder may not evident until late 30. Course is variable that follows continual remission and relapse . . . leading to serial crises. This also gives rise to patients who believe that they can "control" their use. If a person can effectively control their use, then he or she should not be given a diagnosis of alcohol withdrawal.

But now that we have wandered onto the topic of alcohol withdrawal, let's think about it for a moment. Alcohol use disorders have those famous 11 criteria. Alcohol intoxication and withdrawal subcategories have different criteria. So, it goes like this. First, you make a decision on whether there is an alcohol use disorder. All you need are two of the criteria over a 12 month period. No problem at all . . . everyone now has an alcohol use disorder. But the second part of the decision making is to try to figure out intoxication or withdrawal. Basically, intoxication requires whatever you'd do if you were nailed for a DUI. That's about it although driving and being in an alcoholic stupor probably isn't good for you or innocent pedestrians. Alcohol withdrawal is much more serious and that's the point. The writers of DSM-5 tried to make a big distinction between the two subcategories. Unfortunately, intoxication is way too sensitive a category since everyone gets the diagnosis of alcohol use disorders and intoxication. Would you like to be saddled with a psychiatric disorder in your medical records?

Here are the criteria (APA, 2013) for *alcohol intoxication*

   A. Recent ingestion of alcohol.
   B. Clinically significant problematic behavioral or psychological changes (e.g., inappropriate sexual or aggressive behavior, mood lability, impaired judgment) that developed during, or shortly after, alcohol ingestion.
   C. One (or more) of the following signs or symptoms developing during, or shortly after, alcohol use:
      1. Slurred speech.
      2. Incoordination.
      3. Unsteady gait.
      4. Nystagmus.
      5. Impairment in attention or memory.
      6. Stupor or coma.
   D. The signs or symptoms are not attributable to another medical condition and are not better explained by another mental disorder, including intoxication with another substance.

Let's consider the prevalence, differentials, comorbidity, and so on. The answer is that it happens a lot in campuses, hard to give differentials and it's comorbid with lots of things. By themselves, not much interesting. However, but also remember that alcohol use with driving is a lethal combination, suicide is heavily correlated with alcohol dependency (whoops, alcohol withdrawal, gotta keep up with the times), it is common in flamboyant displays of aggression (i.e., mean drunks).

Here are the criteria (APA, 2013) for *Alcohol Withdrawal*

   A. Cessation of (or reduction in) alcohol use that has been heavy and prolonged.
   B. Two (or more) of the following, developing within several hours to a few days after the cessation of (or reduction in) alcohol use described in Criterion A:
      1. Autonomic hyperactivity (e.g., sweating or pulse rate greater than 100 bpm).
      2. Increased hand tremor.
      3. Insomnia.
      4. Nausea or vomiting.
      5. Transient visual, tactile, or auditory hallucinations or illusions.
      6. Psychomotor agitation.
      7. Anxiety.
      8. Generalized tonic-clonic seizures.
   C. The signs or symptoms in Criterion B cause clinically significant distress or impairment in social, occupational, or other important areas of functioning.
   D. The signs or symptoms are not attributable to another medical condition and are not better explained by another mental disorder, including intoxication or withdrawal from another substance.

Again, there isn't a lot that is surprising on the prevalence, course and differentials of alcohol withdrawal although it can become part of a neurocognitive disorder (i.e., alcohol-induced dementia). But mostly, on a continuum, alcohol withdrawal begins to move toward psychotic disorders!

The remaining substances: caffeine, cannabis, phencyclidine, other hallucinogens, inhalants, opioids, sedative/hypnotic/anxiolytics, stimulants, and tobacco generally follow the same structure. First, a use disorder, and then a determination on whether it's intoxication or withdrawal. There are some exceptions: phencyclidines don't have withdrawal states, and tobacco doesn't have intoxication. There are of course a whole bunch of "other" and "unspecified" substances. Once you wander into that rose garden, you'll never get out. Anything that has "other," "unspecified" or the ol' NOS is just plain cheating. Anything can weasel out of making a diagnosis that saying "unspecified" this or "other" that. Go for broke. Make a specific diagnosis. You'll probably be wrong, but you won't be a weasel.

Caffeine

Let's go through each substance use disorders. The first one is . . . *coffee*. Did you realize that your friendly Starbucks clerk really was a dealer? Enabled your habit? Caused you a psychiatric disorder? And mostly charged way too much for a cup of coffee? Before you say "yes" to those questions, look carefully at the criteria. Those criteria almost resemble someone who is on some sort of manic episode while watching a reality show. Nervousness, insomnia, rambling flow of thought, GI problems and so on. To have a caffeine intoxication, the person must have 250 mg or about 19 oz of coffee. That's about 4 or 5 cups on any one day. OK, that probably means that a number of you are at a grave risk of having a caffeine use disorder.

Before you check yourself into a psych ward, be sure to examine Criteria C and D. Remember, the stuff must really be causing you a lot of problems. Being flushed or restless just aren't disorders. But it's fun to say that you are intoxicated on Starbucks or your favorite Jolt Cola energy drink.

- A. Recent consumption of caffeine (typically a high dose well in excess of 250 mg).
- B. Five (or more) of the following signs or symptoms developing during, or shortly after, caffeine use:
    - Restlessness.
    - Nervousness.
    - Excitement.
    - Insomnia.
    - Flushed face.
    - Diuresis.
    - Gastrointestinal disturbance.
    - Muscle twitching.
    - Rambling flow of thought and speech.
    - Tachycardia or cardiac arrhythmia.

- Periods of inexhaustibility.
- Psychomotor agitation.
C. The signs or symptoms in Criterion B cause clinically significant distress or impairment in social, occupational, or other important areas of functioning.
D. The signs or symptoms are not attributable to another medical condition and are not better explained by another mental disorder, including intoxication with another substance.

Nothing about prevalence or course really is worthy of much discussion. Just keep in mind that older people are more sensitive to coffee and it may cause sleep impairment (i.e., lower quality sleep). It may be bad for kids.

However, I thought that caffeine intoxication sounded finny so I went to Wikipedia and read up on it. Caffeine binds to adenosine receptors. Normally, adenosine causes drowsiness . . . but remember the caffeine binds to the adenosine receptors so they get the real thing floating in your blood stream. Caffeine causes your blood vessels to constrict causes increased neuron firing, releases hormones that activate the adrenal glands and results in a "fight or flight" reaction. So, pupils dilate, airways open up, heart beats faster, muscles tighten up and so on.

At this point, let's lower our voice and say quietly, "no, it's gone way beyond intoxication, it's caffeine withdrawal. (Gasps from family members). We will do what we can but caffeine withdrawal is a serious disorder. A new 28-day rehab center has been built to help those suffering from it." Serious stuff, huh? It's either serious or a bad soap opera. Does that make your friendly Starbucks barista an evil pusher in disguise?

A. Prolonged daily use of caffeine.
B. Abrupt cessation of or reduction in caffeine use, followed within 24 hours by three (or more) of the following signs or symptoms:
 1. Headache.
 2. Marked fatigue or drowsiness.
 3. Dysphoric mood, depressed mood, or irritability.
 4. Difficulty concentrating.
 5. Flu-like symptoms (nausea, vomiting, or muscle pain/stiffness).
C. The signs or symptoms in Criterion B cause clinically significant distress or impairment in social, occupational, or other important areas of functioning.
D. The signs or symptoms are not associated with the physiological effects of another medical condition (e.g., migraine, viral illness) and are not better explained by another mental disorder, including intoxication or withdrawal from another substance.

Again, the withdrawal prevalence, course and so aren't remarkable. Just remember that too many bottles of energy drink can make a person really, really twitchy

Cannabis

Let's move onto *Weed*. "Reefer Madness" (great cult movie among drunken undergrads). It also represents a changing opinion of marijuana. In the fifties, it was considered terrible; in the sixties and seventies, it wasn't considered all that serious; today, there is concern because it highly associated with vulnerable teens' amotivational syndrome and a possible gateway to schizophrenia or other severe disorders. It's highly correlated with diminished executive functioning.

Cannabis use disorder pretty much means that a person must have evidence of a couple of the 11 criteria (i.e., remember those four subgroupings). That means that a person can be diagnosed as having a cannabis use disorder without too many problems. Other ways to describe it as "having a low clinical threshold of a diagnosis" or "highly sensitive measure of impairment." Basically, what you have to worry about is that it's really too easy to say that a person has a cannabis use disorder. So, go easy on saying that a person has a cannabis use disorder. Make sure that the person really is encountering problems before giving him or her (although mostly males) a diagnosis of a cannabis use disorder. As in all these substance use disorders, the specifiers are "early" or "late" remission. Early remission is defined as having 3 to 12 months of no symptoms. Late remissions are 12 or more months. Severity is defined as mild (2-3 symptoms), moderate (4-5), or severe (6 or more). The features, prevalence and course aren't remarkable. It's probably the most widely used drug (although alcohol use is more common, it's just not a disorder). Kids, pregnant ladies, and old folks shouldn't use it. Besides, it's illegal and that causes a socioemotional problem when a client is nabbed by the cops.

Here are the criteria (APA, 2013) for cannabis intoxication. Once again, you may be seeing a pattern. Recent use and not attributable to other medical and mental disorders.is a criterion across all substances. Blood shot eyes, munchies, dry mouth, and racing heart rate are also seen across people who have either used too much or are using for the first time.

A. Recent use of cannabis.
B. Clinically significant problematic behavioral or psychological changes (e.g., impaired motor coordination, euphoria, anxiety, sensation of slowed time, impaired judgment, social withdrawal) that developed during, or shortly after, cannabis use.
C. Two (or more) of the following signs or symptoms developing within 2 hours of cannabis use:
    1. Conjunctival injection.
    2. Increased appetite.
    3. Dry mouth.
    4. Tachycardia.
D. The signs or symptoms are not attributable to another medical condition and are not better explained by another mental disorder, including intoxication with another substance.

Onto *Cannabis Withdrawal*

A. Cessation of cannabis use that has been heavy and prolonged (i.e., usually daily or almost daily use over a period of at least a few months).

B. Three (or more) of the following signs and symptoms develop within approximately 1 week after Criterion A:
   1. Irritability, anger, or aggression.
   2. Nervousness or anxiety.
   3. Sleep difficulty (e.g., insomnia, disturbing dreams).
   4. Decreased appetite or weight loss.
   5. Restlessness.
   6. Depressed mood.
   7. At least one of the following physical symptoms causing significant discomfort: abdominal pain, shakiness/tremors, sweating, fever, chills, or headache.
C. The signs or symptoms in Criterion B cause clinically significant distress or impairment in social, occupational, or other important areas of functioning.
D. The signs or symptoms are not attributable to another medical condition and are not better explained by another mental disorder, including intoxication or withdrawal from another substance.

Comparing Intoxication to Withdrawal shows that there is more of an emotional "hit" such as weight loss, depressed mood and so on. Basically, it sounds like a person is "sad" about no longer using weed. I guess when a person gets used to feeling mellow, it's hard to live without the sensation. Not really surprising, is it? The key is that the use of weed has become an integral part of the person's life. It's going back to the impaired control and social problems subgroups of the use disorders. Course, prevalence, and features are pretty much what you'd expect. Starts with teens, gets worse for a lot of people, and gets better for a lot of people. The one notable fact is that heavy use is associated with conduct disorders and antisocial personality disorders. Yeah, heavy use of weed is associated with badass-kind of guys.

Phencyclidine

Next are the *Phencyclidine Use Disorders*. They are a type of hallucinogen-related disorders. It is among other hallucinogen that includes LSD, MDMA (i.e., Ecstasy), psilocybin and other hallucinogens. Some of the *Diagnostic Features*: feelings of dissociation, vulnerable person may experience psychotic episode, extended time until drug is completely metabolized. Interesting sidenote: DSM does not include phencyclidine withdrawal. PCP use ('angel dust") is relatively rare. Like many drugs, PCP is a young males' drug. It is also associated with uncontrolled aggression that leads to injuries. Heavy use may result in memory loss. May include seizures, dystonia, and catalepsy.

Hallucinogens are usually taken orally although other forms have been reported. One feature is that they have a long half-life and recovery may take hours and even days. Before we can feel assured that everyone will dissociate a long time, recovery from other hallucinogens is relatively rapid. Cross-tolerance is also possible (using one drug leads to tolerance in another drug. Bummer).

Here as the criteria (APA, 2013) for phencyclidine intoxication

A. Recent use of phencyclidine (or a pharmacologically similar substance).
B. Clinically significant problematic behavioral changes (e.g., belligerence, assaultiveness, impulsiveness, unpredictability, psychomotor agitation, impaired judgment) that developed during, or shortly after, phencyclidine use.
C. Within 1 hour, two (or more) of the following signs or symptoms:

Note: When the drug is smoked, "snorted," or used intravenously, the onset may be particularly rapid.

1. Vertical or horizontal nystagmus.
2. Hypertension or tachycardia.
3. Numbness or diminished responsiveness to pain.
4. Ataxia.
5. Dysarthria.
6. Muscle rigidity.
7. Seizures or coma.
8. Hyperacusis.

D. The signs or symptoms are not attributable to another medical condition and are not better explained by another mental disorder, including intoxication with another substance.

A special class of Hallucinogen disorders is the Hallucinogen Persisting Perception Disorder. This is important because it represents the "flashbacks" that occur when a person is sober (i.e., not under the influence). Because the visual perception experiences can be disturbing to people, it is probably a good idea to have medical reasons for these perceptual experiences to be ruled out.

Inhalant Use Disorders

Probably not surprising that 10% of kids have sniffed glue (or other volatile substances) at least once although few progress to intoxication. It's not a rite of passage but it's not surprising that a patient with other problems has inhaled inhalants. Inhalants are comprised of a wide array of substances. I googled inhalants and quickly four or five common inhalants: volatile solvents (i.e., paint thinners, dry-cleaner fluids), aerosols (deodorant sprays, vegetable oil sprays), gases (i.e., butane lighter fluids, propane tanks), nitrites (e.g., amyl nitrites).

Intoxication
A. Recent intended or unintended short-term, high-dose exposure to inhalant substances, including volatile hydrocarbons such as toluene or gasoline.
B. Clinically significant problematic behavioral or psychological changes (e.g., belligerence, assaultiveness, apathy, impaired judgment) that developed during, or shortly after, exposure to inhalants.
C. Two (or more) of the following signs or symptoms developing during, or shortly after, inhalant use or exposure:
- Dizziness.
- Nystagmus.
- Incoordination.

- Slurred speech.
- Unsteady gait.
- Lethargy.
- Depressed reflexes.
- Psychomotor retardation.
- Tremor.
- Generalized muscle weakness.
- Blurred vision or diplopia.
- Stupor or coma.
- Euphoria

B. The signs or symptoms are not attributable to another medical condition and are not better explained by another mental disorder, including intoxication with another substance.

I don't know about you but a lot of these symptoms look those of alcohol and every other drug that is a depressant. Differential diagnoses can become a challenge. However, there is usually a rash around the nose where the solvents have irritated the skin.

Opioid Use Disorder

Just as caffeine use disorders are hard to take too seriously, opioid use disorders must be taken just the opposite. This lecture will not do justice to the multi-faceted dilemma that is posed by opioid use disorders. With that caveat, let's delve into opioid use disorders. Here are some opioids:

Natural opiates:
  Codeine
  Morphine

Semi-Synthetic opioids:

  Hydrocodone
  Oxycodone
  Heroin
  Hydromorphone
  Oxymorphone
  Buprenorphine

Synthetic opioids:

  Meperidine
  Fentanyl
  Methadone

Yes, it reads like a villains' lineup of drugs. However, not all these drugs are necessarily problematic. For example, morphine is used in end of life when people are in excruciating pain. It'd be hard to say that morphine when so used is a problem. Further, methadone is a common drug to "replace" heroin. That said, opioid use disorders are characterized by compulsive and prolonged self-administration of opioids. Even though opioids are commonly used to control pain, they are also highly addictive. Once on the merry go round of use and abstinence, the four subgroupings among the 11 criteria are acutely visible (do you remember what the subgroupings are?).

As you might guess, onset is around late teens and early twenties. The course is chronic although there are periods of abstinence. The DSM makes an observation that Vietnam veterans who returned home addicted to opioids almost completely returned to abstinence. The overwhelming return to abstinence provides ample prognostic evidence that recovery is possible. In fact, the prevalence data show that there is an inverse relationship between age and opioid use disorder. This is sometimes known as "maturing" out of the disorder. I guess that you can teach an old dog some new tricks, eh? As you might guess, opioid use is not just for the bad guys. Opioid use is an equal opportunity addiction. Well, it's not equally prevalent among all classes of people, but no one is immune from the threat of becoming dependent on it. Many more male type of people use it than their female counterparts. In other words, it's for boys and not for girls. 3:1 for heroin and 1.5:1 for the other opioids. Ethnicity has Native Americans overrepresented and African Americans underrepresented and with every other group about average. Here's a really interesting fact: young poor folks and wealthy old people get more dependent than other groups. The DSM speculates that it's all about availability.

Suicide risk should always be considered. What makes it tricky is that addicts will use increasing amounts and will accidently overdose. On the other hand, some addicts just flat out try to kill themselves with opioids. You've got to differentiate between the two profiles using a suicide assessment protocol.

You've probably seen movies where there are dramatic moments and sclerosed veins (i.e., tracks), dry mouth and nose, constipation, diminished eyesight, subcutaneous injections (i.e., skin popping), tuberculosis and HIV and Hepatitis C infections become common. In fact, 90% of people who inject opioids contract Hepatitis C infections. As you might guess, opioid use is comorbid with depression and persistent depressive disorder (dysthymia).

Opioid Intoxication, the DSM lists its criteria (APA, 2013) as:

A. Recent use of an opioid.
B. Clinically significant problematic behavioral or psychological changes (e.g., initial euphoria followed by apathy, dysphoria, psychomotor agitation or retardation, impaired judgment) that developed during, or shortly after, opioid use.
C. Pupillary constriction (or pupillary dilation due to anoxia from severe overdose) and one (or more) of the following signs or symptoms developing during, or shortly after, opioid use:
    1. Drowsiness or coma.

    2. Slurred speech.
    3. Impairment in attention or memory.
  D. The signs or symptoms are not attributable to another medical condition and are not better explained by another mental disorder, including intoxication with another substance.

Specify if:
- *With perceptual disturbances:* This specifier may be noted in the rare instance in which hallucinations with intact reality testing or auditory, visual, or tactile illusions occur in the absence of a delirium.

Opioid Withdrawal

Pretty much the same as Opioid Intoxication however the former is clearly more severe than Withdrawal. The criteria specifies several weeks in duration, pervasive physiological reactions and the normal socioemotional consequences.

  A. Presence of either of the following:
    1. Cessation of (or reduction in) opioid use that has been heavy and prolonged (i.e., several weeks or longer).
    2. Administration of an opioid antagonist after a period of opioid use.
  B. Three (or more) of the following developing within minutes to several days after Criterion A:
    1. Dysphoric mood.
    2. Nausea or vomiting.
    3. Muscle aches.
    4. Lacrimation or rhinorrhea.
    5. Pupillary dilation, piloerection, or sweating.
    6. Diarrhea.
    7. Yawning.
    8. Fever.
    9. Insomnia.
  C. The signs or symptoms in Criterion B cause clinically significant distress or impairment in social, occupational, or other important areas of functioning.
  D. The signs or symptoms are not attributable to another medical condition and are not better explained by another mental disorder, including intoxication or withdrawal from another substance.

Sedative-, Hypnotic-, or Anxiolytic-Related Disorders

This category of substances is primarily focused on reducing anxiety. They are also very addictive. The DSM includes benzodiazepines, benzodiazepine-like drugs (e.g., zolpidem, zaleplon), carbamates (e.g., glutethimide, meprobamate), barbiturates (e.g., secobarbital), and barbiturate-like hypnotics (e.g., glutethimide, methaqualone). This class of substances includes all prescription sleeping medications and almost all prescription antianxiety medications. Nonbenzodiazepine antianxiety agents (e.g., buspirone, gepirone) are not included in this class because they do not appear to be associated with significant misuse.

Craving is a common feature of this category of drugs. But it is also used to come down from amphetamines. The basic idea is that a person is trying to get the right mixture of uppers and downers. When a person is feeling jittery from taking too much or from detoxing, he or she may take benzodiazepines. However, there's a real danger here. Because tolerance to these drugs develops quickly, people will take increasing amounts of them. However, the brain stem doesn't develop the same tolerance. In other words, the brain can't handle the increasing amounts of drugs that are being used to achieve some effect. Because they are a depressant, taking a lot of them may lead to suicidal ideation and attempts. Bummer.

As usual, prevalence is greatest with young people in their twenties and least with old people. Not surprisingly, people who seek novelty or are impulsive are most likely to use this class of drugs. For once, women are more likely than men to be users. I was getting a complex and was thinking that only men are vulnerable to drugs. Nope. Makes me feel a whole lot better now.

S, H, or A Intoxication (l was getting tired of writing out the entire class of drugs)

A. Recent use of a sedative, hypnotic, or anxiolytic.
B. Clinically significant maladaptive behavioral or psychological changes (e.g., inappropriate sexual or aggressive behavior, mood lability, impaired judgment) that developed during, or shortly after, sedative, hypnotic, or anxiolytic use.
C. One (or more) of the following signs or symptoms developing during, or shortly after, sedative, hypnotic, or anxiolytic use:
    1. Slurred speech.
    2. Incoordination.
    3. Unsteady gait.
    4. Nystagmus.
    5. Impairment in cognition (e.g., attention, memory).
    6. Stupor or coma.
D. The signs or symptoms are not attributable to another medical condition and are not better explained by another mental disorder, including intoxication with another substance.

If you look at the criteria (APA, 2013), you'll notice that they look a lot like other depressants, most notably alcohol. The only difference? AOB (i.e., alcohol on breath).

S, H, or A Withdrawal

OK, as you might guess, these lists of criteria are going to look a lot more severe. Basically, intoxication just consists of some acute physiological symptoms that cause some problems. That's about it. SHA Withdrawal is another ballgame. Intoxication results in unsteady gait; by comparison, Withdrawal results in "hallucinations." Or, for example, Intoxication results memory problems while Withdrawal is associated with grand mal seizures. Make no mistake: Withdrawal only occurs if the person is already dependent on the drug.

A. Cessation of (or reduction in) sedative, hypnotic, or anxiolytic use that has been prolonged.
B. Two (or more) of the following, developing within several hours to a few days after the cessation of (or reduction in) sedative, hypnotic, or anxiolytic use described in Criterion A:
    1. Autonomic hyperactivity (e.g., sweating or pulse rate greater than 100 bpm).
    2. Hand tremor.
    3. Insomnia.
    4. Nausea or vomiting.
    5. Transient visual, tactile, or auditory hallucinations or illusions.
    6. Psychomotor agitation.
    7. Anxiety.
    8. Grand mal seizures.
C. The signs or symptoms in Criterion B cause clinically significant distress or impairment in social, occupational, or other important areas of functioning.
D. The signs or symptoms are not attributable to another medical condition and are not better explained by another mental disorder, including intoxication or withdrawal from another substance.

Specify if:
- *With perceptual disturbances:* This specifier may be noted when hallucinations with intact reality testing or auditory, visual, or tactile illusions occur in the absence of a delirium.

Stimulant Use Disorder

Stimulants (e.g., amphetamines, amphetamine-like drugs, cocaine) include a broad array of drugs that augment the level of norepinephrine and dopamine. They include drugs that are commonly used as treatment for many medical disorders. They also include powerful psychoactive recreational drugs. They include other drugs that have the same effects but are completely different such methyphenidate (e.g., Ritalin). All stimulants, legal or illegal, are used medically or recreationally. To make things more difficult, they are used for many disorders such as counteracting lethargy and fatigue throughout the day, reduce sleepiness, treat narcolepsy, decrease appetite, promote weight loss (e.g., treat obesity), improve concentration, and treat attentional disorders (e.g., treat ADHD).

They have different forms of administration that and different levels of purity. They are taken as pills, "snorted" as powder through nostrils, and injected intravenously. OK, got enough?

They have a high potential for tolerance and withdrawal effects. Taken in excess, they are commonly associated with multiple medical consequences including stroke, heart attacks, hypersomnia, and depression. OK, I get it: you're tired, you use it; you're obese, you use it; you're studying a lot, you use it. But it's also used because it results in a feeling of well-being, confidence, and euphoria. But then again, long term or excessive use results in chaotic behavior, social isolation, aggressive behavior, sexual dysfunction, and seizures (how's that for good DSM language?). And there is of course, the problem that the effects of intoxication are the opposite of those in withdrawal. I look at it as a big uphill spike and an equally steep crash. They also are associated with hallucinations and paranoid ideation. In terms of the big picture, think manic episodes in terms of risky behaviors.

It's equally prevalent in men and women older than 17; before that age, there is a 3:1 ratio (i.e., 12-17 years). Men inject it 3:1 more than women, whites and African-Americans use it about the same and everyone else not much as all. But here is the really startling number: about a third of college student use prescription stimulants of one sort or another. And as you might guess, it's used a lot with kids for ADHD and obesity. But in general, it's an equal opportunity danger to class, gender, and culture. All in all, stimulants are a really badass category of drugs.

Alright, here are the criteria (APA, 2013) for stimulant intoxication. Like I said above, these symptoms will be a lot like those that you'll see with clients who are having a manic episode only their reactions will be exaggerated. Read the DSM to get the full range of symptoms under "Stimulation Intoxication. As I was reading through the list, I got a sense of the charisma that a person might show or experience.

A. Recent use of an amphetamine-type substance, cocaine, or other stimulant.
B. Clinically significant problematic behavioral or psychological changes (e.g., euphoria or affective blunting; changes in sociability; hypervigilance; interpersonal sensitivity; anxiety, tension, or anger; stereotyped behaviors; impaired judgment) that developed during, or shortly after, use of a stimulant.
C. Two (or more) of the following signs or symptoms, developing during, or shortly after, stimulant use:
    1. Tachycardia or bradycardia.
    2. Pupillary dilation.
    3. Elevated or lowered blood pressure.
    4. Perspiration or chills.
    5. Nausea or vomiting.
    6. Evidence of weight loss.
    7. Psychomotor agitation or retardation.
    8. Muscular weakness, respiratory depression, chest pain, or cardiac arrhythmias.
    9. Confusion, seizures, dyskinesia, dystonia, or coma.
D. The signs or symptoms are not attributable to another medical condition and are not better explained by another mental disorder, including intoxication with another substance.

Specify the specific intoxicant (i.e., amphetamine-type substance, cocaine, or other stimulant)

When you look at the criteria for Stimulant Withdrawal, they don't look all that dissimilar from Stimulant Intoxication. Just remember, that Withdrawal is the downward crash while Intoxication is the upward spiral. The criteria don't mention it but be alert for suicidal ideation or attempts during acute withdrawal.

A. Cessation of (or reduction in) prolonged amphetamine-type substance, cocaine, or other stimulant use.
B. Dysphoric mood and two (or more) of the following physiological changes, developing within a few hours to several days after Criterion A:
    1. Fatigue.
    2. Vivid, unpleasant dreams.
    3. Insomnia or hypersomnia.
    4. Increased appetite.
    5. Psychomotor retardation or agitation.
C. The signs or symptoms in Criterion B cause clinically significant distress or impairment in social, occupational, or other important areas of functioning.
D. The signs or symptoms are not attributable to another medical condition and are not better explained by another mental disorder, including intoxication or withdrawal from another substance.

Specify the specific substance that causes the withdrawal syndrome (i.e., amphetamine-type substance, cocaine, or other stimulant).

Tobacco Use Disorder

After reading and writing about stimulants, I felt tired so I went out and had a cigarette. Well, actually, that was a lie because I don't smoke. I smoked a half-cigarette when I was 11 or 12 (okay, it was a long time ago so I don't remember the date) but I didn't inhale. That made it okay, right? President Clinton once made that statement of using marijuana and said that he never smoked it again. Me and Bill.

About 30% of people smoke cigarettes and of those about 15% will experience increasingly severe medical consequences. Cancer of all sorts is the most common medical consequences of smoking cigarettes. Few questions are asked more frequently than "Do you now or in the past smoke cigarettes?" It's because it is a killer.

Nicotine generally creates a feeling of well-being and is a mild stimulant. Many symptoms of stimulant are simulated when smoking. By the way, nicotine withdrawal is a real bear and one common symptom is craving for sweets. It is ironic that cigarette use may promote weight loss, but cravings during withdrawal will promote weight gain. The DSM has all the pertinent information so there's no reason to go through it here. Key facts: cigarettes are stimulants, are highly addictive, and are medically catastrophic.

OK, this has been about 25 pages of stuff about substance use. To summarize:

Most drugs can be categorized as "uppers," "downers" and "other." The last category includes hallucinogens, inhalants, sedatives and a couple others. But the main villains are uppers and downers. They pretty much are the opposite of each other. Uppers and downers are really medically and psychologically addictive. Downers are associated with depression; uppers are associated with manic behaviors. Always assess for them before making psychiatric diagnoses. 4hat's about it.

I would be remiss if I didn't talk a little bit about a family systems understanding of drug abuse and dependency. OK, until now, the discussion has pretty much concentrated on the individual's experience of substance use, abuse, and dependency. But as I mentioned earlier, the real action occurs when there are substance using systems. By "substance using and abusing systems," I'm referring to collaterals around someone who is using and abusing substances. There is a rich and controversial on this topic. I can't do it justice here, but I'll give you a beginning presentation.

I'm drawing a lot of my stuff from Gregory Bateson's understanding of cybernetics and from 12-Step groups. Let's start with how substances affect one person. Eventually, unwise substance use will adversely affect a person. With these adverse effects, a person's performance in society will be adversely affected. When a person can't do as well in their ordinary tasks, what happens? If that person has loving collaterals, then they will help the using and abusing person. That is, they will make up for that person's decreased functioning. Out of a desire to care and support a loved person in need, they will take over part of the functioning that defines the user/abuser. Some call this "enabling." If the user/abuser have people who love him or her, then

>One person's use leads to others' accommodation.

But that's not all. Remember, people are wonderfully flexible; they will try to adapt to their context, no matter how hostile. So, people accommodating the frailties of a loved one aren't cause for newspaper headlines. The question does arise, however, as to how much can people accommodate a user/abuser's unwise use of substances. They key is that

>Everyone adapts to some extent; not a matter <u>if</u>, only a matter of <u>how much.</u>

>Thus, more use, more accommodation

So, why is this important? Let's consider, usually accommodation has resulted from the necessity of making a lifestyle change. How much accommodation depends on how significant the change in lifestyle? When people accustomed to a "perfect household" (i.e., two cars, white picket fence, 2.4 kids, a cat and two dogs) have their lifestyle changed (cars broken down, picket fence half gone, kids are runaways, and many cats and dogs abound), there will be some repercussions. People just don't like their comfortable life being completely disrupted. So, there is a balance between what love will make collaterals do and how much sacrifice is entailed by their love. How much sacrifice is too much sacrifice? This is the sad story that we've all seen played out in books, movies and in our lives. Accommodation in this discussion may be equated with sacrifice.

Before we come to the conclusion that use and abuse will inevitably result in families breaking down, let's consider further. Stable families have moderate use, moderate accommodation. Why is this so? Many stable families can have moderate use because it is not likely to cause a major change in their lifestyle. What does stability mean in this context? It means that unwise substance use/abuse can be masked by others' care and resources. Thus, a father who is unable to mow the lawn because of a hangover may compel his daughter to do so. OK, not a big deal because daughter is dutiful and doesn't mind helping out the old man. Accommodation is a small price to pay when families are able to help out each other. The family is stable and has enough loving bonds that will endure these gentle buffets. What happens when the buffets become less gentle? Stability is lessened, lifestyle changes, and love is tested to the max.

When love is tested to the max, when families can no longer accommodate the unwise substance use of any particular member and the family unit begins the slow process of disintegration. When individuals use too much, their body dies; when a family member uses too much, their family breaks apart. Unstable families may need extreme crisis for a family member to "hit bottom." Hitting bottom means that options are limited and that a lifestyle change for everyone is inevitable. Life or death options. Families who are not in a loving relationship are more likely to "hit bottom" because the nurturing relationship may accommodate lifestyle changes and mask the consequences arising from immoderate use. Crisis is desirable in alcoholic family systems because little else may persuade the drug-dependent person that there are no other options.

1. Hitting bottom is like heartworm treatment. Anyone know about heartworm treatment? Kill or cure.
2. The very crisis that may persuade a drug dependent person to abstain from drugs may cause the other spouse to give up hope.
3. Humberto Maturana calls this the "passion for living together". When it's gone, it's hard for a family to have any reason for living together. There's simply no reason to accommodate the other person.

When families become accustomed to substance abusers, a significant change may cause the family to break apart.

1. People develop a whole lifestyle that includes drug use; without drug use, their patterns of interaction are no longer recognizable.
2. People may truly desire to stay together, but a relationship that was centered on one person's drug use will lose meaning when the drug use ceases.
3. For couples, marriages of former drug users become highly stressed: they have the rationale for staying together.
4. To stay together, they have to develop a new marital contract--perhaps one without drug use; this frequently means that each person will have to adopt new roles and new behaviors. Frequently, this task is beyond people who have few resources and a history of failure.
5. However, the courtship is muddied by memories of the past. Past disappointments and failures come back to haunt current attempts to revive the relationship.
6. For families, the key is in their children.
   a. Sometimes, the presence of children will act to keep the family together at all costs.
   b. Sometimes, the presence of children will create enough emotional and financial crises that the family will not be able to stay together.
7. Although it's true that alcoholic parents are a risk, it is not clear at all that children of alcoholics are permanently scarred by their experiences. Children are a lot more resilient than many people might give them credit. Interestingly, the experiences of children around key holidays may make a lasting impression that will lead to later problems.
8. If families become too chaotic because of substance abuse, then social services begins to

play a role. The role played by social services can be seen as example of triangles. The triangles created by substance abuse is replicated by unwise intervention by social services

9. Remember, you represent a triangle. Control is always the issue in triangles. Do you really want the burden of having people give up a lifestyle? Do you know enough to be sure of yourself? Families need to trust you before they're willing to give up a lifestyle. Understand their ambivalence; respect it; admire it and remain humbled by the daily courage that it takes to make a decision and act on it.

10. It all depends on the readiness of the family to make a change; the leadership of individual family members when faced with the crisis. Remember Prochaska's understanding of the readiness for change. Chances are that the substance abuse/dependent person is not ready for change.

11. Spirituality is sometimes the only solace that reluctant families have. Spirituality is the ultimate in giving up control which is why it's so important in any discussion of lifestyles and readiness for change.

12. Remember, some families are in danger of someone dying. Imminent danger creates moral dilemmas and forces therapists to carefully consider their options.

Some afternotes:

Substance use and abuse of some kind will probably be the single most common disorder that you'll see in practice. Although it is easy enough to know the criteria, you should also understand the worldview of people who are abusing or depending on drugs.

Gambling Disorder

But wait, there's more to this chapter. Yup, gambling. You know, your Aunt Betty's Bingo games or otherwise known as "Gambling Disorder." Hmm, I wonder if there's such a thing as Bingo Disorder.

With *Gambling Disorder*, there is a full-blown addiction (whatever that means). With this disorder, patients encounter the same degree of socioeconomic disruption as with any substance dependency. Patients are constantly in search of gambling opportunities, lie to friends and families, and jeopardize their employment and personal finances, and manic-like grandiosity.

Another feature of this disorder is the type of restlessness that can be found in patients diagnosed with *Antisocial Personality Disorders*. However, pathological gamblers may develop somatic problems and report high levels of stress. A significant characteristic is the manic-like tendencies in which grandiosity is juxtaposed with suicidal ideations and attempts. From this description and profile, it's pretty clear that pathological gamblers are labile in their affect and actions. In addition, there is frequently a comorbid diagnosis of substance dependency.

But wait, does that mean that my aunt (well, maybe not my aunt, but a friend's aunt) who played bingo was a pathological gambler? I think not although she never seemed to win and she was diligent about getting some regular bingo action. The difference is that the gambling had predetermined amounts of loss (and she did always seem to lose (have I already said that?)) and it appeared to be more of a social outlet with friends and acquaintances. In addition, there was nothing secretive about bingo at her church; I'm sure that the priests were even involved in some of the bingo action.

In addition, professional gamblers may be high stakes and involve high risks, but they are disciplined in their gambling. If they were not disciplined, then they would soon be unable to continue in this sport. I suppose if gamblers continued to lose and they devoted more and more time and money, then they would begin to be at risk to be diagnosed as a pathological gambler.

Apparently, one third of individuals with this disorder are women but there is wide variability in different cultures and geographical locations (yes, you're safe; my friend's aunt lived in Milwaukee). The DSM makes an interesting distinction: pathological women gamblers are more prone to depression and are underrepresented in treatment in part because of the stigma associated with having Gambling Disorder. Although adolescent boys have an early onset, women can develop significant problems later on.

The course of *Gambling Disorder* is reminiscent of addiction as well. Early social onset of gambling may lead to its abrupt significant and pathological development. The DSM notes that legalized gambling or social gambling may well lead to *Gambling Disorder*. That development seems intuitively reasonable: what started out as a social outing with friends may develop into a fantasy world of bright lights and continued entertainment. The only escape from the fantasy world of legalized gambling is the discipline that professional gambler show. Enjoy the ride but know when to cut your losses.

SESSION #7
Theme: Anxiety Disorders, Separation Anxiety Disorder, Selective Mutism, Phobias, Panic Disorders, Agoraphobia, GAD

Well, haven't you ever been anxious? Aren't you a just a little bit anxious on what's going to be on a test? I suppose that anxiety is something that everyone has experienced. But just because everyone has experienced it doesn't make it clinical state of anxiety. Basically, it goes back to the concept that the symptoms of anxiety must disrupt your client's socioeconomic functioning. And exactly what are the core concepts of anxiety? Basically, it's what you'd figure it would be: anxiety, worry, apprehension. In addition, however, there is a corollary to these concepts. Clients will develop patterns of avoidance, ritual acts, or repetitive thoughts as means of protecting against the symptoms of anxiety, worry, and apprehension. So, at the heart of the matter is a lot of worry and people's reactions to the worry. In many cases, the reactions to the worry are more problematic than the actual effects of the worry itself!

Before you come to the conclusion that your client has an anxiety disorder, you've got to rule out that the symptoms are not due to either legal or illegal substances, medical disorders, or another psychiatric disorder. This last point can be sticky. You've got to essentially make a judgment call: you rule out anxiety disorders if there are other psychiatric disorders that better account for your client's presentation of symptoms. And of course, your client must have significant impairment to their socioeconomic functioning. The last four items will be repeated for nearly every single psychiatric disorder: a) are symptoms due to legal or illegal substances; b) are symptoms due to a medical disorder; c) are symptoms better accounted for by another psychiatric disorder; d) is there significant impairment in your client's socioeconomic functioning? Remember these four items because they will recur over and over again in virtually every psychiatric disorder.

Within the Anxiety Disorders, we'll examine *Separation Anxiety Disorder, Selective Mutism, Specific Phobia, Social Phobia, Panic Disorder, Agoraphobia, Generalized Anxiety Disorder*, and a couple others.

Separation Anxiety Disorders

Separation Anxiety Disorders are a natural place to start because they are developmentally the first anxiety disorder that can occur. Here are the DSM-5 criteria (APA, 2013):

A. Developmentally inappropriate and excessive fear or anxiety concerning separation from those to whom the individual is attached, as evidenced by at least three of the following:

1. Recurrent excessive distress when anticipating or experiencing separation from home or from major attachment figures.

2. Persistent and excessive worry about losing major attachment figures or about possible harm to them, such as illness, injury, disasters, or death.

3. Persistent and excessive worry about experiencing an untoward event (e.g., getting lost, being kidnapped, having an accident, becoming ill) that causes separation from a major attachment figure.

4. Persistent reluctance or refusal to go out, away from home, to school, to work, or elsewhere because of fear of separation.

5. Persistent and excessive fear of or reluctance about being alone or without major attachment figures at home or in other settings.

6. Persistent reluctance or refusal to sleep away from home or to go to sleep without being near a major attachment figure.

7. Repeated nightmares involving the theme of separation.

8. Repeated complaints of physical symptoms (e.g., headaches, stomachaches, nausea, vomiting) when separation from major attachment figures occurs or is anticipated.

B. The fear, anxiety, or avoidance is persistent, lasting at least 4 weeks in children and adolescents and typically 6 months or more in adults.

C. The disturbance causes clinically significant distress or impairment in social, academic, occupational, or other important areas of functioning.

D. The disturbance is not better explained by another mental disorder, such as refusing to leave home because of excessive resistance to change in autism spectrum disorder; delusions or hallucinations concerning separation in psychotic disorders; refusal to go outside without a trusted companion in agoraphobia; worries about ill health or other harm befalling significant others in generalized anxiety disorder; or concerns about having an illness in illness anxiety disorder.

Anyone with kids probably had to confront separation anxiety in one form or another. In some cases, the parents probably showed more separation anxiety than the child. However, Separation Anxiety Disorder (SAD) is directed at kids and not at anxious parents. Kids with SAD have a lot of worry and refusal to do this or that and clinginess and being kidnapped and so on. They worry a lot about death and injury to their attachment figures. They're sad bundles of worry.

Before we go any further, let's talk a little bit about "attachment figures." Most of you have probably been introduced to Maslow's monkeys. I saw the old grainy black and white film about baby being traumatized by not having furry figures and instead had skeletal aluminum ones. Nothing like cold steel (well, it was aluminum but "cold steel" sounds better) to traumatize a newborn.

At any rate, babies who had the steely attachment figures (i.e., mothers) didn't do as well as their brethren who had furry attachment figures. The reasoning was that babies need some cuddling to make them feel secure. With adequate security, the baby can venture out and explore because they're not fearful. So, the idea is that kids who have furry mommies will be able to detach from them (i.e., not be clingy).

OK, now back to the 21st century. Attachment anxiety results from fear that mom and dad (or other attachment) won't be around. When kids have had a rotten babyhood, they may feel insecure about their parents' willingness to stick around. So, parental anxiety about entrusting their cherubs may result in cherubic separation anxiety. For most kids, it may be temporarily uncomfortable to have mom and dad scurry away, but they are secure in their attachment to their parents so they won't be panicky. For those with SAD, they may alternate between sadness and being demanding. And of course family members may eventually become frustrated with their anxious little on.

By and large, kids with SAD are equally distributed by gender. Younger kids probably aren't able to articulate their specific fear while older kids are able to say what exact monster is hiding around the corner. The DSM did make an ironic comment that parents with this disorder are those who are panicky about leaving their cherubs at a daycare. Having made fun about panicky parents, there can be a lot of real problems about substandard daycare settings. For those parents, anxiety is realistic. I apologize.

Selective Mutism

Hmm, I know a lot of parents who wish their kids would practice some selective mutism. But babbling voices of babies (doesn't that sound poetic?) should give way to children speaking in social situations. In other words, from a developmental perspective, babbling is only for babies. The other side of speaking is that someone should be listening. Basically, the idea is that kids should be able to respond when someone talks to them. Selective Mutism basically means that the kid doesn't talk in social situations. Usually, the kids don't have any communication disorder; it's anxiety that is keeping the kids from talking. As you might guess, if the kid remains mute for too long, his or her peers will want to play with more vocal kids. Here are the criteria (APA, 2013):

   A. Consistent failure to speak in specific social situations in which there is an expectation for speaking (e.g., at school) despite speaking in other situations.

   B. The disturbance interferes with educational or occupational achievement or with social communication.

   C. The duration of the disturbance is at least 1 month (not limited to the first month of school).

   D. The failure to speak is not attributable to a lack of knowledge of, or comfort with, the spoken language required in the social situation.

   E. The disturbance is not better explained by a communication disorder (e.g., childhood-onset fluency disorder) and does not occur exclusively during the course of autism spectrum disorder, schizophrenia, or another psychotic disorder.

Panic Disorders

The Panic Disorders have *Panic Attacks* as their "building blocks." Although *Panic Attacks* are not a diagnosable disorder, they form the foundation on what constitutes a Panic Disorder. *Panic Attacks* are best likened to having a heart attack. Shortness of breath, a sense of being smothered, palpitations, a feeling of choking are all symptoms of a *Panic Attack*. *Panic Attacks* are basically a cluster of symptoms that occur in panic disorders, phobias, and the trauma disorders. More generally, they can occur in any anxiety disorder. *Panic Attacks* have symptoms that develop abruptly, last several minutes and peak within 10 minutes. To be considered a Panic Attack, at least 4 of the following list of symptoms must occur:

   a. Palpitations, pounding or accelerated heart rate
   b. Sweating
   c. Trembling or shaking
   d. Sensations of shortness of breath or smothering
   e. Feeling of choking
   f. Chest pain or discomfort
   g. Nausea or abdominal distress
   h. Feeling dizzy, unsteady, lightheaded or faint
   i. Derealization (feelings of unreality) or depersonalization (being detached from oneself)
   j. Fear of losing control or going crazy
   k. Fear of dying
   l. Parathesias (numbness or tingling sensations)
   m. Chills or hot flashes

Just so you know: a couple students told me that they believed that these were symptoms from menopause. I took their word for it.

Phobias

Now, let's go onto phobias in general. Phobias are defined as a persistent and irrational fear of an object or situation that leads to attempts to avoid it. Let's examine Agoraphobia and see how it works. As stated previously, there are several different types of agoraphobia. Agoraphobia with Panic Disorders and Agoraphobia without Panic Disorders with the difference being the presence of the Panic Disorders. Agoraphobia without History of Panic Disorders is similar to Panic Disorder with Agoraphobia except that your client's fear is focused on the panic-like symptoms versus a full panic attack. As you might guess, to diagnose Agoraphobia without History of Panic Disorder, you have to rule out that your clients have experienced a full panic attack. The criteria (APA, 2013) for Agoraphobia is anxiety about being in places or situations from which escape may be difficult (or embarrassing) or in which help may not be available, usually associated with clusters of situations like being outside the home alone, being in a crowd or standing in line, on a bridge or public transportation. The situational trigger is being in a place or situation from which escape may be difficult or embarrassing. As you might imagine, Agoraphobia with Panic Disorders is especially debilitating. First, the individual suffers from *Panic Attacks* when confronted with situations or places from which escape is difficult. Imagine the sense of a having a heart attack in a crowded line at work and you get the idea. But the secondary debilitation is that your client will resort to extreme measures to try to avoid being placed in situations or places from which escape is difficult. That might mean avoiding being in a crowded place (e.g., waiting in lines, elevators), in public transportation (e.g., trains, airplanes), on bridges or even just being alone outside a personal residence. I'd say that your client might experience "significant impairment in their socioeconomic functioning;" wouldn't you agree? That's why Agoraphobia without Panic Disorders can be just as debilitating as Agoraphobia with Panic Disorders. Here are the DSM-5 criteria (APA, 2013):

A. Marked fear or anxiety about two (or more) of the following five situations:
   1. Using public transportation (e.g., automobiles, buses, trains, ships, planes).
   2. Being in open spaces (e.g., parking lots, marketplaces, bridges).
   3. Being in enclosed places (e.g., shops, theaters, cinemas).
   4. Standing in line or being in a crowd.
   5. Being outside of the home alone.

B. The individual fears or avoids these situations because of thoughts that escape might be difficult or help might not be available in the event of developing panic-like symptoms or other incapacitating or embarrassing symptoms (e.g., fear of falling in the elderly; fear of incontinence).

C. The agoraphobic situations almost always provoke fear or anxiety.

D. The agoraphobic situations are actively avoided, require the presence of a companion, or are endured with intense fear or anxiety.

E. The fear or anxiety is out of proportion to the actual danger posed by the agoraphobic situations and to the sociocultural context.

F. The fear, anxiety, or avoidance is persistent, typically lasting for 6 months or more.

G. The fear, anxiety, or avoidance causes clinically significant distress or impairment in social, occupational, or other important areas of functioning.

H. If another medical condition (e.g., inflammatory bowel disease, Parkinson's disease) is present, the fear, anxiety, or avoidance is clearly excessive.

I. The fear, anxiety, or avoidance is not better explained by the symptoms of another mental disorder—for example, the symptoms are not confined to specific phobia, situational type; do not involve only social situations (as in social anxiety disorder); and are not related exclusively to obsessions (as in obsessive-compulsive disorder), perceived defects or flaws in physical appearance (as in body dysmorphic disorder), reminders of traumatic events (as in posttraumatic stress disorder), or fear of separation (as in separation anxiety disorder).

Prevalence data have a couple points to remember. First, women are twice as likely as men to experience agoraphobia. On the other hand, men have higher rates of comorbid substance use (they drink/drug AND are an agoraphobe; bummer for men). It can have an onset in childhood although it's more likely to have an onset in late teens/early adulthood. Interestingly, Agoraphobia without Panic Attacks can have an onset in last twenties. So, the interpretation is that Panic Attacks with Agoraphobia have a worse prognosis because of early onset. That's a common pattern: the earlier the onset of anything, the worse the prognosis. About half (in clinic samples) of people diagnosed as agoraphobic also have Panic Attacks. Finally, people with agoraphobia are likely to also be comorbid with other anxiety disorders.

Let's move onto Specific Phobias. Now, specific phobias can be a client's phobic reactions to just about anything. You got a thing, then there's probably a phobia attached to it. Whether it's animate or inanimate, it really doesn't seem to matter. What matters is the following: your client has a persistent and irrational fear of an object or situation that leads to attempts to avoid it. Remember that it must be persistent and that it must be irrational or it doesn't count as a phobia. Phobias are ego-dystonic in that even your clients will acknowledge that their fear is irrational. Furthermore, the fear generally varies as a function of the closeness to the feared object or situation and the extent to which escape is limited. In many cases, clients will remember what precipitated the fear and the resulting phobic reactions, but that doesn't stop them from having the subsequent persistent and irrational fear. What is usually problematic is the client's extreme efforts to avoid the object or situation. What might be an example of phobias? Well, there are phobias about dogs. Imagine for a moment that a gentle dog whose only threats to peoplekind are that it might slobber a little too much, eat way too much, live to go on a walk through the neighborhood and basically think that all people are good, kindly souls. Having a persistent fear of such a dog is probably irrational unless you don't like dog slobber. Generalizing a fear of dogs to all dogs is probably irrational. On the other hand, having a similar fear of evil and foul-tempered dogs (even those that do not slobber and eat too much) is probably not a phobia although it could be. Under what circumstances could you have a fear of evil and foul-tempered dogs that is not a phobia?

Social Anxiety

Social Anxiety (formerly, Social Phobia in DSM-IV TR) is a common phobia characterized by a marked and persistent fear of social or performance situations where embarrassment might occur, exposure to the situation elicits an immediate anxiety response, and recognition that the fear is irrational. Furthermore, clients usually end up avoiding the fear situation. As you might expect, there must be a significant impairment to clients' socioeconomic functioning (haven't you heard that one before?) or marked distress. For kids under 18, symptoms must have been documented for at least 6 months. Finally, the fear or avoidance should not be better accounted for by another disorder, is not due to drug use, and is not due to a medical disorder. With Social Anxiety, clients just avoid the feared situations although they sometimes will just endure them with lots and lots of dread. As you might also guess, clients with Social Phobias will be a tad sensitive to criticism, not terribly assertive, have feelings of low self-esteem, have limited social skills, have a history of underachievement (well, what else would you expect if you avoided performing where you might be embarrassed at the outcome?), and have limited social networks. People with social phobias are not happy with life because of the misery that they endure. Here are the DSM-5 criteria (APA, 2013):

A. Marked fear or anxiety about one or more social situations in which the individual is exposed to possible scrutiny by others. Examples include social interactions (e.g., having a conversation, meeting unfamiliar people), being observed (e.g., eating or drinking), and performing in front of others (e.g., giving a speech).

Note: In children, the anxiety must occur in peer settings and not just during interactions with adults.

B. The individual fears that he or she will act in a way or show anxiety symptoms that will be negatively evaluated (i.e., will be humiliating or embarrassing; will lead to rejection or offend others).

C. The social situations almost always provoke fear or anxiety.

- Note: In children, the fear or anxiety may be expressed by crying, tantrums, freezing, clinging, shrinking, or failing to speak in social situations.

D. The social situations are avoided or endured with intense fear or anxiety.

E. The fear or anxiety is out of proportion to the actual threat posed by the social situation and to the sociocultural context.

F. The fear, anxiety, or avoidance is persistent, typically lasting for 6 months or more.

G. The fear, anxiety, or avoidance causes clinically significant distress or impairment in social, occupational, or other important areas of functioning.

H. The fear, anxiety, or avoidance is not attributable to the physiological effects of a substance (e.g., a drug of abuse, a medication) or another medical condition.

I. The fear, anxiety, or avoidance is not better explained by the symptoms of another mental disorder, such as panic disorder, body dysmorphic disorder, or autism spectrum disorder.

J. If another medical condition (e.g., Parkinson's disease, obesity, disfigurement from burns or injury) is present, the fear, anxiety, or avoidance is clearly unrelated or is excessive.

Specify if:

- Performance only: If the fear is restricted to speaking or performing in public.

Onset is in early teens and 75% are between 8 and 15 years at age of onset. Another interesting tidbit: onset can be insidious or it can occur because of a traumatic social event. I wonder if it might be "Post Traumatic Social Disorder" then again, maybe not. It probably isn't surprising that people with Social Anxiety come across as shy and wimpy. You know, right? Rigid posture, no eye contact, and soft voice (starting to sound a little creepy). This is one of those disorders where Cognitive-Behavior Therapy (CBT) would be a good idea. Then again, some folks would use alcohol or benzodiazepines to prepare for a social event. CBT is probably a better course of action unless you have a fine single-malt.

Panic Disorder

To have a Panic Disorder, a client must have at least two uncued Panic Attacks. "Uncued" means that nothing in particular precipitated the Panic Attacks. It's as if the Panic Attack happened out of the blue. Cues are usually defined as situational triggers as in what happens with Phobias. Thus, if Panic Attacks are cued by something, then in all likelihood, it's a phobia of some sort. If you remember this distinction, then it makes sense that there are Panic Disorders with Agoraphobia and Panic Disorders Without Agoraphobia. One has a situational trigger and one doesn't. More about Agoraphobia in a minute.

Panic Attacks can present themselves in some cultures as an intense fear of witchcraft or magic. The course of Panic Attacks is usually between late adolescence and the mid-thirties although it varies considerably. The normal course is chronic with ups and downs. Remember, when I say the "course of a disorder," I'm referring to the beginning, middle, and end of disorder. In short, I'm referring to the pattern of a disorder as it presents itself. The lifetime prevalence is between 1.5% and 5% with a 1-year prevalence rate between 1% and 2%. There is some evidence to support the idea that having close relatives with panic disorders makes your client more vulnerable to also having them. First degree biological relatives with Panic Disorder have a four to seven times greater chance of developing Panic Disorder than non-relatives.

Some key diagnostic points are that Panic Attacks can occur in a number of anxiety disorders in addition to panic disorder; the diagnosis of panic disorder requires the presence of recurrent, unexpected Panic Attacks; uncued Panic Attacks can progress, over time, to the cued attacks of specific or social phobia. Here are the criteria (APA, 2013) for Panic Disorders: Recurrent unexpected Panic Attacks. A panic attack is an abrupt surge of intense fear or intense discomfort that reaches a peak within minutes and during which time four (or more) of the following symptoms occur:

Note: The abrupt surge can occur from a calm state or an anxious state.

Palpitations, pounding heart, or accelerated heart rate.

- Sweating.

- Trembling or shaking.

- Sensations of shortness of breath or smothering.

- Feelings of choking.

- Chest pain or discomfort.

- Nausea or abdominal distress.

- Feeling dizzy, unsteady, light-headed, or faint.

- Chills or heat sensations.

- Paraesthesia (numbness or tingling sensations).

- Derealization (feelings of unreality) or depersonalization (being detached from oneself).
- Fear of losing control or "going crazy."
- Fear of dying.
  - Note: Culture-specific symptoms (e.g., tinnitus, neck soreness, headache, uncontrollable screaming or crying) may be seen. Such symptoms should not count as one of the four required symptoms.

B. At least one of the attacks has been followed by 1 month (or more) of one or both of the following:

1. Persistent concern or worry about additional Panic Attacks or their consequences (e.g., losing control, having a heart attack, "going crazy").

2. A significant maladaptive change in behavior related to the attacks (e.g., behaviors designed to avoid having Panic Attacks, such as avoidance of exercise or unfamiliar situations).

C. The disturbance is not attributable to the physiological effects of a substance (e.g., a drug of abuse, a medication) or another medical condition (e.g., hyperthyroidism, cardiopulmonary disorders).

D. The disturbance is not better explained by another mental disorder (e.g., the Panic Attacks do not occur only in response to feared social situations, as in social anxiety disorder; in response to circumscribed phobic objects or situations, as in specific phobia; in response to obsessions, as in obsessive-compulsive disorder; in response to reminders of traumatic events, as in posttraumatic stress disorder; or in response to separation from attachment figures, as in separation anxiety disorder).

Whites and Native Americans have been reported with higher prevalence than other ethnicities. The course is chronic and waxes and wanes. Onset can occur in childhood with "fearful spells." Older adults have a different pattern than other age groups. Lower prevalence. Hybrid of Panic Attacks and generalized anxiety disorders. More likely to attribute panic to specific social events. Older folks then don't report Panic Attacks but when they do, it's part of a Generalized Anxiety Disorder; they don't show much insight on what is causing their Panic Attacks. Older folks are searching for a plausible reason for their panicky feelings. Probably no difference in gender distributions. Overall, there is considerable variability among ages and ethnicities on panic disorders.

Generalized Anxiety Disorder

Generalized Anxiety Disorder is characterized by (would you guess?) excessive anxiety and worry for 6 months about a couple of events or activities, difficulty in controlling the worry, additional symptoms (i.e., restlessness, fatigue, problems in concentrating, irritability, muscular tension, or disturbed sleep), ruling out other anxiety and somatization disorders like phobias, Panic Attacks, obsessive-compulsive disorders, post-traumatic stress disorders, hypochondriasis, and other disorder related disorders, significant impairment in socioeconomic functioning, and of course the usual precautions that the symptoms are not due to medical disorders, substance abuse/prescription drugs, or other psychiatric or developmental disorders. Generalized Anxiety Disorders are frequently accompanied by depression, exaggerated startle response (kinda twitchy, I guess), and muscle aches. Again, kids with Generalized Anxiety Disorders probably are punctual to a fault, worry a whole lot about their performance, catastrophize, and may be overconforming, perfectionist, and unsure of themselves. Here are the criteria (APA, 2013):

- A. Excessive anxiety and worry (apprehensive expectation), occurring more days than not for at least 6 months, about a number of events or activities (such as work or school performance).

- B. The individual finds it difficult to control the worry.

- C. The anxiety and worry are associated with three (or more) of the following six symptoms (with at least some symptoms having been present for more days than not for the past 6 months):

    - Note: Only one item is required in children.

2. Restlessness or feeling keyed up or on edge.

3. Being easily fatigued.

4. Difficulty concentrating or mind going blank.

5. Irritability.

6. Muscle tension.

7. Sleep disturbance (difficulty falling or staying asleep, or restless, unsatisfying sleep).

- D. The anxiety, worry, or physical symptoms cause clinically significant distress or impairment in social, occupational, or other important areas of functioning.

- E. The disturbance is not attributable to the physiological effects of a substance (e.g., a drug of abuse, a medication) or another medical condition (e.g., hyperthyroidism).

- F. The disturbance is not better explained by another mental disorder (e.g., anxiety or worry about having *Panic Attacks* in panic disorder, negative evaluation in social anxiety disorder [social phobia], contamination or other obsessions in obsessive-compulsive disorder, separation from attachment figures in separation anxiety disorder, reminders of traumatic events in posttraumatic stress disorder, gaining weight in anorexia nervosa, physical complaints in somatic symptom disorder, perceived appearance flaws in body dysmorphic disorder, having a serious illness in illness anxiety disorder, or the content of delusional beliefs in schizophrenia or delusional disorder).

Women are more likely than men to have GAD; their comorbid disorders are likely to be anxiety and depression disorders while men have substance abuse. OK, that means that GAD men use drugs and GAD women are depressed and anxious.

The symptoms of the last three anxiety disorders are caused by general medical disorders, substances, and a disorder not otherwise specified. What the first two mean is that the symptoms of anxiety disorders can be caused by general medical disorders or substances. Remember that the other anxiety disorders must rule out that the symptoms are predominantly caused by medical disorders or substances. Anxiety Disorders, Not Otherwise Specified (NOS) basically means that you believe that your client has an anxiety disorder but that it doesn't fit neatly into any of the other disorders. Why do you suppose that NOS disorders present a problem with the DSM-IVTR diagnostic schema in general and the Axis I disorders in particular?

For any of the anxiety disorders, you'll need to have access to a variety of clinical information that include current and past history of anxiety, feelings of derealization, depersonalization, or emotional numbing, fears of losing control or going crazy, sleep disturbance or bad dreams, history of medical disorders, somatic symptomology, previous and current psychiatric disorders, current medications and abused substances, current or past traumatic events or stressors, compulsive behaviors or rituals, obsessive, intrusive thoughts and phobic fears and the context in which they occur.

Some ideas on treatment:

The behavioral technique of flooding is an effective treatment for agoraphobia and has proved superior to all other treatment modalities. The technique exposes the patient to the feared stimulus for brief but intense periods. Flooding is rapidly effective in reducing symptoms, but for the most sustained results the exposure should be evenly spaced and regularly repeated. The goal of flooding is extinction--the elimination of the dysfunctional response to the feared stimulus. Ideally, this technique should be used in conjunction with psychopharmacological interventions.

SESSION #8
Theme: Obsessive-Compulsive Disorders, Body Dysmorphic Disorder, Hoarding Disorder, Trichotillomania, and Excoriation

Reality show, anyone? Primetime show, I'm the MC. I introduce a contest in which contestants pick at their hair, skin, repeatedly inspect what they have pulled out, critically examine the overall effect and then hoard the fruits of their labor. Aren't you glad that you're in psychopathology? Where else would you be able to have those images burned into your mind? Getting away from reality shows, what's the theme in this session? I think that it revolves around obsessions. That's the commonality among all the disorders. Obsess and act on the obsessions. Definitely not something to diagnose before lunch.

Obsessive-Compulsive Disorders (OCD)

So, have you ever obsessed about anything . . . say, about passing a class or two? Losing weight? Trying to look good? I hate to tell you but those really aren't obsessions although they could be. Obsessions are recurrent, intrusive and anxiety-provoking thoughts, impulses or images. They are ego-dystonic, that is, the person really, really doesn't like having these recurrent thoughts, impulses, or images. The most common obsessions are those around contamination (leading to lots of hand washing), repeated doubts (checking those locks a bunch of times), focus on the order of objects (gotta keep that asymmetry under control), aggressive or horrific impulses (shouting obscenities at your mild-mannered, lovable instructor), and sexual imagery (recurrent pornographic images). Given your client's abhorrence for these thoughts, impulses, or images, they engage in compulsive behaviors. Compulsions are defined as repetitive behavior or mental acts that a person feels driven to perform. You might reasonably ask "what is the relationship between the obsessions and compulsions?" Basically, the compulsions try to "undo" the ego-dystonic obsessions and thus to reduce the anxiety experienced around them. For example, while driving away, your clients might have an image that their house is going to be burglarized. Your clients would then have to drive back to their house and check every door, window, and other means of access. Or before going to bed, they might fear a break in. So, they'd basically check every possible means by which a burglar might break in. This ritual might last several hours if they check, re-check, and re-re-check everything many, many times. And that's why it significantly impairs their socioeconomic functioning. There is a sense of paralysis that occurs because your clients are attempting to cope with the thoughts, impulses, or images that keep them anxious. Here are the criteria (APA, 2013):

    A. Presence of obsessions, compulsions, or both:

        o Obsessions are defined by (1) and (2):

2.   Recurrent and persistent thoughts, urges, or images that are experienced, at some time during the disturbance, as intrusive and unwanted, and that in most individuals cause marked anxiety or distress.

3. The individual attempts to ignore or suppress such thoughts, urges, or images, or to neutralize them with some other thought or action (i.e., by performing a compulsion).

    - Compulsions are defined by (1) and (2):

    5. Repetitive behaviors (e.g., hand washing, ordering, checking) or mental acts (e.g., praying, counting, repeating words silently) that the individual feels driven to perform in response to an obsession or according to rules that must be applied rigidly.

    6. The behaviors or mental acts are aimed at preventing or reducing anxiety or distress, or preventing some dreaded event or situation; however, these behaviors or mental acts are not connected in a realistic way with what they are designed to neutralize or prevent, or are clearly excessive.

        - Note: Young children may not be able to articulate the aims of these behaviors or mental acts.

    B. The obsessions or compulsions are time-consuming (e.g., take more than 1 hour per day) or cause clinically significant distress or impairment in social, occupational, or other important areas of functioning.

    C. The obsessive-compulsive symptoms are not attributable to the physiological effects of a substance (e.g., a drug of abuse, a medication) or another medical condition.

    D. The disturbance is not better explained by the symptoms of another mental disorder (e.g., excessive worries, as in generalized anxiety disorder; preoccupation with appearance, as in body dysmorphic disorder; difficulty discarding or parting with possessions, as in hoarding disorder; hair pulling, as in trichotillomania [hair-pulling disorder]; skin picking, as in excoriation [skin-picking] disorder; stereotypies, as in stereotypic movement disorder; ritualized eating behavior, as in eating disorders; preoccupation with substances or gambling, as in substance-related and addictive disorders; preoccupation with having an illness, as in illness anxiety disorder; sexual urges or fantasies, as in paraphilic disorders; impulses, as in disruptive, impulse-control, and conduct disorders; guilty ruminations, as in major depressive disorder; thought insertion or delusional preoccupations, as in schizophrenia spectrum and other psychotic disorders; or repetitive patterns of behavior, as in autism spectrum disorder).

I like OCD as a disorder. It is so central to most psychiatric disorders. It has unhealthy beliefs and actions; it has a little bit of mania to them, a little bit of delusions, a little of social anxiety; maybe even a little of depression. It covers the whole range of nuttiness that comprises people's psychiatric life. For treatment purposes, look at one sentence from DSM-5: In OCD, beliefs can include an inflated sense of responsibility and the tendency to overestimate threat; perfectionism and intolerance of uncertainty; and over-importance of thoughts (e.g., believing that having a forbidden thought is as bad as acting on it) and the need to control thoughts. This is like your nightmare supervisor or even an unpleasant in-law. It also represents a lot of good images for treatment.

Although compulsions differ widely, here are some examples that occur frequently: Cleaning, checking, ordering, and counting. Fighting against taboo thoughts and preventing perceived harm.

Check out the comorbidity prevalence rates. OCD seems to be comorbid with everything at high rates, going from 30% to 70% on various disorders. In terms of prevalence, kids' OCD is more variable than adults. I suppose that it's because kids are growing up and are in a process of changing whereas adults are stuck with what they have. As you might expect, kids worry about harm to parents, men are more likely to have OCD (with comorbidity with substances). The DSM mentions that gender differences exist in the type of obsessions. It says something about women having cleaning obsessions while men have obsessions about taboo topics. I guess that the men are feeling guilty about all the porn that they watch and buy.

Body Dysmorphic Disorder

Body Dysmorphic Disorder is basically a preoccupation with an imagined defect in appearance or excessive concern about a minor physical anomaly that causes significant impairment in socioeconomic functioning and that cannot be accounted for by another mental disorder. The symptoms are myriad: your clients may complain about acne, wrinkles, hair thinning, and on and on and on. We're not talking about major psychopathology here although your clients will be distressed by their appearance. Your clients will generally have a localized area of concern but won't specify the defects because of their level of distress. So, you have to be sensitive to their level of distress. It might not seem like such a big deal to you but to your client, a wart is not a rose by any other name. You might wonder how a wart or any other minor defect might cause significant impairment. Imagine a person who becomes somewhat obsessive about that one body part. Like the classical obsessive-compulsive client, the impairment occurs in how your client attempts to reduce the anxiety around the defect; avoiding mirrors, excessive dieting, hiding the bodily part in question and so on. These efforts can take quite a bit of effort and result in impaired socioeconomic functioning. The course generally begins in adolescence with a gradual or abrupt onset. Here are the DSM-5 criteria (APA, 2013):

A. Preoccupation with one or more perceived defects or flaws in physical appearance that are not observable or appear slight to others.

B. At some point during the course of the disorder, the individual has performed repetitive behaviors (e.g., mirror checking, excessive grooming, skin picking, reassurance seeking) or mental acts (e.g., comparing his or her appearance with that of others) in response to the appearance concerns.

C. The preoccupation causes clinically significant distress or impairment in social, occupational, or other important areas of functioning.

D. The appearance preoccupation is not better explained by concerns with body fat or weight in an individual whose symptoms meet *Diagnostic Criteria* for an eating disorder.

Specify if:

- With muscle dysmorphia: The individual is preoccupied with the idea that his or her body build is too small or insufficiently muscular. This specifier is used even if the individual is preoccupied with other body areas, which is often the case.

Specify if:

- Indicate degree of insight regarding body dysmorphic disorder beliefs (e.g., "I look ugly" or "I look deformed").

- With good or fair insight: The individual recognizes that the body dysmorphic disorder beliefs are definitely or probably not true or that they may or may not be true.

- With poor insight: The individual thinks that the body dysmorphic disorder beliefs are probably true.

- With absent insight/delusional beliefs: The individual is completely convinced that the body dysmorphic disorder beliefs are true.

Let's go through this disorder. There is a lot interesting observations within DSM-5. The key to the disorder is excessive worry about the inadequacy or imperfection of one part of the body. In men, it's probably their musculature or genitalia; in women, it's either something being too much or too little. In both cases, there is a delusion of reference (i.e., the belief that other people notice the imagined flaws. How narcissistic!) Onset is in early to midteens and has a chronic course. Note that there is an increased suicide risk with body dysmorphic disorder.

Hoarding

Hmmm, ever watch the reality show "Hoarders?" Great way to waste time. It is also a great way to see hoarding in action. Here are the criteria (APA, 2013):

A. Persistent difficulty discarding or parting with possessions, regardless of their actual value.

B. This difficulty is due to a perceived need to save the items and to distress associated with discarding them.

C. The difficulty discarding possessions results in the accumulation of possessions that congest and clutter active living areas and substantially compromises their intended use. If living areas are uncluttered, it is only because of the interventions of third parties (e.g., family members, cleaners, authorities).

D. The hoarding causes clinically significant distress or impairment in social, occupational, or other important areas of functioning (including maintaining a safe environment for self and others).

E. The hoarding is not attributable to another medical condition (e.g., brain injury, cerebrovascular disease, Prader-Willi syndrome).

F. The hoarding is not better explained by the symptoms of another mental disorder (e.g., obsessions in obsessive-compulsive disorder, decreased energy in major depressive disorder, delusions in schizophrenia or another psychotic disorder, cognitive deficits in major neurocognitive disorder, restricted interests in autism spectrum disorder).

Specify if:

- With excessive acquisition: If difficulty discarding possessions is accompanied by excessive acquisition of items that are not needed or for which there is no available space.

Specify if:

- With good or fair insight: The individual recognizes that hoarding-related beliefs and behaviors (pertaining to difficulty discarding items, clutter, or excessive acquisition) are problematic.

- With poor insight: The individual is mostly convinced that hoarding-related beliefs and behaviors (pertaining to difficulty discarding items, clutter, or excessive acquisition) are not problematic despite evidence to the contrary.

I wondered how people start hoarding. It probably started with a little bit too much QVC action. It progresses to senseless internet purchases (Amazon rejoices), then goes to scoring some free items on the curbs and ends up with stealing stuff. Here's what to expect in hoarding. Lots of anxiety about reducing the amount of stuff; it usually takes third party interventions. But there is the other side as well. Valuable and junky stuff are mixed together. Animal and human products are mixed together. In short, it's possessions by the pound with no effort to organize or to recycle unneeded or unwanted items. It's probably not rocket science to discern that decision-making is impaired in hoarders. Hoarders have a hard time in making decisions. Nearly three quarters of hoarders are comorbid with other anxiety disorders.

I was interested in this disorder because onset can be in preteens and progress for decades even unto older people. So, it's a chronic and progressive disorder that starts in preteens. Women and men are equal opportunity hoarders although women use purchasing power as their preferred method of acquiring stuff. All I can say is that credit card companies love hoarders. But lots of other people don't much care for hoarders. There are health code problems, animal control problems, homeowners' covenants, risk for fire or injury, and difficulty in repairing or replacing nonfunctioning appliances.

Trichotillomania

Easy for you to say . . . this disorder involves pulling out hair. Kind of an endorphin release. No, not because patients are frustrated by life's problems, but because the tension characteristic of impulse control disorders is relieved by pulling out hair. The DSM notes that tension is experienced either before the act of pulling out hair or the impulse to not pull out hair. Yes, you know it is Trichotillomania because there are odd patches where hair is absent. I suppose that male pattern baldness can be an indication of Trichotillomania. However, it seems to me that most men do not experience pleasure from a lack of hair although there may be tension for a man not to be hairy. The key in Trichotillomania is the tension before the hair pulling and the relief after removing the hair. If in fact, male pattern baldness was the usual result of Trichotillomania, then the sales of Rogaine would be negligible (which it isn't). The next time that you see a balding guy, tell him that he doesn't have a psychiatric disorder that involves being bald. However, I doubt that he'll be amused.

Trichotillomania resembles eating disorders in its secretive nature although family members are typically aware of the activities. What is somewhat odd is that patients with this disorder may try to remove other people's hair. What is not odd is that patients may be somewhat surreptitious in trying to remove other people's hair. In fact, these patients may pull hairs from pets, dolls or anything with hair. Hmm, when Fido comes bounding toward you, carefully inspect him for hair loss. He may be a victim of others' Trichotillomania. Seriously though, I image that this disorder is painful to people who have this disorder. In that sense, it is like an eating disorder. That suggests that is probably co-morbid with OCD and Alcohol Dependency. I imagine that it is somewhat like cutting. There is pain attached with pulling out hair and with cutting, but it's controlled by the patient. At least, that's the idea until the cutting and pulling gets out of control. It may well be that there is a constellation of Obsessive-Compulsive Disorders of which Trichotillomania is one.

In terms of other considerations, males and females are equally represented among children although among adults, females more often present with this disorder. The DSM makes a good observation in that this gender imbalance may result with men's discomfort in asking psychiatric assistance with their hair loss. In terms of course and prevalence, onset can begin in early childhood or become a chronic condition in adulthood. It can be abrupt and end soon, or it may come and go for years. It's hard to know precisely when Trichotillomania begins and when it ends.

In terms of differential diagnosis, the DSM has a notation that it's important to rule out or at least consider as a comorbid disorder, other disorders such as Obsessive-Compulsive Disorder. In addition, when children exhibit Trichotillomania, diagnosis should not be given because they might outgrow the habit. Here are the criteria (APA, 2013) for Trichotillomania:

A. Recurrent pulling out of one's hair, resulting in hair loss.

B. Repeated attempts to decrease or stop hair pulling.

C. The hair pulling causes clinically significant distress or impairment in social, occupational, or other important areas of functioning.

D. The hair pulling or hair loss is not attributable to another medical condition (e.g., a dermatological condition).

E. The hair pulling is not better explained by the symptoms of another mental disorder (e.g., attempts to improve a perceived defect or flaw in appearance in body dysmorphic disorder).

Excoriation

Skin-picking. Not much more to be said. Just remember skin-picking is not finger licking good. Here are the criteria (APA, 2013).

A. Recurrent skin picking resulting in skin lesions.

B. Repeated attempts to decrease or stop skin picking.

C. The skin picking causes clinically significant distress or impairment in social, occupational, or other important areas of functioning.

D. The skin picking is not attributable to the physiological effects of a substance (e.g., cocaine) or another medical condition (e.g., scabies).

E. The skin picking is not better explained by symptoms of another mental disorder (e.g., delusions or tactile hallucinations in a psychotic disorder, attempts to improve a perceived defect or flaw in appearance in body dysmorphic disorder, stereotypies in stereotypic movement disorder, or intention to harm oneself in non-suicidal self-injury).

Just for the sake of being complete, a few gory details are good grist for telling others what you've learned in this class. Skin picking is completed using fingernails, tweezers, toothpicks and other implements. But wait, that's not all. Skin pickers also rub, bite and squeeze their skin or pimples. Alright, that's about enough especially before dinner. But it's not all fun and games. Skin picking can result in lesions that may result in bacterial infections. It can result in disfigurement that will require dermatological treatment. So, it really is an OCD which deserves serious consideration. But skin-picking?

SESSION #9
Theme: Dissociative Disorders, Somatic Disorders, Factitious Disorder

Dissociative Disorders include
- Dissociative Amnesia
- Dissociative Fugue
- Dissociative Identity Disorder
- Depersonalization Disorder

Somatic Disorders include
- Somatic Symptom Disorder
- Illness Anxiety Disorder
- Conversion Disorder (Functional Neurological Symptom Disorder)
- Psychological Factors Affecting Other Medical Conditions
- Factitious Disorder

Dissociative Disorders

Dissociative Disorders are basically a temporary disruption in the normally integrated functions of memory, identity, or consciousness, leading to amnesia, feelings of depersonalization, or multiple distinct personalities in the same individual. There will be several criteria that will be common with most if not all dissociative disorders: significant impairment of socioeconomic functioning, symptoms can't be better explained by a medical condition (including some type of neurological condition), symptoms can't be better explain by use of prescription drugs and/or abused substances, and symptoms can't be better accounted for by another psychiatric disorder.

Because of the exotic nature of some of these disorders, some definitions are in order:
1. Anterograde amnesia - inability to form new memories after the condition causing the amnesia occurs
2. Dissociation - the splitting off of a group of mental processes from conscious awareness
3. Ego-dystonic - thoughts, affect and behavior elements of an individual's personality that are considered unacceptable and inconsistent with the individual's total personality or self-identify
4. Fugue - a period of amnesia during which the individual appears to be conscious and makes rational decisions. The individual has no memory of the period on recovery
5. Retrograde amnesia - a loss of memory for events that occurred before the onset of the amnesia and the condition causing it.

Within Dissociative Disorders, some of the necessary clinical history to obtain are mood swings or changes; unexplained changes in handwriting; periods of amnesia; episodes of unusual and uncharacteristic behavior; unexplained, sudden or extended trips; time distortions or lapses; erratic behavior; appearance of two or more distinct identities or personality states. Questions to consider include whether your client reports recurrent experiences of time distortion, lapses, unusual or ego-dystonic behavior, depersonalization or amnesia; whether symptoms be produced by drugs or a nonpsychiatric illness; and whether there are repeated experiences of feeling detached from one's own thoughts or body, or episodes of amnesia?

Normally, people have an integration of consciousness, memory, identity, emotion, perception, body representation, minor motor control and behavior. To some degree, Dissociative Disorders represent a rupture of these spheres of functioning. Dissociation is also associated with trauma states.

Dissociative Identity Disorder

Dissociative Identity Disorder (DID) is characterized by two or more distinct personalities that have a relatively enduring pattern of perceiving, relating to and thinking about the environment and self; at least two of these personalities recurrently take control of the person's behavior; inability to recall personal info during these episodes that is too extensive to be explained by forgetfulness; and disturbance is not caused by substances, a general medical condition. Although DSM does not state that DID also has a significant impairment in socioeconomic functioning, disruption of a client's life is typical. DID were formerly called Multiple Personality Disorder and there is a rich professional and popular literature about clients with multiple personalities. Most of the popular literature can be safely considered as useful for entertainment but little else. The popular literature tends to be sensationalistic with exhibitions and claims that are better suited for daytime talk shows. The professional literature suggests that DID clients failed to integrate aspects of their identity, memory, and consciousness. There is a competition among the different personalities each with distinct names, personal histories, self-images, and identities. The primary identity is not typically dominant and the alternate identities will assume control. It's like having a nasty family all in one body. One of the typical symptoms is that clients will report gaps in their memory. Clients with DID frequently report severe physical and sexual abuse sustained when they were children. Controversy exists with such memories because of the "false memory" syndrome. You'll recall that the false memory syndrome occurs when clinicians accidentally plant ideas into highly suggestible clients. Notwithstanding this concern, there does appear to be evidence that clients with DID sustain a traumatic personal history. The course of the DID is chronic and recurrent. Here are the criteria (APA, 2013):

Diagnostic Criteria

Disruption of identity characterized by two or more distinct personality states, which may be described in some cultures as an experience of possession. The disruption in identity involves marked discontinuity in sense of self and sense of agency, accompanied by related alterations in affect, behavior, consciousness, memory, perception, cognition, and/or sensory-motor functioning. These signs and symptoms may be observed by others or reported by the individual.

- A. Recurrent gaps in the recall of everyday events, important personal information, and/or traumatic events that are inconsistent with ordinary forgetting.

- B. The symptoms cause clinically significant distress or impairment in social, occupational, or other important areas of functioning.

- C. The disturbance is not a normal part of a broadly accepted cultural or religious practice.

- o Note: In children, the symptoms are not better explained by imaginary playmates or other fantasy play.
- D. The symptoms are not attributable to the physiological effects of a substance (e.g., blackouts or chaotic behavior during alcohol intoxication) or another medical condition (e.g., complex partial seizures).

Dissociative Amnesia

The first and most critical criterion is the inability to recall important personal information, usually of a traumatic nature, that is too extensive to be explained by ordinary forgetfulness; second, the symptoms doesn't occur exclusively during another disorder and is not due to a medical condition or drug use; and finally, the symptoms cause clinically significant impairment in socioeconomic functioning. DSM lists two types of memory disturbance: localized amnesia (i.e., failure to recall event right after a traumatic event) and selective amnesia (i.e., recall of parts but not all of a traumatic event) that are most commonly reported with Dissociative Amnesia. Three other types of amnesia have been reported: Generalized amnesia (i.e., failure to recall a client's entire life), continuous amnesia (i.e., inability to recall events before a certain time up to and including the present), and systematic amnesia (i.e., inability to recall information about certain categories of information including members of a client's family). DSM reports that the latter three types of amnesia don't occur often and if they do, will eventually end up being diagnosed as another disorder (e.g., Dissociative Identity Disorder). The course of the disorder can occur in any age group with both acute and chronic presentation of gaps in their retrospective recall of events or people. Here are the criteria:

Diagnostic Criteria

- A. An inability to recall important autobiographical information, usually of a traumatic or stressful nature, that is inconsistent with ordinary forgetting.
    - o Note: Dissociative amnesia most often consists of localized or selective amnesia for a specific event or events; or generalized amnesia for identity and life history.
- B. The symptoms cause clinically significant distress or impairment in social, occupational, or other important areas of functioning.
- C. The disturbance is not attributable to the physiological effects of a substance (e.g., alcohol or other drug of abuse, a medication) or a neurological or other medical condition (e.g., partial complex seizures, transient global amnesia, sequelae of a closed head injury/traumatic brain injury, other neurological condition).
- D. The disturbance is not better explained by dissociative identity disorder, posttraumatic stress disorder, acute stress disorder, somatic symptom disorder, or major or mild neurocognitive disorder.

Specify if:

- *With dissociative fugue*: Apparently purposeful travel or bewildered wandering that is associated with amnesia for identity or for other important autobiographical information.

Depersonalization Disorder

Depersonalization Disorder is characterized by persistent or recurrent experiences of feeling detached from own body; intact reality testing during the experience; significant impairment of socioeconomic functioning; symptoms do not occur exclusively during the course of another mental disorder, is not due to a physiological condition, and is not due to a substance. You know, about 30 years ago, people used to pay a lot of money to achieve this state of consciousness! And now, it's a mental disorder. Well, the times, they are a changin'... Depersonalization Disorder is typically chronic, can wax and wane, and has been experienced by 1/3 of people exposed to life-threatening situations. Here are the criteria galore:

Diagnostic Criteria

A. The presence of persistent or recurrent experiences of depersonalization, derealization, or both:

1. Depersonalization: Experiences of unreality, detachment, or being an outside observer with respect to one's thoughts, feelings, sensations, body, or actions (e.g., perceptual alterations, distorted sense of time, unreal or absent self, emotional and/or physical numbing).

2. Derealization: Experiences of unreality or detachment with respect to surroundings (e.g., individuals or objects are experienced as unreal, dreamlike, foggy, lifeless, or visually distorted).

B. During the depersonalization or derealization experiences, reality testing remains intact.

C. The symptoms cause clinically significant distress or impairment in social, occupational, or other important areas of functioning.

D. The disturbance is not attributable to the physiological effects of a substance (e.g., a drug of abuse, medication) or another medical condition (e.g., seizures).

E. The disturbance is not better explained by another mental disorder, such as schizophrenia, panic disorder, major depressive disorder, acute stress disorder, posttraumatic stress disorder, or another dissociative disorder.

Somatic Disorders

The central concepts within somatic disorders include persistent or recurring complaints of physical symptoms that are not supported by lab findings and other somatic diagnostics, persistent worry about having a physical illness that are not supported by findings and diagnostics, exaggerated concern about minor or imagined physical defects in an otherwise normal appearing person, and symptoms commonly appear to be associated with psychological factors. The usual suspects are also present: symptoms are not caused by substances or other psychiatric disorders, and that the disorders cause impairment in the socioeconomic functioning.

As you read this lecture, please consider how somatic disorders are essentially a diagnosis of exclusion after all physical etiologies are ruled out, how psychological symptoms usually are applied in retrospect, whether substance related, medical or other mental disorder could better account for the symptoms, whether clients worry excessively about having a serious illness or defect in appearance despite contrary medical evidence, whether clients complain exclusively of pain, or symptoms affecting voluntary motor or sensory function, or of multiple physical symptoms? Basically, somatization disorders imply that your clients' pain is all in their "head" and that the physical symptoms are just a way of talking about their pain. Can you see a problem or two with this diagnosis?

DSM-5 cleaned up a lot of the murkiness that existed in the DSM-IV version of somatic disorders. There are now fewer disorders without the type of stigma that was associated with them in the past. One key difference is that Somatic Disorders focuses on what is present versus speculating on what is not present. Past editions used somatization disorders as a fallback. If a somatic cause for a disorder could not be located, it was assumed to be a psychiatric problem. Look at the criteria (APA, 2013) for Somatic Symptom Disorder.

A. One or more somatic symptoms that are distressing or result in significant disruption of daily life.
B. Excessive thoughts, feelings, or behaviors related to the somatic symptoms or associated health concerns as manifested by at least one of the following:
 1. Disproportionate and persistent thoughts about the seriousness of one's symptoms.
 2. Persistently high level of anxiety about health or symptoms.
 3. Excessive time and energy devoted to these symptoms or health concerns.
C. Although any one somatic symptom may not be continuously present, the state of being symptomatic is persistent (typically more than 6 months).

Specify if:
- With predominant pain (previously pain disorder): This specifier is for individuals whose somatic symptoms predominantly involve pain.

Specify if:
- Persistent: A persistent course is characterized by severe symptoms, marked impairment, and long duration (more than 6 months).

Specify current severity:
- Mild: Only one of the symptoms specified in Criterion B is fulfilled.
- Moderate: Two or more of the symptoms specified in Criterion B are fulfilled
- Severe: Two or more of the symptoms specified in Criterion B are fulfilled, plus there are multiple somatic complaints (or one very severe somatic symptom).

Basically, the disorder is that a person worries excessively about their medical symptoms. Yup, that's right. Just worries too much about an unexplained medical problem. Don't know what is crazier: the patient or the diagnostic category. Not much else really is all that important.

Illness Anxiety Disorder

I preferred the old name: Hypochrondiasis. Yeah, I know that it was hard to pronounce the word, but it sounded so neat. Basically, it's a person who loves WebMD, watches a lot of TV shows on medicine and probably is a nuisance to physicians. Take a gander at the criteria (APA, 2013):

Diagnostic Criteria
   A. Preoccupation with having or acquiring a serious illness.
   B. Somatic symptoms are not present or, if present, are only mild in intensity. If another medical condition is present or there is a high risk for developing a medical condition (e.g., strong family history is present), the preoccupation is clearly excessive or disproportionate.
   C. There is a high level of anxiety about health, and the individual is easily alarmed about personal health status.
   D. The individual performs excessive health-related behaviors (e.g., repeatedly checks his or her body for signs of illness) or exhibits maladaptive avoidance (e.g., avoids doctor appointments and hospitals).
   E. Illness preoccupation has been present for at least 6 months, but the specific illness that is feared may change over that period of time.
   F. The illness-related preoccupation is not better explained by another mental disorder, such as somatic symptom disorder, panic disorder, generalized anxiety disorder, body dysmorphic disorder, obsessive-compulsive disorder, or delusional disorder, somatic type.

Specify whether:
- Care-seeking type: Medical care, including physician visits or undergoing tests and procedures, is frequently used.
- Care-avoidant type: Medical care is rarely used.

Illness Anxiety Disorder isn't a real fancy title but I think that you have probably heard of or even referred to people as "people with illness anxiety disorders." The criteria for Hypochondriasis are that your clients have a preoccupation with fears or beliefs in having a serious disorder based on misinterpretation of symptomology, refuse to accept reassurance from medical personnel and lab findings, are not delusional, have a significant impairment in their socioeconomic functioning, have had the symptoms for at least 6 months, and have symptoms that can't be better explained by another disorder. What else do we know about people with illness anxiety disorders? Well, they may be preoccupied with bodily functions, minor physical abnormalities, or vague and minor physical sensations. And of course the preoccupations are what create the socioeconomic impairments. People with illness anxiety disorders have a lot of fears of aging and death, but don't necessarily exercise or eat healthily. A common problem is that the frequent somatic complaints will lead to problems with their physicians and insurance companies. Like the kid who cried "wolf" too many times, their physicians may not carefully evaluate people with illness anxiety disorders when they really do have a legitimate somatic disorder. As a clinician, you're frequently caught in the middle of this dance between the client and physician. Be sure to know enough to ascertain when to advocate for an in-depth evaluation. The course is generally chronic with typical onset in early adulthood.

Conversion Disorder

Time for a history lesson; this diagnosis is a remnant of Sigmund Freud's era! First, let's state what it is: one or more symptoms or deficits affecting voluntary motor or sensory functions, temporal association with psychological stress or conflict, not intentionally produced, cannot be explained by the effects of a substance, a neurological or physical condition or by a culturally sanctioned behavior or experience, causes significant socioeconomic impairment, is not limited to pain or a sexual dysfunction, and you can rule out Somatic Symptom Disorder and other psychiatric disorders. Of course, Sigmund was not as specific (some would say as mechanistic) in his criteria as exist in DSM. Essentially, Sigmund believed that clients' repressed desires or experiences might present themselves through unexplained paralysis of an arm, leg, or a bodily organ (i.e., temporary blindness). The terms "primary gain" and "secondary gain" are useful to remember for this disorder. The conversion disorder allows a primary gain through symbolic resolution to the psychological conflict by keeping it out of awareness and a secondary gain through getting external benefits by being incapacitated (however briefly) or by evading some unpleasant duty. Go ahead and figure out some primary and secondary gains for Freud's client (i.e., "Anna") when she had a "hysterical paralysis" (i.e., conversion disorder). The term "hysterical" actually has some present day relevance: an associated feature of conversion disorder is histrionic symptoms, with more women represented than men among clinical populations. People with this disorder generally have an acute, early onset between ages 10 and 35 years.

Having said all that, let's look at the *Diagnostic Criteria* (APA, 2013):

Diagnostic Criteria
A. One or more symptoms of altered voluntary motor or sensory function.
B. Clinical findings provide evidence of incompatibility between the symptom and recognized neurological or medical conditions.
C. The symptom or deficit is not better explained by another medical or mental disorder.
D. The symptom or deficit causes clinically significant distress or impairment in social, occupational, or other important areas of functioning or warrants medical evaluation.

Specify symptom type:
- With weakness or paralysis
- With abnormal movement (e.g., tremor, dystonic movement, myoclonus, gait disorder)
- With swallowing symptoms
- With speech symptom (e.g., dysphonia, slurred speech)
- With attacks or seizures
- With anesthesia or sensory loss
- With special sensory symptom (e.g., visual, olfactory, or hearing disturbance)
- With mixed symptoms

Specify if:
- Acute episode: Symptoms present for less than 6 months.
- Persistent: Symptoms occurring for 6 months or more.

Specify if:
- With psychological stressor *(specify stressor)*
- Without psychological stressor

Factitious Disorders

Factitious Disorders are essentially an attempt by your client through deception to feign physical or mental illness in order to assume the role of patient. Now, I know that you're saying that clients don't do such things (you know, the glass half-full idea), but I assure you that such things do happen. However, before I don't want you to become cynical so this diagnosis will allow you to ascertain which clients are faking and which ones aren't. Well, sorta anyway. Like the Pain Disorder, Factitious have three subtypes: predominant psychological factors, predominant physical factors, and combined factors. More about these later. First, let's examine what is common among these subtypes. Clients are intentionally feigning physical and/or psychological symptoms and that there are no external incentives for the behavior.

Some of the necessary history that you'll need include previous inconclusive hospitalizations, repeated, unexplained physical or psychological symptoms, evidence that the client is lying about some part of history, multiple surgical scars, especially on the abdomen, client is or has been a health worker, client experienced a serious illness as a child, client has a fever without other evidence of active disease, repeated tests and evaluations yield no identifiable cause for the symptoms. Some questions to consider include whether your client is consciously and intentionally faking a medical condition for the sole purpose of maintaining the role of patient; assessing whether symptoms disappear when client is under constant observation or does not have access to personal belongings; whether client is excessively knowledgeable about the symptoms, tests and procedures of their illness; whether psychiatric symptoms are unresponsive to standard treatment; and whether your client is vague or elusive about important elements of history or abusive of staff when confronted. Any mental disorder that accounts for the deceptive behavior takes precedence over this diagnosis. I was somewhat amused at how seriously DSM takes Factitious Disorders. I guess it's like saying that Mother Nature doesn't like to be fooled. To not be fooled, the criteria (APA, 2013) are here for your enjoyment:

Factitious Disorder Imposed on Self

Diagnostic Criteria:
A. Falsification of physical or psychological signs or symptoms, or induction of injury or disease, associated with identified deception.
B. The individual presents himself or herself to others as ill, impaired, or injured.
C. The deceptive behavior is evident even in the absence of obvious external rewards.
D. The behavior is not better explained by another mental disorder, such as delusional disorder or another psychotic disorder.

Specify:
- Single episode
- Recurrent episodes (two or more events of falsification of illness and/or induction of injury)

Factitious Disorder Imposed on another Person (Previously Factitious Disorder by Proxy)

　　A. Falsification of physical or psychological signs or symptoms, or induction of injury or disease, in another, associated with identified deception.
　　B. The individual presents another individual (victim) to others as ill, impaired, or injured.
　　C. The deceptive behavior is evident even in the absence of obvious external rewards.
　　D. The behavior is not better explained by another mental disorder, such as delusional disorder or another psychotic disorder.

Note: The perpetrator, not the victim, receives this diagnosis.

Specify:
- Single episode
- Recurrent episodes (two or more events of falsification of illness and/or induction of injury)

Well, onto to the actual subtype criteria. Factitious Disorders with psychological signs describe a clinical presentation in which psychological symptoms (i.e., mental disorder) predominate. As you might, some clients will be very cooperative and others, not so much so. By comparison, Factitious Disorders with physical signs describe a clinical presentation in which physical symptoms (i.e., medical disorder) predominate. Clients may feign or produce all sorts of conditions including infections, complaints of pain, anemia, rashes, vomiting and so on. Factitious Disorders with combined psychological and physical signs include a clinical presentation in which neither psychological nor physical symptoms predominate.

SESSION #10
Theme: Trauma-related Disorders

Session 9 includes the trauma disorders. Lots of interesting stuff to go over.

Trauma-related disorders include
- Reactive Attachment Disorder
- Disinhibited Social Engagement Disorder
- PTSD
- ASD
- Adjustment Disorders

And a couple substances induced this or that.

Trauma Cluster of Disorders

This is an important grouping if for nothing else that it includes PTSD and its brethren.

Reactive Attachment Disorder

Before we get there, let's start with Reactive Attachment Disorder (RAD). In this developmental sequence, it starts with kid end. In RAD, the child (between 9 months and 5 years) doesn't show much fondness or interest in their primary caretaker. What a brat! On the other hand, the DSM speculates that the kid probably had a pretty grim babyhood for him or her to refuse to show much caring for their caretakers. It just isn't normal. Here are the criteria (APA, 2013).

   A. A consistent pattern of inhibited, emotionally withdrawn behavior toward adult caregivers, manifested by both of the following:
      1. The child rarely or minimally seeks comfort when distressed.
      2. The child rarely or minimally responds to comfort when distressed.
   B. A persistent social and emotional disturbance characterized by at least two of the following:
      1. Minimal social and emotional responsiveness to others.
      2. Limited positive affect.
      3. Episodes of unexplained irritability, sadness, or fearfulness that are evident even during nonthreatening interactions with adult caregivers.
   C. The child has experienced a pattern of extremes of insufficient care as evidenced by at least one of the following:
      1. Social neglect or deprivation in the form of persistent lack of having basic emotional needs for comfort, stimulation, and affection met by caregiving adults.
      2. Repeated changes of primary caregivers that limit opportunities to form stable attachments (e.g., frequent changes in foster care).
      3. Rearing in unusual settings that severely limit opportunities to form selective attachments (e.g., institutions with high child-to-caregiver ratios).

D. The care in Criterion C is presumed to be responsible for the disturbed behavior in Criterion A (e.g., the disturbances in Criterion A began following the lack of adequate care in Criterion C).
E. The criteria are not met for autism spectrum disorder.
F. The disturbance is evident before age 5 years.
G. The child has a developmental age of at least 9 months.

Specify if:
- Persistent: The disorder has been present for more than 12 months.

Specify current severity:
- Reactive attachment disorder is specified as severe when a child exhibits all symptoms of the disorder, with each symptom manifesting at relatively high levels.

One last note. Kids who are diagnosed with an Autism Spectrum Disorder also have limited interest in social interactions. However, ASD has a much wider range of symptoms. Everything is pretty much normal except for the kids' fondness for social interactions for their parents. By comparison, ASD kids have widespread deficits.

Disinhibited Social Engagement Disorder

Hmmm, this is pretty much the opposite of RAD although the disinhibition is with everyone not just parents. Let's start by examining the DSM criteria (APA, 2013):

A. A pattern of behavior in which a child actively approaches and interacts with unfamiliar adults and exhibits at least two of the following:
   1. Reduced or absent reticence in approaching and interacting with unfamiliar adults.
   2. Overly familiar verbal or physical behavior (that is not consistent with culturally sanctioned and with age-appropriate social boundaries).
   3. Diminished or absent checking back with adult caregiver after venturing away, even in unfamiliar settings.
   4. Willingness to go off with an unfamiliar adult with minimal or no hesitation.
B. The behaviors in Criterion A are not limited to impulsivity (as in attention-deficit/hyperactivity disorder) but include socially disinhibited behavior.
C. The child has experienced a pattern of extremes of insufficient care as evidenced by at least one of the following:
   1. Social neglect or deprivation in the form of persistent lack of having basic emotional needs for comfort, stimulation, and affection met by caregiving adults.
   2. Repeated changes of primary caregivers that limit opportunities to form stable attachments (e.g., frequent changes in foster care).
   3. Rearing in unusual settings that severely limit opportunities to form selective attachments (e.g., institutions with high child-to-caregiver ratios).
D. The care in Criterion C is presumed to be responsible for the disturbed behavior in Criterion A (e.g., the disturbances in Criterion A began following the pathogenic care in Criterion C).
E. The child has a developmental age of at least 9 months.

Specify if:

- Persistent: The disorder has been present for more than 12 months.

Specify current severity:
- Disinhibited social engagement disorder is specified as severe when the child exhibits all symptoms of the disorder, with each symptom manifesting at relatively high levels.

Child welfare folks probably are familiar with these kids. Usually, a serious lack of affection and caring early on diminishes normal boundaries. Thus, the kids aren't real sure about what is or is not okay social behavior. Remember, for this diagnosis, there should be some evidence of severe past neglect. Second, the lack of inhibition must really be over the top for the kid to deserve the diagnosis.

PTSD

To do this topic justice, let's start by looking at the criteria (APA, 2013):

Diagnostic Criteria

- Note: The following criteria apply to adults, adolescents, and children older than 6 years. For children 6 years and younger, see corresponding criteria below.
- A. Exposure to actual or threatened death, serious injury, or sexual violence in one (or more) of the following ways:
    1. Directly experiencing the traumatic event(s).
    2. Witnessing, in person, the event(s) as it occurred to others.
    3. Learning that the traumatic event(s) occurred to a close family member or close friend. In cases of actual or threatened death of a family member or friend, the event(s) must have been violent or accidental.
    4. Experiencing repeated or extreme exposure to aversive details of the traumatic event(s) (e.g., first responders collecting human remains; police officers repeatedly exposed to details of child abuse).
        - Note: Criterion A4 does not apply to exposure through electronic media, television, movies, or pictures, unless this exposure is work related.
- B. Presence of one (or more) of the following intrusion symptoms associated with the traumatic event(s), beginning after the traumatic event(s) occurred:
    1. Recurrent, involuntary, and intrusive distressing memories of the traumatic event(s).
        - Note: In children older than 6 years, repetitive play may occur in which themes or aspects of the traumatic event(s) are expressed.
    2. Recurrent distressing dreams in which the content and/or affect of the dream are related to the traumatic event(s).
        - Note: In children, there may be frightening dreams without recognizable content.
    3. Dissociative reactions (e.g., flashbacks) in which the individual feels or acts as if the traumatic event(s) were recurring. (Such reactions may occur on a continuum, with the most extreme expression being a complete loss of awareness of present surroundings.)
        - Note: In children, trauma-specific reenactment may occur in play.

4. Intense or prolonged psychological distress at exposure to internal or external cues that symbolize or resemble an aspect of the traumatic event(s).
5. Marked physiological reactions to internal or external cues that symbolize or resemble an aspect of the traumatic event(s).

C. Persistent avoidance of stimuli associated with the traumatic event(s), beginning after the traumatic event(s) occurred, as evidenced by one or both of the following:
   1. Avoidance of or efforts to avoid distressing memories, thoughts, or feelings about or closely associated with the traumatic event(s).
   2. Avoidance of or efforts to avoid external reminders (people, places, conversations, activities, objects, situations) that arouse distressing memories, thoughts, or feelings about or closely associated with the traumatic event(s).

D. Negative alterations in cognitions and mood associated with the traumatic event(s), beginning or worsening after the traumatic event(s) occurred, as evidenced by two (or more) of the following:
   1. Inability to remember an important aspect of the traumatic event(s) (typically due to dissociative amnesia and not to other factors such as head injury, alcohol, or drugs).
   2. Persistent and exaggerated negative beliefs or expectations about oneself, others, or the world (e.g., "I am bad," "No one can be trusted," "The world is completely dangerous," "My whole nervous system is permanently ruined").
   3. Persistent, distorted cognitions about the cause or consequences of the traumatic event(s) that lead the individual to blame himself/herself or others.
   4. Persistent negative emotional state (e.g., fear, horror, anger, guilt, or shame).
   5. Markedly diminished interest or participation in significant activities.
   6. Feelings of detachment or estrangement from others.
   7. Persistent inability to experience positive emotions (e.g., inability to experience happiness, satisfaction, or loving feelings).

E. Marked alterations in arousal and reactivity associated with the traumatic event(s), beginning or worsening after the traumatic event(s) occurred, as evidenced by two (or more) of the following:
   1. Irritable behavior and angry outbursts (with little or no provocation) typically expressed as verbal or physical aggression toward people or objects.
   2. Reckless or self-destructive behavior.
   3. Hypervigilance.
   4. Exaggerated startle response.
   5. Problems with concentration.
   6. Sleep disturbance (e.g., difficulty falling or staying asleep or restless sleep).

F. Duration of the disturbance (Criteria B, C, D, and E) is more than 1 month.

G. The disturbance causes clinically significant distress or impairment in social, occupational, or other important areas of functioning.

H. The disturbance is not attributable to the physiological effects of a substance (e.g., medication, alcohol) or another medical condition.

Specify whether:

- With dissociative symptoms: The individual's symptoms meet the criteria for posttraumatic stress disorder, and in addition, in response to the stressor, the individual experiences persistent or recurrent symptoms of either of the following:
    1. Depersonalization: Persistent or recurrent experiences of feeling detached from, and as if one were an outside observer of, one's mental processes or body (e.g., feeling as though one were in a dream; feeling a sense of unreality of self or body or of time moving slowly).
    2. Derealization: Persistent or recurrent experiences of unreality of surroundings

Let's start by reducing this diagnosis into its component parts. There are basically four different areas: Intrusion, Avoidance, Negative Mood and Affect, Arousal that are the result of some form of actual or threatened injury, death, or sexual violence and must have been occurring for more than a month. In PTSD, the actual event or events have widened over the years. PTSD was just defined trauma resulting from combat. However, a wide variety of experience that has been adjudged to be traumatic can be the precipitant for a trauma. Car accidents are commonly used as the trauma for PTSD. Or being drug users being woken up by shouting and rapidly moving police officers in the middle of night can be traumatic. However, it may be more traumatic for the spouses of the drug users. But any startling and frightening event or events can be enough to be traumatic. The bad part: anything can be asserted to be traumatic. This is a problem because there actually may be no trauma. It may just be a fraudulent claim.

Intrusiveness is the first major area. This causes problems in part because a person can't relax. They can't sleep because of disruptive dreams and flashbacks. Dissociation may occur. In this context, dissociation refers to reliving one or more scenes that last a long time. Finally, some type of startle event that comes from re-experiencing events through some form of internal or external cue.

Avoidance is the second area. Avoidance can also be seen as flight away from memories. PTSD is all about traumatic memories that can be triggered by internal and external reminders of the precipitating trauma. Fleeing is therefore a logical albeit tragic response to the pain that results from intrusive memories.

The third area concerns negative mood and affect. Mood and affect are the most common indicators in an interviewing room. Negative and blunted affect is a normal reaction to chronic fear and dread. Because the patient continually re-experiences a deadly scenario from which they cannot escape, they descend into a helpless/hopeless state of mind. *Distortions and delusions* are a natural response to helplessness and hopelessness. These symptoms result in the well- known numbness that is recounted by clients and clinicians alike.

Arousal states is the fourth area. They can almost seem like someone who is strung out on uppers. If you reread (or maybe just read the substance abuse lecture for the first time. . .) the chapter on substance use, you see that someone who is overdosing on uppers will have exaggerated startle responses, hypervigilance, and paranoid ideation. In combination with the negative mood and anxiety, this might be seen as *anxious depression*.

The kid version of PTSD is very much like the adult variety. The dreams and retelling may be different but the reactions to trauma are similar. Because there is typically no substance dependency, kids can't escape the prison of their memories. Here a couple other notes regarding PTSD. Although the presentation of PTSD is that there is an abrupt onset, that's not always the case. In fact, there may be an appearance of some symptoms of PTSD but the complete onset may not occur for an extended period of time. Second, although the duration of PTSD is longer among women than men, the prevalence is about the same for both genders.

A last note about PTSD. Some writers also warn against secondary trauma. This form of trauma is potentially problematic for clinicians. Imagine that a clinician repeatedly listens to horrific stories from multiple clients. The mixture of caring outreach, emotional vulnerability and unprepared personal preparation may hasten burnout. That's why boundaries and well-established behavioral mechanisms are necessary to prevent burnout.

ASD or Acute Stress Disorder.

This is pretty much prodromal to PTSD (well, maybe anyway). PTSD starts after a month while ASD symptoms show up 3 days to a month after the precipitating event or events. Without a good history or a good memory, it not be clear on whether it's PTSD or ASD. The key question is whether ASD is nothing more than the beginning of PTSD.

I'm not sure that it really matters much. The treatment will be the same regardless of whether it's ASD or PTSD.

Adjustment Disorders

This pretty much the diagnosis given to people who need something to be covered by insurance. It is also handy if there is a (relatively mild) stressor. The criteria (APA, 2013) below pretty much define what it is.
   A. The development of emotional or behavioral symptoms in response to an identifiable stressor(s) occurring within 3 months of the onset of the stressor(s).
   B. These symptoms or behaviors are clinically significant, as evidenced by one or both of the following:
      1. Marked distress that is out of proportion to the severity or intensity of the stressor, taking into account the external context and the cultural factors that might influence symptom severity and presentation.
      2. Significant impairment in social, occupational, or other important areas of functioning.
   C. The stress-related disturbance does not meet the criteria for another mental disorder and is not merely an exacerbation of a pre-existing mental disorder.
   D. The symptoms do not represent normal bereavement.
   E. Once the stressor or its consequences have terminated, the symptoms do not persist for more than an additional 6 months.

Specify whether:
- With depressed mood: Low mood, tearfulness, or feelings of hopelessness are predominant.

- With anxiety: Nervousness, worry, jitteriness, or separation anxiety is predominant.
- With mixed anxiety and depressed mood: A combination of depression and anxiety is predominant.
- With disturbance of conduct: Disturbance of conduct is predominant.
- With mixed disturbance of emotions and conduct: Both emotional symptoms (e.g., depression, anxiety) and a disturbance of conduct are predominant.
- Unspecified: For maladaptive reactions that are not classifiable as one of the specific subtypes of adjustment disorder.

SESSION #11
Theme: Sleeping and Eating Disorders

There are a lot of sleeping disorders in the DSM. Here is the listing from the DSM. insomnia disorder, hypersomnolence disorder, narcolepsy, breathing-related sleep disorders, circadian rhythm sleep-wake disorders, non–rapid eye movement (NREM) sleep arousal disorders, nightmare disorder, rapid eye movement (REM) sleep behavior disorder, restless legs syndrome, and substance/medication-induced sleep disorder. Generally speaking, the presenting complaints are around the quality, timing, and amount of sleep. Complicating any discussion of sleep disorders are the co-occurrence of many medical disorders with them. Let's start with insomnia that is probably the best known sleep disorder.

Insomnia

A. A predominant complaint of dissatisfaction with sleep quantity or quality, associated with one (or more) of the following symptoms:

1. Difficulty initiating sleep. (In children, this may manifest as difficulty initiating sleep without caregiver intervention.)

2. Difficulty maintaining sleep, characterized by frequent awakenings or problems returning to sleep after awakenings. (In children, this may manifest as difficulty returning to sleep without caregiver intervention.)

3. Early-morning awakening with inability to return to sleep.

B. The sleep disturbance causes clinically significant distress or impairment in social, occupational, educational, academic, behavioral, or other important areas of functioning.

C. The sleep difficulty occurs at least 3 nights per week.

D. The sleep difficulty is present for at least 3 months.

E. The sleep difficulty occurs despite adequate opportunity for sleep.

F. The insomnia is not better explained by and does not occur exclusively during the course of another sleep-wake disorder (e.g., narcolepsy, a breathing-related sleep disorder, a circadian rhythm sleep-wake disorder, a parasomnia).

G. The insomnia is not attributable to the physiological effects of a substance (e.g., a drug of abuse, a medication).

H. Coexisting mental disorders and medical conditions do not adequately explain the predominant complaint of insomnia.

Specify if:

- With non–sleep disorder mental comorbidity, including substance use disorders

- With other medical comorbidity
- With other sleep disorder

Specify if:

- Episodic: Symptoms last at least 1 month but less than 3 months.
- Persistent: Symptoms last 3 months or longer.
- Recurrent: Two (or more) episodes within the space of 1 year.

Note: Acute and short-term insomnia (i.e., symptoms lasting less than 3 months but otherwise meeting all criteria with regard to frequency, intensity, distress, and/or impairment) should be coded as another specified insomnia disorder.

There are several types of insomnia: initial and middle insomnia. The first entails getting to sleep and the other one entails staying asleep. The other form of insomnia is nonrestorative sleep in which quality overrides the quantity in feeling rested. The DSM lists difficulty in getting to sleep as "sleep latency" of 20 to 30 minutes and middle insomnia includes periods of time between 20 to 30 minutes. The irony is that the greater the effort to get to or maintain sleep, the less likely there will be success to do so. The consequences are daytime sleepiness, poor concentration, poor attention, decreased energy, and moodiness. Alright, got it? If you don't get enough sleep, you'll fall asleep listening to me lecture.

Women are more likely than men to have insomnia and about 1/3 of all people have insomnia symptoms. Worse yet, insomnia usually means that there is something else around that is contributing to the lack of sleep. Onset is usually in young adult although it can have onset at any time especially during late life when other medical problems may exacerbate poor sleep hygiene. Insomnia has a chronic course.

Hypersomnolence Disorder

How do I say it except that a person is sleeping a lot (as in too much each night, several nights per week)? Again, this complements insomnia. Here, it's too much of low quality sleep. Hey, but I love the term, "sleep drunkenness." Try for moment using the 11 criteria of substance use to describe sleep drunkenness. I think that I might tolerance and withdrawal symptoms of sleep drunkenness. Someone with this disorder probably takes daytime naps and falls asleep during obnoxious TV shows (i.e., poor plotlines and lots of used car commercials). The quantity of sleep for insomnia is less 6.5 hours; for insomnia, it's more than 9.5 hours. Onset is in young adulthood and the course that worsens and is chronic. Here are the criteria (APA, 2013).

A. Self-reported excessive sleepiness (hypersomnolence) despite a main sleep period lasting at least 7 hours, with at least one of the following symptoms:

1. Recurrent periods of sleep or lapses into sleep within the same day.
2. A prolonged main sleep episode of more than 9 hours per day that is nonrestorative (i.e., unrefreshing).

3. Difficulty being fully awake after abrupt awakening.

B. The hypersomnolence occurs at least three times per week, for at least 3 months.

C. The hypersomnolence is accompanied by significant distress or impairment in cognitive, social, occupational, or other important areas of functioning.

D. The hypersomnolence is not better explained by and does not occur exclusively during the course of another sleep disorder (e.g., narcolepsy, breathing-related sleep disorder, circadian rhythm sleep-wake disorder, or a parasomnia).

E. The hypersomnolence is not attributable to the physiological effects of a substance (e.g., a drug of abuse, a medication).

F. Coexisting mental and medical disorders do not adequately explain the predominant complaint of hypersomnolence.

Specify if:

- With mental disorder, including substance use disorders
- With medical condition
- With another sleep disorder

Specify if:

- Acute: Duration of less than 1 month.
- Subacute: Duration of 1–3 months.
- Persistent: Duration of more than 3 months.

Specify current severity: Specify severity based on degree of difficulty maintaining daytime alertness as manifested by the occurrence of multiple attacks of irresistible sleepiness within any given day occurring, for example, while sedentary, driving, visiting with friends, or working.

- Mild: Difficulty maintaining daytime alertness 1–2 days/week.
- Moderate: Difficulty maintaining daytime alertness 3–4 days/week.
- Severe: Difficulty maintaining daytime alertness 5–7 days/week.

Narcolepsy

Here are the criteria (APA, 2013)

A. Recurrent periods of an irrepressible need to sleep, lapsing into sleep, or napping occurring within the same day. These must have been occurring at least three times per week over the past 3 months.

B. The presence of at least one of the following:

1. Episodes of cataplexy, defined as either (a) or (b), occurring at least a few times per month:

    a. In individuals with long-standing disease, brief (seconds to minutes) episodes of sudden bilateral loss of muscle tone with maintained consciousness that are precipitated by laughter or joking.

    b. In children or in individuals within 6 months of onset, spontaneous grimaces or jaw-opening episodes with tongue thrusting or a global hypotonia, without any obvious emotional triggers.

2. Hypocretin deficiency, as measured using cerebrospinal fluid (CSF) hypocretin-1 immunoreactivity values (less than or equal to one-third of values obtained in healthy subjects tested using the same assay, or less than or equal to 110 pg/mL). Low CSF levels of hypocretin-1 must not be observed in the context of acute brain injury, inflammation, or infection.

3. Nocturnal sleep polysomnography showing rapid eye movement (REM) sleep latency less than or equal to 15 minutes, or a multiple sleep latency test showing a mean sleep latency less than or equal to 8 minutes and two or more sleep-onset REM periods.

Specify current severity:

- Mild: Infrequent cataplexy (less than once per week), need for naps only once or twice per day, and less disturbed nocturnal sleep.

- Moderate: Cataplexy once daily or every few days, disturbed nocturnal sleep, and need for multiple naps daily.

- Severe: Drug-resistant cataplexy with multiple attacks daily, nearly constant sleepiness, and disturbed nocturnal sleep (i.e., movements, insomnia, and vivid dreaming).

Say what? Narcolepsy as in sudden urge and subsequent nap 3 times per week over a three-month period. I thought that it was a joke. I thought that irresistible need to sleep only occurred when you're forced to listen to someone droning on. But it's for real. A couple years, someone brought in a YouTube clip of a dog with narcoplexy with cataplexy complications. Dog was happily walking and then fell flat on their snout and went to sleep. Cataplexy is "loss of muscle tone precipitated by strong emotional response." Basically, it's when someone falls down after hearing a good joke. Probably makes the joke teller proud of their ability and joke listener embarrassed at their cataplectic tendencies. DSM says something about the ability of someone with narcoplexy being able to perform easy tasks in a robotic fashion. Sounds like narcoleptic zombies to me. Interesting double onset; first at ages 15-25 and other at ages 30-35.

Obstructive Sleep Apnea Hypopnea and Sleep-Related Hypoventilation

Ever sleep in a tent with a bunch of old men? Sounds like something from an X-rated movie, doesn't it? Actually, I did so as a scoutmaster. There were four or five fat old men sleeping on cots in a 5 x 6 tent. Not only was it cozy, it was incredibly noisy. Given the crescendo of sounds that resulted in tidal volume, it was a wonder that I got any sleep. By the way, the terms "crescendo" and "tidal volume" are from DSM. The writers understood my plight. You really don't need to know much about these diagnoses except for the definition of the terms.

Circadian Rhythm Sleep-Wake Disorders

OK, this diagnosis is more interesting. Basically, we're used to having a regular night and day in which we sleep at night and work during the day. Yeah, I know that there are times in your life where play happens at day and night or work happens at night and so on. But bear with me. Basically, we have a certain rhythm of when we're awake and we sleep. When that gets all screwed up, then problems can occur. It's probably another way of saying that the human body craves routine. Routine food, routine exercise.

Things like shift work, flying commercial jets, vacations, and newborns disrupt your sleeping rhythm. After a while, you crave sleep much the way that an alcoholic craves EtOH. Here are the criteria (APA, 2013).

Diagnostic Criteria

A. A persistent or recurrent pattern of sleep disruption that is primarily due to an alteration of the circadian system or to a misalignment between the endogenous circadian rhythm and the sleep–wake schedule required by an individual's physical environment or social or professional schedule.

B. The sleep disruption leads to excessive sleepiness or insomnia, or both.

C. The sleep disturbance causes clinically significant distress or impairment in social, occupational, and other important areas of functioning.

Specify whether:

- Delayed sleep phase type: A pattern of delayed sleep onset and awakening times, with an inability to fall asleep and awaken at a desired or conventionally acceptable earlier time.

    1. *Specify* if:

        - Familial: A family history of delayed sleep phase is present.

    2. *Specify* if:

        - Overlapping with non-24-hour sleep-wake type: Delayed sleep phase type may overlap with another circadian rhythm sleep-wake disorder, non-24-hour sleep-wake type.

- Advanced sleep phase type: A pattern of advanced sleep onset and awakening times, with an inability to remain awake or asleep until the desired or conventionally acceptable later sleep or wake times.

- *Specify* if:
  - Familial: A family history of advanced sleep phase is present.
- Irregular sleep-wake type: A temporally disorganized sleep-wake pattern, such that the timing of sleep and wake periods is variable throughout the 24-hour period.

Here are my comments in being irregular: bad sleep hygiene; feeling lonely; bored; on vacation. Think airline pilots.

- Non-24-hour sleep-wake type: A pattern of sleep-wake cycles that is not synchronized to the 24-hour environment, with a consistent daily drift (usually to later and later times) of sleep onset and wake times.

Here are my comments on non-24 hour sleep-wake type: Think someone living in Alaska that doesn't have a routine nighttime and daytime.

- Shift work type: Insomnia during the major sleep period and/or excessive sleepiness (including inadvertent sleep) during the major awake period associated with a shift work schedule (i.e., requiring unconventional work hours).

Here are my comments on shift work: Think bad fast food restaurant where your client gets all the really undesirable patchwork of shifts. Now, imagine that they are frying up your food. McD's anyone?

- Unspecified type

This is another one of those, "Who knows?" kind of diagnosis.

Specify if:

- Episodic: Symptoms last at least 1 month but less than 3 months.
- Persistent: Symptoms last 3 months or longer.
- Recurrent: Two or more episodes occur within the space of 1 year.

Non-Rapid Eye Movement Sleep Arousal Disorders

A. Recurrent episodes of incomplete awakening from sleep, usually occurring during the first third of the major sleep episode, accompanied by either one of the following:

1. Sleepwalking: Repeated episodes of rising from bed during sleep and walking about. While sleepwalking, the individual has a blank, staring face; is relatively unresponsive to the efforts of others to communicate with him or her; and can be awakened only with great difficulty.

2. Sleep terrors: Recurrent episodes of abrupt terror arousals from sleep, usually beginning with a panicky scream. There is intense fear and signs of autonomic arousal, such as mydriasis (i.e., excessive dilations of the pupils), tachycardia, rapid breathing, and sweating, during each episode. There is relative

>   unresponsiveness to efforts of others to comfort the individual during the episodes.

B. No or little (e.g., only a single visual scene) dream imagery is recalled.

C. Amnesia for the episodes is present.

D. The episodes cause clinically significant distress or impairment in social, occupational, or other important areas of functioning.

E. The disturbance is not attributable to the physiological effects of a substance (e.g., a drug of abuse, a medication).

F. Coexisting mental and medical disorders do not explain the episodes of sleepwalking or sleep terrors.

Two types here: sleepwalking and sleep terrors. In both subtypes, the problem is an incomplete arousal from sleep. Basically, the client doesn't quite wake up. Almost awake but not quite. Duration is a couple minutes although the DSM lists something about an hour! DSM defines sleepwalking as complex motor behaviors. These behaviors can result in walking around (hence, sleepwalking). As you might guess, once awake, the person has no memory about walking around. People who wrote the DSM do have a sense of humor. They mention eating and sex as complex motor behaviors. Who knew? Sleep terrors are different. Here, a person suddenly wakes up, terrified. No nightmare, just dread and wakes up screaming. Almost sounds like one of those slasher movies, doesn't it? Another observation; this sleep disorder is not comorbid with other disorders. It just happens.

Nightmare Disorders

Let's start with the criteria (APA, 2013):

Diagnostic Criteria

A. Repeated occurrences of extended, extremely dysphoric, and well-remembered dreams that usually involve efforts to avoid threats to survival, security, or physical integrity and that generally occur during the second half of the major sleep episode.

B. On awakening from the dysphoric dreams, the individual rapidly becomes oriented and alert.

C. The sleep disturbance causes clinically significant distress or impairment in social, occupational, or other important areas of functioning.

D. The nightmare symptoms are not attributable to the physiological effects of a substance (e.g., a drug of abuse, a medication).

E. Coexisting mental and medical disorders do not adequately explain the predominant complaint of dysphoric dreams.

Specify if:

- During sleep onset

Specify if:

- With associated non-sleep disorder, including substance use disorders
- With associated other medical condition
- With associated other sleep disorder

Specify if:

- Acute: Duration of period of nightmares is 1 month or less.
- Subacute: Duration of period of nightmares is greater than 1 month but less than 6 months.
- Persistent: Duration of period of nightmares is 6 months or greater.

Specify current severity:

- Severity can be rated by the frequency with which the nightmares occur:
- Mild: Less than one episode per week on average.
- Moderate: One or more episodes per week but less than nightly.
- Severe: Episodes nightly.

Night Terrors don't have nightmare; Nightmare Disorders do have nightmares (aren't you glad that I spelled this out for you?). Nightmare Disorders have an escape plotline (i.e., patient is trying to escape some dreadful zombie or event). Nightmares usually happen during later phase of the sleep cycle. What that means is that nightmares usually take place later in the night or even near morning. Prevalence increases from ages 10 to 13 for both males and females but continues to increase to ages 20-29 for females but not males. Can be as much as twice as much for women as for men. Prevalence decreases steadily with age for both sexes, but the gender difference remains about the same.

Rapid Eye Movement Sleep Disorder

As usual, first the criteria (APA, 2013).

Diagnostic Criteria

A. Repeated episodes of arousal during sleep associated with vocalization and/or complex motor behaviors.

B. These behaviors arise during rapid eye movement (REM) sleep and therefore usually occur more than 90 minutes after sleep onset, are more frequent during the later portions of the sleep period, and uncommonly occur during daytime naps.

C. Upon awakening from these episodes, the individual is completely awake, alert, and not confused or disoriented.

D. Either of the following:

1. REM sleep without atonia on polysomnographic recording.

2. A history suggestive of REM sleep behavior disorder and an established synucleinopathy diagnosis (e.g., Parkinson's disease, multiple system atrophy).

E. The behaviors cause clinically significant distress or impairment in social, occupational, or other important areas of functioning (which may include injury to self or the bed partner).

F. The disturbance is not attributable to the physiological effects of a substance (e.g., a drug of abuse, a medication) or another medical condition.

G. Coexisting mental and medical disorders do not explain the episodes.

Well, this is not a way to get a good night's sleep. With this disorder, your bed partner wakes up, completely aroused, loudly cursing and thrashing about him (or her). DSM calls it a "dream enactment." The person is able to recall the dream. You may wonder about REM sleep behavior. Well, it's all part of a cycle. Think of it as "Pre-sleep, mid-sleep, almost-awake." On the other hand, there is a more scientific way of looking at it:

I went to something called helpguide.org It was a pretty clear description of sleep. . .it didn't put me to sleep.

"During the night, your sleep follows a predictable pattern, moving back and forth between deep restorative sleep (deep sleep or non-REM sleep) and more alert stages and dreaming (REM sleep). Together, the stages of REM and non-REM sleep form a complete sleep cycle. Each cycle typically lasts about 90 minutes and repeats four to six times over the course of a night. The amount of time you spend in each stage of sleep changes as the night progresses. For example, most deep sleep occurs in the first half of the night. Later in the night, your REM sleep stages become longer, alternating with light Stage N2 sleep. This is why if you are sensitive to waking up in the middle of the night, it is probably in the early morning hours, not immediately after going to bed."

I tried to paraphrase it but found that this made the most sense. But okay, let's see how this plays into psychopathology. Overall, people need several sleep cycles to feel restored. Part of this restoration is to feel mentally alert and relaxed. Imagine what happens when depression results in sleep disruption: a person doesn't feel mentally all there. That might result in negative self-statements and so on. Further, the disrupted sleep cycles may cause may make a person feel increasingly unwell that causes depression and so on. So, there is a domino effect in sleep disruptions.

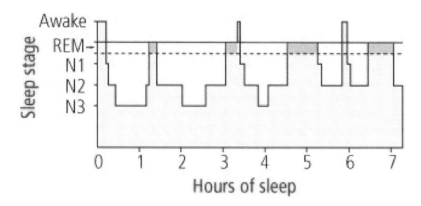

Restless Legs Syndrome

A. An urge to move the legs, usually accompanied by or in response to uncomfortable and unpleasant sensations in the legs, characterized by all of the following:

  1. The urge to move the legs begins or worsens during periods of rest or inactivity.

  2. The urge to move the legs is partially or totally relieved by movement.

  3. The urge to move the legs is worse in the evening or at night than during the day, or occurs only in the evening or at night.

B. The symptoms in Criterion A occur at least three times per week and have persisted for at least 3 months.

C. The symptoms in Criterion A are accompanied by significant distress or impairment in social, occupational, educational, academic, behavioral, or other important areas of functioning.

D. The symptoms in Criterion A are not attributable to another mental disorder or medical condition (e.g., arthritis, leg edema, peripheral ischemia, leg cramps) and are not better explained by a behavioral condition (e.g., positional discomfort, habitual foot tapping).

E. The symptoms are not attributable to the physiological effects of a drug of abuse or medication (e.g., akathisia).

Restless Legs Syndrome (RLS) is a sensorimotor, neurological sleep disorder. OK, that sounds good, but what does it mean? Thank you for asking, grasshopper. It basically means that it's movement that is dictated by something happening in the brain. Basically, the movement can't be explained except that it happens. RLS happens when a person is at rest at night although it can also occur during the daytime when relaxed. Usually, the movements are precipitated by an intense burning or urge. Women are more likely than men to have RLS and it increases with age. Sounds like most everything bad happens when you're old. RLS is comorbid with most psychiatric stress disorders. RLS can be seen in kids especially when they've been sitting a long while at school. Hmmm, sounds like an excuse to me. "Mr. Johnson, I had to get up because I have RLS." How can a principal say "no" to RLS?

There are six or seven more sleep disorders that have to do unspecified this or unspecified that. It also includes substance-induced sleep disorders. These disorders are pretty standard. They usually mean that the disorders don't quite fit the formal but they still cause problems. Substance-induced is pretty straightforward. Some type of substance can be inferred as having caused the symptom.

Feeding and Eating Disorders

I'd better put away junk food as I write this lecture. It's going to make me feel way too guilty. We'll be covering eight feeding and eating disorders today. The disorders are Pica, Rumination Disorder, Avoidant/Restrictive Food Intake Disorder, Anorexia Nervosa, Bulimia Nervosa, Binge-Eating Disorder, Other Specified Feeding or Eating Disorder, Unspecified Feeding or Eating Disorder. OK, let's start.

Pica

Let's start with the criteria (APA, 2013).

Diagnostic Criteria
A. Persistent eating of nonnutritive, nonfood substances over a period of at least 1 month.
B. The eating of nonnutritive, nonfood substances is inappropriate to the developmental level of the individual.
C. The eating behavior is not part of a culturally supported or socially normative practice.
D. If the eating behavior occurs in the context of another mental disorder (e.g., intellectual disability [intellectual developmental disorder], autism spectrum disorder, schizophrenia) or medical condition (including pregnancy), it is sufficiently severe to warrant additional clinical attention.

OK, this is as simple as it gets. A person eats nonnutritive, nonfood items that is not in keeping with developmental age. Basically, someone is eating nonfood who should know better than to do so. But pica is alive and well. Just go to McD's and you'll see pica in action. Pica occurs in males and females and has onset in childhood.

Rumination Disorder

Diagnostic Criteria
A. Repeated regurgitation of food over a period of at least 1 month. Regurgitated food may be re-chewed, re-swallowed, or spit out.
B. The repeated regurgitation is not attributable to an associated gastrointestinal or other medical condition (e.g., gastroesophageal reflux, pyloric stenosis).
C. The eating disturbance does not occur exclusively during the course of anorexia nervosa, bulimia nervosa, binge-eating disorder, or avoidant/restrictive food intake disorder.
D. If the symptoms occur in the context of another mental disorder (e.g., intellectual disability [intellectual developmental disorder] or another neurodevelopmental disorder), they are sufficiently severe to warrant additional clinical attention.

Specify if:
- In remission: After full criteria for rumination disorder were previously met, the criteria have not been met for a sustained period of time.

Alright, I first thought that this was some sort of mad cow disease but then I remember that mad cow is a neurocognitive and not a eating disorder. But it does relate to cows, doesn't it? I can Elsie the Cow, chewing her cud, ruminating away.

But what happens in the rumination disorder? Yeah, you guessed it: repeated regurgitation of food over a period of at least 1 month. No, silly, they don't chew and rechew the piece of food for a month! No, rumination occurs a couple times each week, maybe even daily for at least a month. Because the food is left undigested, a person will not benefit from it. The regurgitation serves as a method of restricting food intake. People with the rumination disorder will understandably be secretive about their behavior. Onset can occur at any time. Malnutrition is the probable outcome.

Avoidant/Restrictive Food Intake Disorder

Let's eat the criteria (APA, 2013) (ugh)

A. An eating or feeding disturbance (e.g., apparent lack of interest in eating or food; avoidance based on the sensory characteristics of food; concern about aversive consequences of eating) as manifested by persistent failure to meet appropriate nutritional and/or energy needs associated with one (or more) of the following:
   1. Significant weight loss (or failure to achieve expected weight gain or faltering growth in children).
   2. Significant nutritional deficiency.
   3. Dependence on enteral feeding or oral nutritional supplements.
   4. Marked interference with psychosocial functioning.
B. The disturbance is not better explained by lack of available food or by an associated culturally sanctioned practice.
C. The eating disturbance does not occur exclusively during the course of anorexia nervosa or bulimia nervosa, and there is no evidence of a disturbance in the way in which one's body weight or shape is experienced.
D. The eating disturbance is not attributable to a concurrent medical condition or not better explained by another mental disorder. When the eating disturbance occurs in the context of another condition or disorder, the severity of the eating disturbance exceeds that routinely associated with the condition or disorder and warrants additional clinical attention.

Specify if:
- In remission: After full criteria for avoidant/restrictive food intake disorder were previously met, the criteria have not been met for a sustained period of time.The first question that I asked myself was how to differentiate this disorder from anorexia. Both disorders involve restricting food intake, right? The DSM makes an interesting distinction. With ARFID (I just love acronyms, don't you?), a person dislikes food but isn't focused on self-image or identity so much. With ARFID, the person is the opposite of a "foodie." They just plain don't like food. Little kids are the target population as opposed to teenage girls. The little kids are called "picky" eaters and object to a whole

host of variables around food. Wrong color, flavor, aroma, temperature and so on. I guess that's why they're called picky eaters. Nothing really surprising. It's a disorder that just covers the bases for infants and little kids. But now onto Anorexia, that's the granddaddy of eating disorders.

Anorexia Nervosa

Well, we're finally at Anorexia. It's a fascinating disorder with all the drama of any psychiatric disorder. It impacts identity, family, medical emergency, psychiatric diagnosis. It is widespread and people have died from it. Yes, this disorder is for real and it needs careful attention and here are the criteria (APA, 2013)

Diagnostic Criteria
   A. Restriction of energy intake relative to requirements, leading to a significantly low body weight in the context of age, sex, developmental trajectory, and physical health. *Significantly low weight* is defined as a weight that is less than minimally normal or, for children and adolescents, less than that minimally expected.
   B. Intense fear of gaining weight or of becoming fat, or persistent behavior that interferes with weight gain, even though at a significantly low weight.
   C. Disturbance in the way in which one's body weight or shape is experienced, undue influence of body weight or shape on self-evaluation, or persistent lack of
   Specify whether:
   - Restricting type: During the last 3 months, the individual has not engaged in recurrent episodes of binge eating or purging behavior (i.e., self-induced vomiting or the misuse of laxatives, diuretics, or enemas). This subtype describes presentations in which weight loss is accomplished primarily through dieting, fasting, and/or excessive exercise.
   - Binge-eating/purging type: During the last 3 months, the individual has engaged in recurrent episodes of binge eating or purging behavior (i.e., self-induced vomiting or the misuse of laxatives, diuretics, or enemas).

Specify if:
- In partial remission: After full criteria for anorexia nervosa were previously met, Criterion A (low body weight) has not been met for a sustained period, but either Criterion B (intense fear of gaining weight or becoming fat or behavior that interferes with weight gain) or Criterion C (disturbances in self-perception of weight and shape) is still met.
- In full remission: After full criteria for anorexia nervosa were previously met, none of the criteria have been met for a sustained period of time.

Specify current severity:
The minimum level of severity is based, for adults, on current body mass index (BMI) (see below) or, for children and adolescents, on BMI percentile. The ranges below are derived from World Health Organization categories for thinness in adults; for children and adolescents, corresponding BMI percentiles should be used. The level of severity may be increased to reflect clinical symptoms, the degree of functional disability, and the need for supervision.

- Mild: BMI ≥ 17 kg/m²
- Moderate: BMI 16–16.99 kg/m²
- Severe: BMI 15–15.99 kg/m²
- Extreme: BMI < 15 kg/m²

As the criteria above document, the three areas of focus are food restriction, fear of fat, and disturbed self-image. Anorexia is unique in having a visible measure of the severity of the disorder in terms of BMI (body mass index). However, there are any numbers of people who complain about how inane BMI is as an absolute measure. These kinds of measures can be misleading to girls who are already sensitive to any indicator of their body weight. Anorexia becomes a form of self-starvation with all the nutritional consequences of doing so. At some point, it becomes an acute medical problem in addition to the original psychiatric concern.

Obsession about food is common as are compulsions that may accompany them. The DSM describes anorexics as seeking control, as having inflexible thinking, limited social spontaneity, and restrained emotional expression. I think of anorexics as being "shut down." With the desperate efforts to maintain complete control over image, it's not surprising that emotional spontaneity would be absent. Another form of anorexia shows itself as engaging in excessive physical activity. Although this form doesn't restrict food, it has the same semi-starvation look as a result. Misuse of prescription drugs also occurs as a method of reducing weight. More ominous thoughts. Most problems associated with anorexia are reversible but conditions like loss of bone density will not be easily remedied.

Anorexia varies considerably worldwide although Asians are particularly prone to it. It does appear to be more common in industrialized countries; it does not appear to be as common with ethnic minorities in the United States. Ironically, voluntary self-starvation occurs while involuntary starvation is occurring in many parts of the world. Suicide risk is elevated and medical frailty should also be considered. Bipolar, depression, and anxiety disorders are frequently comorbid with anorexia. OCD and alcoholism are other disorders that are commonly associated with anorexia.

Bulimia Nervosa

Once again, let's start with an examination of the criteria (APA, 2013).

Diagnostic Criteria

A. Recurrent episodes of binge eating. An episode of binge eating is characterized by both of the following:
1. Eating, in a discrete period of time (e.g., within any 2-hour period), an amount of food that is definitely larger than what most individuals would eat in a similar period of time under similar circumstances.
2. A sense of lack of control over eating during the episode (e.g., a feeling that one cannot stop eating or control what or how much one is eating).

B. Recurrent inappropriate compensatory behaviors in order to prevent weight gain, such as self-induced vomiting; misuse of laxatives, diuretics, or other medications; fasting; or excessive exercise.
C. The binge eating and inappropriate compensatory behaviors both occur, on average, at least once a week for 3 months.
D. Self-evaluation is unduly influenced by body shape and weight.
E. The disturbance does not occur exclusively during episodes of anorexia nervosa.

Specify if:
- In partial remission: After full criteria for bulimia nervosa were previously met, some, but not all, of the criteria have been met for a sustained period of time.
- In full remission: After full criteria for bulimia nervosa were previously met, none of the criteria have been met for a sustained period of time.

Specify current severity:
The minimum level of severity is based on the frequency of inappropriate compensatory behaviors (see below). The level of severity may be increased to reflect other symptoms and the degree of functional disability.
- Mild: An average of 1–3 episodes of inappropriate compensatory behaviors per week.
- Moderate: An average of 4–7 episodes of inappropriate compensatory behaviors per week.
- Severe: An average of 8–13 episodes of inappropriate compensatory behaviors per week.
- Extreme: An average of 14 or more episodes of inappropriate compensatory behaviors per week.

So, how best to describe a bulimic? Uncontrolled binging that is compensated through self-induced vomiting; misuse of laxatives; fasting, or excessive exercise. The dynamic is that the lack of control over eating is remedied by the hypercontrol of weight regulation (through laxatives, regurgitation, etc.).

The *Diagnostic Criteria* states that there must be a discrete period of time that they assert is 2 hours. So, the binging event must occur over a 2-hour period of time. DSM makes an interesting distinction about the lack of control over binging. The bulimic cannot control eating when a phone rings but will do so when someone arrives unexpectedly. This speaks to the secretive nature of bulimia that is typically caused by shame. Food intake does continue until the bulimic can no longer eat. Bulimics present most consistently with negative affect (i.e., depressed). Precipitants for binging might be boredom, interpersonal stressors, availability of food, renewed assessment of body image and other negative feelings. Self-critical depression is the most common mood and affect of a bulimic.

Some compensatory techniques such vomiting will cause tooth enamel to be eroded. Such eroded tooth enamel may result in decay; stomach acid may also discolor skin. The DSM has some discussion on the eventual goals of a bulimic: one goal will be to vomit. Oddly, a bulimic will eat in order to vomit. Although vomiting might have started as a way to compensate for binging, it becomes a desirable goal in itself.

Onset is in midteens to early adulthood by women. Course is chronic but intermittent. Suicide risk is high for bulimics. Much like anorexics, the comorbid symptoms are found in depressive and anxiety disorders. The DSM notes that the mood disorders precede the onset of bulimia.

Binge-Eating Disorder

This disorder is similar to bulimia except that it doesn't include compensatory behaviors such as vomiting. These folks also aren't as focused on body image as are bulimics. Finally, they are most likely to benefit from treatment as opposed to bulimics. The criteria (APA, 2013) are given below.

> A. Recurrent episodes of binge eating. An episode of binge eating is characterized by both of the following:
>   1. Eating, in a discrete period of time (e.g., within any 2-hour period), an amount of food that is definitely larger than what most people would eat in a similar period of time under similar circumstances.
>   2. A sense of lack of control over eating during the episode (e.g., a feeling that one cannot stop eating or control what or how much one is eating).
> B. The binge-eating episodes are associated with three (or more) of the following:
>   1. Eating much more rapidly than normal.
>   2. Eating until feeling uncomfortably full.
>   3. Eating large amounts of food when not feeling physically hungry.
>   4. Eating alone because of feeling embarrassed by how much one is eating.
>   5. Feeling disgusted with oneself, depressed, or very guilty afterward.
> C. Marked distress regarding binge eating is present.
> D. The binge eating occurs, on average, at least once a week for 3 months.
> E. The binge eating is not associated with the recurrent use of inappropriate compensatory behavior as in bulimia nervosa and does not occur exclusively during the course of bulimia nervosa or anorexia nervosa.

Specify if:
- In partial remission: After full criteria for binge-eating disorder were previously met, binge eating occurs at an average frequency of less than one episode per week for a sustained period of time.
- In full remission: After full criteria for binge-eating disorder were previously met, none of the criteria have been met for a sustained period of time.

Specify current severity:
The minimum level of severity is based on the frequency of episodes of binge eating (see below). The level of severity may be increased to reflect other symptoms and the degree of functional disability.
- Mild: 1–3 binge-eating episodes per week.

Moderate: 4–7 binge-eating episodes per week.

SESSION #12
Theme: Depressive Disorders

Theme: Bipolar and Depressive Disorders. Disorders include Bipolar I and II, Cyclothymia, Disruptive Mood Dysregulation, Major Depressive Disorder, Persistent Depressive Disorder, Premenstrual Dysphoric Disorder, Substance/Medication Induced Depressive Disorder, and Specifiers for Depressive Disorders.

Bipolar Disorders: Introduction

You've got to know this stuff cold . . .err, well, something like that. Because I'll be using a lot of terminology, let me define some terms before we go much further. Anhedonia is the loss of interest or pleasure in everyday activities that are typically enjoyed. Catalepsy is a condition of diminished responsiveness and continually maintained immobile position whereas cataplexy is a loss of muscle tone with accompanying weakness. Catatonia is a classically psychotic syndrome characterized by muscle rigidity and lack of response to outside stimuli. Hypersomnia means that a client is sleeping for periods significantly longer than usual whereas insomnia means clients are having difficulty falling or staying asleep. Mood is a pervasive and sustained emotion. Mood-congruent psychotic features are delusions or hallucinations whose content are consistent with clients' typical depressive or manic themes. Mood-incongruent psychotic features are delusions or hallucinations not consistent with depressive or manic themes. Psychomotor agitation is an abnormal increase in physical and emotional activity whereas psychomotor retardation - abnormal slowing of physical and emotional responses. Rapid cycling signifies an occurrence of a least 4 episodes of a mood disturbance in the last 12 months that met criteria for manic, hypomanic or major depressive episodes. Episodes are demarcated by a switch to an episode of opposite polarity.

With no further ado, let's start with the concept of mood episodes. Think of them as the building blocks of mood disorders. It's analogous to the role of *Panic Attacks* within anxiety disorders. For a client to have a Major Depressive Episode, five or more of the following nine criteria must have been present during a two-week period and represent a change from previous functioning. Furthermore, one of the symptoms must be either depressed mood or anhedonia. The criteria include depressed mood, every day, most of the day; anhedonia every day, most of the day; significant weight loss or weight gain and/or increase/decrease in appetite; insomnia or hypersomnia; psychomotor agitation or retardation; fatigue or loss of energy nearly every day; feelings of worthlessness or lots of unnecessary guilt nearly every day; diminished ability to concentrate or be decisiveness nearly every day; recurrent thoughts of death. Some of the other typical criteria also apply. Clients are experiencing a significant impairment in the socioeconomic functioning; symptoms are not due to substance use or a general medical condition; symptoms are not better accounted for by another psychiatric disorder. One last symptom is exclusionary: to be considered a Major Depressive Episode, the client's symptoms can't meet those for a Mixed Episode (more about this later). To reiterate, to have a Major Depressive Episode, your clients should have two weeks of a blue funk in which their eating, sleeping, and pleasure taking are significantly changed or reduced. The eating and sleeping are sometimes called vegetative functioning and their impairment is highly correlated with serious mood disorders. Other characteristic of a Major Depressive Episode is the inability to concentrate, lots of guilt, preoccupation with death, and fatigue. Don't you get tired just thinking about it? Just imagine experiencing one or two or many of them. That's why these episodes shouldn't be taken lightly. It's not just a matter of telling someone to get up and do something. If they could, they would. There is also a spiraling effect. The more disrupted their sleeping and eating become, the fewer reserves that they'll have to be able to snap out of their depressive episode. And of course the more depressive episodes that they experience, the more disrupted that their sleeping and eating will become. As they lose interest in friends, hobbies, work, sex, they may lose interest in life itself. These episodes pervade nearly all areas of your clients' life, much like a cancer.

If you don't like a construction analogy, think fast food. "We'll have one of the Manic Episodes and hold the Depressive Episodes and the fries." That combo value meal is called a Bipolar I Disorder, Single Manic Episode. Although it's called Bipolar I Disorder, it doesn't really entail a mood swing into depression. That's probably the confusing part of this disorder. However, it does suggest the method by which the Bipolar I Disorders are all organized. If there is a manic or mixed episode, then it's a Bipolar I Disorder; if there's no manic or mixed episode, then it's probably a Bipolar II Disorder. More about Bipolar II Disorders in a moment. For now, just remember that the flavor just depends on what combo value meal that you've ordered. Finally, the usual criteria for Mood Disorders are also present: clients are experiencing a significant impairment in the socioeconomic functioning; symptoms are not due to substance use or a general medical condition; symptoms are not better accounted for by Schizoaffective Disorder or other psychotic disorders

Five Things to Remember about Mood Disorders.

Common problems in diagnosing Mood Disorders include clients almost but don't quite fulfilling *Diagnostic Criteria*; clients fulfilling criteria for more than one mood disorder and clients' mood symptoms being comorbid (i.e., being associated) with other psychiatric disorders. To assist you in making diagnosing, here are some pointers. Consider whether the mood is abnormal? If so, does the client's behavior, affect, and cognition fit one or more of the four main syndromes (i.e., Major Depressive Disorder, Persistent Depressive Disorder, Bipolar Disorders, and Cyclothymic Disorder).

Second, could the symptoms be a result of a substance or nonpsychiatric illness?

Third, consider whether there are symptoms of psychosis (i.e., delusions, hallucinations, thought insertion, thought broadcasting)? If no currently, exclude schizoaffective, schizophrenia, schizophreniform, delusional and psychotic disorder. If yes, but not in past 2 weeks in absence of mood symptoms, exclude schizoaffective disorder. If yes, but only in presence of mood symptoms, diagnosis can be either Major Depressive Disorder, Bipolar I Disorder or Bipolar II Disorder.

Fourth, is there any history of manic, hypomanic or mixed episodes? If client currently or in past experienced criteria for manic, mixed, or hypomanic episode, exclude all depressive disorders. If client experienced currently or in past experienced criteria for a current manic, hypomanic or mixed episode, exclude Bipolar I Disorder, Single Manic Episode, Most Recent Hypomanic Episode, Most Recent Episode, Most Recent Manic, and Most Recent Mixed. If there has never been a Manic, Hypomanic or Mixed Episode, exclude Bipolar I Disorder, Most Recent Depressed and Most Recent Unspecified.

Fifth, consider whether the current mood is depressed. If criteria of a Major Depressive Episode are met and there are no previous Manic Episodes, the diagnosis is Major Depressive Disorder. If criteria of Major Depressive Episode are met and there has been a previous Manic or Hypomanic Episode, all depressive diagnoses are excluded. If criteria for Major Depressive and Dysthymic Disorders are both met, give both diagnoses if the dysthymic disorder has been established for at least two years before the major depressive disorder.

This is the granddaddy of depressive disorders: Bipolar I. Here are the criteria. By the way, I also included the criteria for Bipolar II. Note how similar that they are. It makes an accurate diagnosis difficult. I think that DSM-5 has made matters worse.

Bipolar I

Diagnostic Criteria
For a diagnosis of Bipolar I disorder, it is necessary to meet the following criteria (APA, 2013) for a manic episode. The manic episode may have been preceded by and may be followed by hypomanic or major depressive episodes.

Manic Episode
- A. A distinct period of abnormally and persistently elevated, expansive, or irritable mood and abnormally and persistently increased goal-directed activity or energy, lasting at least 1 week and present most of the day, nearly every day (or any duration if hospitalization is necessary).
- B. During the period of mood disturbance and increased energy or activity, three (or more) of the following symptoms (four if the mood is only irritable) are present to a significant degree and represent a noticeable change from usual behavior:
    1. Inflated self-esteem or grandiosity.
    2. Decreased need for sleep (e.g., feels rested after only 3 hours of sleep).
    3. More talkative than usual or pressure to keep talking.
    4. Flight of ideas or subjective experience that thoughts are racing.
    5. Distractibility (i.e., attention too easily drawn to unimportant or irrelevant external stimuli), as reported or observed.
    6. Increase in goal-directed activity (either socially, at work or school, or sexually) or psychomotor agitation (i.e., purposeless non-goal-directed activity).
    7. Excessive involvement in activities that have a high potential for painful consequences (e.g., engaging in unrestrained buying sprees, sexual indiscretions, or foolish business investments).

C. The mood disturbance is sufficiently severe to cause marked impairment in social or occupational functioning or to necessitate hospitalization to prevent harm to self or others, or there are psychotic features.
D. The episode is not attributable to the physiological effects of a substance (e.g., a drug of abuse, a medication, other treatment) or to another medical condition.
    - Note: A full manic episode that emerges during antidepressant treatment (e.g., medication, electroconvulsive therapy) but persists at a fully syndromal level beyond the physiological effect of that treatment is sufficient evidence for a manic episode and, therefore, a bipolar I diagnosis.

Note: Criteria A–D constitute a manic episode. At least one lifetime manic episode is required for the diagnosis of bipolar I disorder.

Hypomanic Episode

A. A distinct period of abnormally and persistently elevated, expansive, or irritable mood and abnormally and persistently increased activity or energy, lasting at least 4 consecutive days and present most of the day, nearly every day.
B. During the period of mood disturbance and increased energy and activity, three (or more) of the following symptoms (four if the mood is only irritable) have persisted, represent a noticeable change from usual behavior, and have been present to a significant degree:
   1. Inflated self-esteem or grandiosity.
   2. Decreased need for sleep (e.g., feels rested after only 3 hours of sleep).
   3. More talkative than usual or pressure to keep talking.
   4. Flight of ideas or subjective experience that thoughts are racing.
   5. Distractibility (i.e., attention too easily drawn to unimportant or irrelevant external stimuli), as reported or observed.
   6. Increase in goal-directed activity (either socially, at work or school, or sexually) or psychomotor agitation.
   7. Excessive involvement in activities that have a high potential for painful consequences (e.g., engaging in unrestrained buying sprees, sexual indiscretions, or foolish business investments).
C. The episode is associated with an unequivocal change in functioning that is uncharacteristic of the individual when not symptomatic.
D. The disturbance in mood and the change in functioning are observable by others.
E. The episode is not severe enough to cause marked impairment in social or occupational functioning or to necessitate hospitalization. If there are psychotic features, the episode is, by definition, manic.
F. The episode is not attributable to the physiological effects of a substance (e.g., a drug of abuse, a medication, other treatment).
    - Note: A full hypomanic episode that emerges during antidepressant treatment (e.g., medication, electroconvulsive therapy) but persists at a fully syndromal level beyond the physiological effect of that treatment is sufficient evidence for a hypomanic episode diagnosis. However, caution is indicated so that one or two symptoms (particularly increased irritability, edginess, or agitation following

antidepressant use) are not taken as sufficient for diagnosis of a hypomanic episode, nor necessarily indicative of a bipolar diathesis.

Note: Criteria A–F constitutes a hypomanic episode. Hypomanic episodes are common in bipolar I disorder but are not required for the diagnosis of bipolar I disorder.

Bipolar II

By comparison, look at the criteria (APA, 2013) for Bipolar II.

Diagnostic Criteria

For a diagnosis of Bipolar II Disorder, it is necessary to meet the following criteria for a current or past hypomanic episode *and* the following criteria for a current or past major depressive episode:

Hypomanic Episode

A. A distinct period of abnormally and persistently elevated, expansive, or irritable mood and abnormally and persistently increased activity or energy, lasting at least 4 consecutive days and present most of the day, nearly every day.
B. During the period of mood disturbance and increased energy and activity, three (or more) of the following symptoms have persisted (four if the mood is only irritable), represent a noticeable change from usual behavior, and have been present to a significant degree:
   1. Inflated self-esteem or grandiosity.
   2. Decreased need for sleep (e.g., feels rested after only 3 hours of sleep).
   3. More talkative than usual or pressure to keep talking.
   4. Flight of ideas or subjective experience that thoughts are racing.
   5. Distractibility (i.e., attention too easily drawn to unimportant or irrelevant external stimuli), as reported or observed.
   6. Increase in goal-directed activity (either socially, at work or school, or sexually) or psychomotor agitation.
   7. Excessive involvement in activities that have a high potential for painful consequences (e.g., engaging in unrestrained buying sprees, sexual indiscretions, or foolish business investments).
C. The episode is associated with an unequivocal change in functioning that is uncharacteristic of the individual when not symptomatic.
D. The disturbance in mood and the change in functioning are observable by others.
E. The episode is not severe enough to cause marked impairment in social or occupational functioning or to necessitate hospitalization. If there are psychotic features, the episode is, by definition, manic.
F. The episode is not attributable to the physiological effects of a substance (e.g., a drug of abuse, a medication or other treatment).
   - Note: A full hypomanic episode that emerges during antidepressant treatment (e.g., medication, electroconvulsive therapy) but persists at a fully syndromal level beyond the physiological effect of that treatment is sufficient evidence for a

hypomanic episode diagnosis. However, caution is indicated so that one or two symptoms (particularly increased irritability, edginess, or agitation following antidepressant use) are not taken as sufficient for diagnosis of a hypomanic episode, nor necessarily indicative of a bipolar diathesis.

Major Depressive Episode

A. Five (or more) of the following symptoms have been present during the same 2-week period and represent a change from previous functioning; at least one of the symptoms is either (1) depressed mood or (2) loss of interest or pleasure.
   o Note: Do not include symptoms that are clearly attributable to another medical condition.
2. Depressed mood most of the day, nearly every day, as indicated by either subjective report (e.g., feels sad, empty, or hopeless) or observation made by others (e.g., appears tearful). (Note: In children and adolescents, can be irritable mood.)
3. Markedly diminished interest or pleasure in all, or almost all, activities most of the day, nearly every day (as indicated by either subjective account or observation).
4. Significant weight loss when not dieting or weight gain (e.g., a change of more than 5% of body weight in a month), or decrease or increase in appetite nearly every day. (Note: In children, consider failure to make expected weight gain.)
5. Insomnia or hypersomnia nearly every day.
6. Psychomotor agitation or retardation nearly every day (observable by others; not merely subjective feelings of restlessness or being slowed down).
7. Fatigue or loss of energy nearly every day.
8. Feelings of worthlessness or excessive or inappropriate guilt (which may be delusional) nearly every day (not merely self-reproach or guilt about being sick).
9. Diminished ability to think or concentrate, or indecisiveness, nearly every day (either by subjective account or as observed by others).
10. Recurrent thoughts of death (not just fear of dying), recurrent suicidal ideation without a specific plan, or a suicide attempt or a specific plan for committing suicide.
   B. The symptoms cause clinically significant distress or impairment in social, occupational, or other important areas of functioning.
   C. The episode is not attributable to the physiological effects of a substance or another medical condition.

Note: Criteria A–C constitutes a major depressive episode. Major depressive episodes are common in bipolar I disorder but are not required for the diagnosis of bipolar I disorder.

Note: Responses to a significant loss (e.g., bereavement, financial ruin, losses from a natural disaster, a serious medical illness or disability) may include the feelings of intense sadness, rumination about the loss, insomnia, poor appetite, and weight loss noted in Criterion A, which may resemble a depressive episode. Although such symptoms may be understandable or considered appropriate to the loss, the presence of a major depressive episode in addition to the normal response to a significant loss should also be carefully considered. This decision inevitably requires the exercise of clinical judgment based on the individual's history and the cultural norms for the expression of distress in the context of loss.

In distinguishing grief from a major depressive episode (MDE), it is useful to consider that in grief the predominant affect is feelings of emptiness and loss, while in MDE it is persistent depressed mood and the inability to anticipate happiness or pleasure. The dysphoria in grief is likely to decrease in intensity over days to weeks and occurs in waves, the so-called pangs of grief. These waves tend to be associated with thoughts or reminders of the deceased. The depressed mood of a MDE is more persistent and not tied to specific thoughts or preoccupations. The pain of grief may be accompanied by positive emotions and humor that are uncharacteristic of the pervasive unhappiness and misery characteristic of a major depressive episode. The thought content associated with grief generally features a preoccupation with thoughts and memories of the deceased, rather than the self-critical or pessimistic ruminations seen in a MDE. In grief, self-esteem is generally preserved, whereas in a MDE, feelings of worthlessness and self-loathing are common. If self-derogatory ideation is present in grief, it typically involves perceived failings vis-à-5is the deceased (e.g., not visiting frequently enough, not telling the deceased how much he or she was loved). If a bereaved individual thinks about death and dying, such thoughts are generally focused on the deceased and possibly about "joining" the deceased, whereas in a major depressive episode such thoughts are focused on ending one's own life because of feeling worthless, undeserving of life, or unable to cope with the pain of depression.

See what I mean about the similarity of the two disorders?

Cyclothymic Disorder

Cyclothymic Disorder is diagnosed when there have been many periods of hypomanic and depressive symptoms for at least 2 years but have not met criteria for major depressive, manic or mixed episode in the first 2 years. Clients with Cyclothymic Disorders should not have experienced relief from the hypomanic and depressive symptoms for more than two months at a time. DSM does put in an aside in which it is stated that after the first two years, if clients can be diagnosed with Manic Episodes, both Bipolar I and Cyclothymic Disorder are diagnosed simultaneously. In addition, DSM also states that after the first two years, if clients can be diagnosed with Major Depressive Episodes, both Bipolar II and Cyclothymic Disorder are diagnosed simultaneously. This is sometimes called a "double depression." Aside from the first three criteria, the usual criteria for Mood Disorders are also present: clients are experiencing a significant impairment in the socioeconomic functioning; symptoms are not due to substance use or a general medical condition; symptoms are not better accounted for by Schizoaffective Disorder or other psychotic disorders.

Here are the actual criteria (APA, 2013)

Diagnostic Criteria

A. For at least 2 years (at least 1 year in children and adolescents) there have been numerous periods with hypomanic symptoms that do not meet criteria for a hypomanic episode and numerous periods with depressive symptoms that do not meet criteria for a major depressive episode.

B. During the above 2-year period (1 year in children and adolescents), the hypomanic and

C. Depressive periods have been present for at least half the time and the individual has not been without the symptoms for more than 2 months at a time.

D. Criteria for a major depressive, manic, or hypomanic episode have never been met.

E. The symptoms in Criterion A are not better explained by schizoaffective disorder, schizophrenia, schizophreniform disorder, delusional disorder, or other specified or unspecified schizophrenia spectrum and other psychotic disorder.

F. The symptoms are not attributable to the physiological effects of a substance (e.g., a drug of abuse, a medication) or another medical condition (e.g., hyperthyroidism).

G. The symptoms cause clinically significant distress or impairment in social, occupational, or other important areas of functioning.

Specify if:

- With anxious distress

Disruptive Mood Dysregulation

OK, lots of jargon but what exactly is "Disruptive Mood Dysregulation?" Sounds like a car misfiring, doesn't it? Well, it is kind of a bratty kid disorder. But it goes beyond bratty kids; it's like a bratty kid on steroids (or maybe PCP). No, no not really, but kids with this diagnosis must be really bratty kids. There are two features: first, frequent temper outbursts and second, chronic, persistently irritable or angry mood between outbursts. Fun, huh?

To understand this disorder, look at the title. "Disruptive" well, that means that the disorder causes disruptions. Duh. That seems self-evident. "Mood" is all about emotions. Think teenage angst. So, the first two words are all about moodiness causes problems. Still a big duh. The last word makes it all come together: "Dysregulation" It's used a lot to mean that a person can't control their emotions. Think of someone in an emotional freefall. DMD means that a person can't control his or her problematic moodiness.

Gotta happen a lot (i.e., three or more times weekly) and the irritability must be present continuously. DMD (now, we start with acronyms) is different from pediatric bipolar disorder (PBD). Now, we get to something interesting. DMD is different from PBD because of the continuity of the mood disruption in DMD. Irritability in kids is equal to depression in adults. So, when kids have irritability as in DMD that is different than PBD. The latter is only diagnosed when the irritability or mood disruption occurs occasionally. PBD must only have periods of mania. Confusing? It seems to me that "continuous" versus "intermittent" is difficult to keep straight. But for right, DMD is continuous with lots of angry mood and temper outbursts.

Prevalence is really not known although it is more likely to happen in adolescent boys than any other group. Onset is before age 10 although DMD should not be diagnosed before age 6. About half of kids with DMD will continue to have it a year later but will rarely progress to PBD or adult bipolar disorder. Not much to say about genetics of DMD; it's a lot like PBD and anxiety disorders. Boys are more likely than girls to be diagnosed with DMD and suicide risk is higher than in normal populations.

In terms of family problems, I mean what do you expect? Yeah, the families of DMD (and PBD for that matter) are screwed up. It's not fair to say that the families cause the DMD; it is fair to say that the family members of kids with DMD don't like them much. Although the DSM-5 doesn't phrase it this way, a psychosocial assessment would show problems throughout most of the areas.

Differential diagnoses are probably the least helpful part of the discussion of DMD. Basically, the whole discussion is differentiating DMD from PBD. Parents should be able to identify distinct periods when the kid wasn't completely irritable. It can "wax and wane" but shouldn't be "episodic." Yup, with DMD, the irritability should be there all the time; with PBD, the parents get some respite. Of course, the kid does occasionally have manic episodes. . ... But, wait, what are manic episodes in kids? Well. . ." elevated or expansive mood and grandiosity." Hmm, not really distinguishing normal kids from kids diagnosed with DMD, does it? Do your best and remember that bratty kids shouldn't be diagnosed as anything but bratty.

OK, next we go onto oppositional defiant disorder (ODD) as a differentiating disorder. Well, here ODD is almost always present in DMD, but not the other way around. It does make sense. With DMD, a kid is throwing temper tantrums all the time. I'd be stunned if the kid wasn't oppositional-defiant. Only 15% of kids diagnosed with ODD meet the criteria for DMD. The key is the irritability. With ADHD and other anxiety disorders, DMD should NOT be diagnosed if the temper tantrums happen during their course. The section on comorbidity basically says that ODD and DMD overlap but they should be considered comorbid. I guess that it's six of one and a half dozen of another. Just remember that DMD is comorbid with most kid psychiatric disorders.

Here are the DSM-5 criteria (APA, 2013):

Diagnostic Criteria
- A. Severe recurrent temper outbursts manifested verbally (e.g., verbal rages) and/or behaviorally (e.g., physical aggression toward people or property) that are grossly out of proportion in intensity or duration to the situation or provocation.
- B. The temper outbursts are inconsistent with developmental level.
- C. The temper outbursts occur, on average, three or more times per week.
- D. The mood between temper outbursts is persistently irritable or angry most of the day, nearly every day, and is observable by others (e.g., parents, teachers, peers).
- E. Criteria A–D have been present for 12 or more months. Throughout that time, the individual has not had a period lasting 3 or more consecutive months without all of the symptoms in Criteria A–D.
- F. Criteria A and D are present in at least two of three settings (i.e., at home, at school, with peers) and are severe in at least one of these.
- G. The diagnosis should not be made for the first time before age 6 years or after age 18 years.

H. By history or observation, the age at onset of Criteria A–E is before 10 years.
I. There has never been a distinct period lasting more than 1 day during which the full symptom criteria, except duration, for a manic or hypomanic episode have been met.
    - Note: Developmentally appropriate mood elevation, such as occurs in the context of a highly positive event or its anticipation, should not be considered as a symptom of mania or hypomania.
J. The behaviors do not occur exclusively during an episode of major depressive disorder and are not better explained by another mental disorder (e.g., autism spectrum disorder, posttraumatic stress disorder, separation anxiety disorder, persistent depressive disorder [dysthymia]).
    - Note: This diagnosis cannot coexist with oppositional defiant disorder, intermittent explosive disorder, or bipolar disorder, though it can coexist with others, including major depressive disorder, attention-deficit/hyperactivity disorder, conduct disorder, and substance use disorders. Individuals whose symptoms meet criteria for both disruptive mood dysregulation disorder and oppositional defiant disorder should only be given the diagnosis of disruptive mood dysregulation disorder. If an individual has ever experienced a manic or hypomanic episode, the diagnosis of disruptive mood dysregulation disorder should not be assigned.
K. The symptoms are not attributable to the physiological effects of a substance or to another medical or neurological condition.

OK, next we go onto oppositional defiant disorder (ODD) as a differentiating disorder. Well, here ODD is almost always present in DMD, but not the other way around. It does make sense. With DMD, a kid is throwing temper tantrums all the time. I'd be stunned if the kid wasn't oppositional-defiant. Only 15% of kids diagnosed with ODD meet the criteria for DMD. The key is the irritability. With ADHD and other anxiety disorders, DMD should NOT be diagnosed if the temper tantrums happen during their course. The section on comorbidity basically says that ODD and DMD overlap but they should be considered comorbid. I guess that it's six of one and a half dozen of another. Just remember that DMD is comorbid with most kid psychiatric disorders.

The criteria (APA, 2013) pretty much are a summary of the above discussion:

A. Lots of temper tantrums that are out of proportion to the precipitating event.
B. But they are way beyond developmental level (i.e., 11-year-old should not act like 7 year olds).
C. Tantrums should have more than 3 times weekly
D. The irritable mood is present most of the time.
E. Must have been present for 12 months with no more than three months when it was NOT present. Basically, no more than a 3-month period in which the mood was not present.
F. Must have been present in two or more settings (i.e., home, school, and playground).
G. Must be between 6 and 18 years
H. Must have onset before 10 years
I. Manic episodes must never have occurred (or at least only one day)

To summarize, the kid with a DMD is between 6 and 18, had onset before 10 years, irritable all the time and has 3 or more major temper tantrums in multiple settings. And all this without expansive and grandiose moods that signify mania.

That's it for DMD.

Major Depressive Disorder

The big D. Yes, we're here, we're depressed or at least we're studying depression. Before we get deep into depression, let's talk about grief. DSM-5 makes a peculiar distinction between grief and MDD or at least grief and a major depressive episode. In grief, the whole thing in grief is a feeling of emptiness and loss while in MDE, it is a persistent depressed mood and an inability to anticipate happiness or pleasure. OK, the distinction sounds reasonable. Grief is focused on a person and the experiences associated with that person. The memories can be both positive and negative. Eventually, the grief decreases. In a MDE, there is a persistent depressed mood and anhedonia and is not tied to any one person. In MDE, the memories are bitter self-critical ruminations. Thoughts of death in grief are focused on the other person; in MDE, it's focused on self.

Now, onto the main event. The Big D. Yes, major depression thing. With no further ado, let's start with the concept of mood episodes. Think of them as the building blocks of mood disorders. It's analogous to the role of *Panic Attacks* within anxiety disorders. Because I'll be using a lot of terminology, let me define some terms before we go much further. Anhedonia is the loss of interest or pleasure in everyday activities that are typically enjoyed. Catalepsy is a condition of diminished responsiveness and continually maintained immobile position whereas cataplexy is a loss of muscle tone with accompanying weakness. Catatonia is a classically psychotic syndrome characterized by muscle rigidity and lack of response to outside stimuli. Hypersomnia means that a client is sleeping for periods significantly longer than usual whereas insomnia means clients are having difficulty falling or staying asleep. Mood is a pervasive and sustained emotion. Mood-congruent psychotic features are delusions or hallucinations whose content are consistent with clients' typical depressive or manic themes. Mood-incongruent psychotic features are delusions or hallucinations not consistent with depressive or manic themes.

Clients are experiencing a significant impairment in the socioeconomic functioning; symptoms are not due to substance use or a general medical condition; symptoms are not better accounted for by another psychiatric disorder. One last symptom is exclusionary: to be considered a Major Depressive Episode, the client's symptoms can't meet those for a Mixed Episode (more about this later).

To reiterate, to have a Major Depressive Episode, your clients should have two weeks of a blue funk in which their eating, sleeping, and pleasure taking are significantly changed or reduced. The eating and sleeping are sometimes called vegetative functioning and their impairment is highly correlated with serious mood disorders. Other characteristics of a Major Depressive Episode are the inability to concentrate, lots of guilt, preoccupation with death, and fatigue.

Don't you get tired just thinking about it? Just imagine experiencing one or two or many of them. That's why these episodes shouldn't be taken lightly. It's not just a matter of telling someone to get up and do something. If they could, they would. There is also a spiraling effect. The more disrupted their sleeping and eating become, the fewer reserves that they'll have to be able to snap out of their depressive episode. And of course the more depressive episodes that they experience, the more disrupted that their sleeping and eating will become. As they lose interest in friends, hobbies, work, sex, they may lose interest in life itself. These episodes pervade nearly all areas of your clients' life, much like a cancer.

One difficulty in diagnosing depression is that it mimics those of a general medical condition. The vegetative problems (i.e., sleeping, eating) are present in medical disorders as is anhedonia. The criteria (APA, 2013) are listed below.

Diagnostic Criteria
   A. Five (or more) of the following symptoms have been present during the same 2-week period and represent a change from previous functioning; at least one of the symptoms is either (1) depressed mood or (2) loss of interest or pleasure.
      o Note: Do not include symptoms that are clearly attributable to another medical condition.
2. Depressed mood most of the day, nearly every day, as indicated by either subjective report (e.g., feels sad, empty, and hopeless) or observation made by others (e.g., appears tearful). (Note: In children and adolescents, can be irritable mood.)
3. Markedly diminished interest or pleasure in all, or almost all, activities most of the day, nearly every day (as indicated by either subjective account or observation).
4. Significant weight loss when not dieting or weight gain (e.g., a change of more than 5% of body weight in a month), or decrease or increase in appetite nearly every day. (Note: In children, consider failure to make expected weight gain.)
5. Insomnia or hypersomnia nearly every day.
6. Psychomotor agitation or retardation nearly every day (observable by others, not merely subjective feelings of restlessness or being slowed down).
7. Fatigue or loss of energy nearly every day.
8. Feelings of worthlessness or excessive or inappropriate guilt (which may be delusional) nearly every day (not merely self-reproach or guilt about being sick).
9. Diminished ability to think or concentrate, or indecisiveness, nearly every day (either by subjective account or as observed by others).
10. Recurrent thoughts of death (not just fear of dying), recurrent suicidal ideation without a specific plan, or a suicide attempt or a specific plan for committing suicide.
   B. The symptoms cause clinically significant distress or impairment in social, occupational, or other important areas of functioning.
   C. The episode is not attributable to the physiological effects of a substance or to another medical condition.

Note: Criteria A–C represent a major depressive episode.

Note: Responses to a significant loss (e.g., bereavement, financial ruin, losses from a natural disaster, a serious medical illness or disability) may include the feelings of intense sadness, rumination about the loss, insomnia, poor appetite, and weight loss noted in Criterion A, which may resemble a depressive episode. Although such symptoms may be understandable or considered appropriate to the loss, the presence of a major depressive episode in addition to the normal response to a significant loss should also be carefully considered. This decision inevitably requires the exercise of clinical judgment based on the individual's history and the cultural norms for the expression of distress in the context of loss.

In distinguishing grief from a major depressive episode (MDE), it is useful to consider that in grief the predominant affect is feelings of emptiness and loss, while in MDE it is persistent depressed mood and the inability to anticipate happiness or pleasure. The dysphoria in grief is likely to decrease in intensity over days to weeks and occurs in waves, the so-called pangs of grief. These waves tend to be associated with thoughts or reminders of the deceased. The depressed mood of MDE is more persistent and not tied to specific thoughts or preoccupations. The pain of grief may be accompanied by positive emotions and humor that are uncharacteristic of the pervasive unhappiness and misery characteristic of MDE. The thought content associated with grief generally features a preoccupation with thoughts and memories of the deceased, rather than the self-critical or pessimistic ruminations seen in MDE. In grief, self-esteem is generally preserved, whereas in MDE feelings of worthlessness and self-loathing are common. If self-derogatory ideation is present in grief, it typically involves perceived failings vis-à-5is the deceased (e.g., not visiting frequently enough, not telling the deceased how much he or she was loved). If a bereaved individual thinks about death and dying, such thoughts are generally focused on the deceased and possibly about "joining" the deceased, whereas in MDE such thoughts are focused on ending one's own life because of feeling worthless, undeserving of life, or unable to cope with the pain of depression.

- D. The occurrence of the major depressive episode is not better explained by schizoaffective disorder, schizophrenia, schizophreniform disorder, delusional disorder, or other specified and unspecified schizophrenia spectrum and other psychotic disorders.
- E. There has never been a manic episode or a hypomanic episode.
  - Note: This exclusion does not apply if all of the manic-like or hypomanic-like episodes are substance-induced or are attributable to the physiological effects of another medical condition.

I tried to summarize this disorder but it's really important stuff so I'll go through what's in DSM-5. Depression kills. Well, that was dramatic, wasn't it? But depression is a significant risk factor in mortality in not only suicide but other medical and psychiatric disorders. You've probably heard about the beneficial aspects of laughter and smiling; the opposite is true as well. Dour and dark thoughts and behaviors hasten illness and death. Prevalence is not surprising: women in their twenties are the most clinical sample at risk. Although onset peaks with clients in their twenties, it can really begin at any age. Although women are more at risk, the course is variable for anyone of any age or gender.

One useful clinical recommendation is to assess the periods of time of at least two months that the client has not experienced depression. The reasoning is that chronicity greatly decreases the chance of a positive outcome. A chronic course is associated with the development of other serious psychiatric disorders such severe anxiety, personality disorders, and alcoholism. There is a substantial genetic contribution in major depressive disorders.

Dysthymia or Persistent Depressive Disorder

What's this, you say? It used to be simply dysthymia which was a long-term sadness without being a major depression. In DSM-5, chronic major depression is being consolidated with dysthymia. What remains consistent is the two-year time frame during which depressed mood is pretty most of the time. Not surprisingly, poor appetite/overeating, insomnia/hypersomnia, low energy/fatigue, problems with concentration or making decisions, and hopelessness are the key to diagnosing dysthymia. Although only two of the above are necessary to diagnose dysthymia, a generalized sense of gloom should be seen. Think of the list as being a definition of gloom. When I say "most of the time," it means that there can't be more than two months at a time when the symptoms aren't present. When doom and gloom are present most of the time, they have to be present most of the time. A little bit isn't enough. Dysthymia must be a "pure" depression without mania/hypomania, schizophrenia, or general medical condition. These are the differential diagnoses that must be ruled out before making a diagnosis of dysthymia. Remember, you've got to rule out those three diagnostic areas before making your diagnosis of dysthymia. The specifications are a royal pain. It's possible to have "anxious distress" while being depressed. That means that a person is depressed and feeling tense, restless, worried, or sense of foreboding. The severity is based on which of the above symptoms are present. A second specifier is called "mixed feature." This is when a depressive episode has periods of elevated or expansive mood, grandiosity, talkativeness, flight of ideas/racing thoughts, increase in energy, risky behaviors and decreased need for sleep. These symptoms are consistent with manic episodes. So, "mixed features" just means that a person is mostly depressed but has periods of almost manic episodes. That's why it is called "mixed." Depression mixed with pleasure or acknowledges the presence of pleasurable stimuli. Basically, melancholic features mean that a person isn't getting much pleasure from life. But the actual symptoms we've heard before: depressed mood, morning time blues, early awakening problems (just "can't get enough sleep."), slowing down, weight loss, and way too much guilt. Melancholic features should be a continuous feature, not just your average bad hair day or week. The fourth specifier is with "atypical features".

This is one of those weird specifiers. I kept reading the description and it doesn't make much sense. But basically it means that a person is sensitive to other people. When a person is rejected, they feel leaden, sleep too much, gain weight, and is increasingly sensitive to criticism/rejection. I mean what is atypical about that? I guess that it means that I'm atypical in feeling rejected. The fifth specifier is important: "with psychotic features." OK, this one is depression with some psychoticism. Anyone for depression with a sprinkling of hallucination and delusions? One interesting change in the DSM-5 is that Persistent Depressive Disorder can have Major Depression Episodes as a specifier. The reasoning was that a person can be depressed but not enough to be diagnosed as having Major Depression but that over the long run, the client does go into a funk that does meet the criteria.

Here are the criteria (APA, 2013):
This disorder represents a consolidation of DSM-IV-defined chronic major depressive disorder and dysthymic disorder.

A. Depressed mood for most of the day, for more days than not, as indicated by either subjective account or observation by others, for at least 2 years.

Note: In children and adolescents, mood can be irritable and duration must be at least 1 year.

B. Presence, while depressed, of two (or more) of the following:
   1. Poor appetite or overeating.
   2. Insomnia or hypersomnia.
   3. Low energy or fatigue.
   4. Low self-esteem.
   5. Poor concentration or difficulty making decisions.
   6. Feelings of hopelessness.

C. During the 2-year period (1 year for children or adolescents) of the disturbance, the individual has never been without the symptoms in Criteria A and B for more than 2 months at a time.

D. Criteria for a major depressive disorder may be continuously present for 2 years.

E. There has never been a manic episode or a hypomanic episode, and criteria have never been met for cyclothymic disorder.

F. The disturbance is not better explained by a persistent schizoaffective disorder, schizophrenia, delusional disorder, or other specified or unspecified schizophrenia spectrum and other psychotic disorder.

G. The symptoms are not attributable to the physiological effects of a substance (e.g., a drug of abuse, a medication) or another medical condition (e.g. hypothyroidism).

H. The symptoms cause clinically significant distress or impairment in social, occupational, or other important areas of functioning.

Note: Because the criteria for a major depressive episode include four symptoms that are absent from the symptom list for persistent depressive disorder (dysthymia), a very limited number of individuals will have depressive symptoms that have persisted longer than 2 years but will not meet criteria for persistent depressive disorder. If full criteria for a major depressive episode have been met at some point during the current episode of illness, they should be given a diagnosis of major depressive disorder. Otherwise, a diagnosis of other specified depressive disorder or unspecified depressive disorder is warranted.

Specify if:
- With anxious distress
- With mixed features
- With melancholic features
- With atypical features
- With mood-congruent psychotic features
- With mood-incongruent psychotic features
- With peripartum onset

Specify if:
- In partial remission
- In full remission

Specify if:
- Early onset: If onset is before age 21 years.
- Late onset: If onset is at age 21 years or older.

Specify if (for most recent 2 years of persistent depressive disorder):

- With pure dysthymic syndrome: Full criteria for a major depressive episode have not been met in at least the preceding 2 years.
- With persistent major depressive episode: Full criteria for a major depressive episode have been met throughout the preceding 2-year period.
- With intermittent major depressive episodes, with current episode: Full criteria for a major depressive episode are currently met, but there have been periods of at least 8 weeks in at least the preceding 2 years with symptoms below the threshold for a full major depressive episode.
- With intermittent major depressive episodes, without current episode: Full criteria for a major depressive episode are not currently met, but there has been one or more major depressive episodes in at least the preceding 2 years.

Premenstrual Dysphoric Disorder

PMS, anyone? I always was uncomfortable with the whole notion of PMS. It seemed like too easy a label to pin on women. I have no doubt that people experienced discomfort, both men and women, during menses (albeit different kinds of discomfort). So, what does PDD mean? Basically, lots of symptoms (5 or more) before menses, improvement during menses, and minimal the week after menses. The symptoms are labile mood (i.e., mood swings). The key however is that the discomfort must be severe enough to meet criteria for Persistent Depressive Disorder. So, that means premenstrual discomfort by itself is not a psychiatric disorder. It can be diagnosed only when the symptoms are severe and it results in socioemotional disruption. Here are the criteria (APA, 2013)

A. In the majority of menstrual cycles, at least five symptoms must be present in the final week before the onset of menses, start to *improve* within a few days after the onset of menses, and become *minimal* or absent in the week postmenses.
B. One (or more) of the following symptoms must be present:
    1. Marked affective lability (e.g., mood swings; feeling suddenly sad or tearful, or increased sensitivity to rejection).
    2. Marked irritability or anger or increased interpersonal conflicts.
    3. Marked depressed mood, feelings of hopelessness, or self-deprecating thoughts.
    4. Marked anxiety, tension, and/or feelings of being keyed up or on edge.
C. One (or more) of the following symptoms must additionally be present, to reach a total of *five* symptoms when combined with symptoms from Criterion B above.
    1. Decreased interest in usual activities (e.g., work, school, friends, and hobbies).
    2. Subjective difficulty in concentration.
    3. Lethargy, easy fatigability, or marked lack of energy.
    4. Marked change in appetite; overeating; or specific food cravings.
    5. Hypersomnia or insomnia.
    6. A sense of being overwhelmed or out of control.
    7. Physical symptoms such as breast tenderness or swelling, joint or muscle pain, a sensation of "bloating," or weight gain.

Note: The symptoms in Criteria A–C must have been met for most menstrual cycles that occurred in the preceding year.

D. The symptoms are associated with clinically significant distress or interference with work, school, usual social activities, or relationships with others (e.g., avoidance of social activities; decreased productivity and efficiency at work, school, or home).
E. The disturbance is not merely an exacerbation of the symptoms of another disorder, such as major depressive disorder, panic disorder, persistent depressive disorder (dysthymia), or a personality disorder (although it may co-occur with any of these disorders).
F. Criterion A should be confirmed by prospective daily ratings during at least two symptomatic cycles. (Note: The diagnosis may be made provisionally prior to this confirmation.)
G. The symptoms are not attributable to the physiological effects of a substance (e.g., a drug of abuse, a medication, other treatment) or another medical condition (e.g., hyperthyroidism).

- Severe: 8–13 binge-eating episodes per week.
- Extreme: 14 or more binge-eating episodes per week.

SESSION #13
Theme: Schizophrenia Spectrum and Other Psychotic Disorders

- Definitions of Terms
- Clinician-Rated Assessment of Symptoms and Related Clinical Phenomena in Psychosis
- Schizotypal (Personality) Disorder
- Delusional Disorder
- Brief Psychotic Disorder
- Schizophreniform Disorder
- Schizophrenia
- Schizoaffective Disorder
- Substance/Medication-Induced Psychotic Disorder
- Psychotic Disorder Due to Another Medical Condition
- Catatonia Associated with Another Mental Disorder (Catatonia Specifier)
- Catatonic Disorder Due to Another Medical Condition
- Unspecified Catatonia
- Other Specified Schizophrenia Spectrum and Other Psychotic Disorder
- Unspecified Schizophrenia Spectrum and Other Psychotic Disorder

I don't know about you, but I was almost looking forward to talking about the "big S family:" Schizophrenia. The core concepts within schizophrenia and other the psychotic disorders include significant distortion in the perception of reality; an impairment in the capacity to reason, speak, and behave rationally or spontaneously; an impairment in the capacity to respond spontaneously with appropriate affect and motivation; and distortions that occur in the absence of impairment in consciousness or memory. Some people mistakenly think that schizophrenics have "split personalities." It's actually closer to "broken" personalities in which there is a lack of integration of the affection, cognition, and behavior. Judgment is lacking although individuals may in fact try to comply with societal demands. During the next several weeks, then, I'll try to provide an overview of schizophrenia and psychotic disorders to provide an appreciation of their dire predicament. Historically, schizophrenics have been described as having "thought disorders," "loss of ego boundaries," "lack of reality testing," "psychotic," and other similar labels. Although there is little doubt that people with the diagnosis of schizophrenia have a major impairment, it's not as clear how to operationalize the disorder. For example, if a clinician was taught that clients with a loss of ego boundaries were schizophrenics, then it might appear that many unruly adolescents were in fact schizophrenics!

Diagnosis of any psychosis requires that the client have delusions, hallucinations, or disorganized speech and thought. Insanity makes no such distinctions. However, for right now, let's see how they correspond with each other. Psychosis is a psychiatric term that fell on the historical spectrum of NORMAL >   NEUROSIS > PSYCHOSIS. Insanity is used in legal settings. If we're normal (please don't smile too much at this assumption!), "neurotics" is an old term that refers to people with maladaptive habits. By the same token, "psychotics" refers to people who have delusions and hallucinations (i.e., have lost touch with reality). There are many terms used to describe the process of becoming psychotic. You might hear the term, "destabilize," "decompensate," or my favorite, "going nuts." The diagnoses given will be those from the Schizophrenia, Delusion and other Psychotic constellation of diagnoses. Generally speaking, psychotropic medication is the treatment of choice although psychoeducational treatment for the identified patient and family members can also help. By contrast, "insanity" is a legal term and refers to the inability to distinguish right from wrong. There is, of course, overlap between the two terms. Someone who has florid symptomology from a psychotic disorder probably won't be able to distinguish right from wrong and could easily be judged to be insane. However, not all people with psychotic disorders are insane, especially those who have successfully been put on medication. Note that courts are interested in distinguishing "right from wrong" while psychiatry is interested in distinguishing "normal from psychotic." Small distinction? Perhaps. But remember that terms like insanity reflect the sociopolitical mores. So, insanity like psychosis as I stated at the beginning of the lecture, may well be a moving target. What was "insane" 25 years ago may not be "insane" today. However, hallucinations and delusions, especially bizarre ones are probably less dependent on sociopolitical mores. So, the psychotic disorders are more likely to remain stable.

Schizoaffective Disorder

Well, what do you expect? Of course, there's going to be schizophrenia with a little major depression sprinkled on it. I mean, let's face it, your life wouldn't be complete unless your clients were both crazy and suicidal. But enough about your life, let's talk Schizoaffective stuff. The name of the disorder pretty much says it all, "schizo" is for the psychosis in the disorder; "affective" is for the major depression in the disorder. The key is that it is primarily a psychotic disorder (i.e., schizophrenia) on which there is periods in which depression and/or mania both are present. The DSM makes a point in saying that the negative symptoms and insight in Schizoaffective Disorders are not as pronounced as in Schizophrenia. There is mention that if Criteria A of Schizophrenia goes into some form of remission, it is likely that some type of Depressive Disorder might become prominent. Again, an interesting point is that the prognosis of Schizoaffective Disorders is somewhat in between mood disorders and schizophrenia. The latter disorder has the worst prognosis. OK, here's the scoop. Schizoaffective is difficult (if not impossible) to make a differential diagnosis from Major Depressive Disorder (with psychotic features), Bipolar I, and Schizophrenia itself.

Schizotypal Personality Disorder

Schizotypal Personality Disorder is a Cluster A personality disorder. It is sometimes considered a promordal indicator of Schizophrenia. It can be considered as Schizophrenia-Lite. The following paragraph is taken from the lecture on personality disorders. "Schizotypal Personality Disorder is a pervasive pattern of deficits marked by discomfort with and reduced capacity for close relationships with cognitive or perceptual distortions and eccentricities of behavior that begin by early adulthood and present in many contexts. Clients with this disorder present with five or more of the following symptoms: ideas of reference; odd beliefs or magical thinking that is inconsistent with cultural norms; unusual perceptual experiences; odd thinking and speech; suspiciousness; inappropriate and/or constricted affect; odd, eccentric, or peculiar behavior; lack of close friends; excessive social anxiety that does diminish with familiarity and is associated with paranoid fears. What can I say? Schizotypal Personality is a lot like

Schizophrenia Lite. A lot of the criteria will be repeated in Schizophrenia only more so. Sometimes, the only difference will be in their intensity. What is clear is that Schizotypal Personality Disorders will present as odd individuals in their appearance, speech, and beliefs. Chances are that they won't have many friends, either. Interestingly enough, DSM reports that relatively few Schizotypal Personality Disorders go on to develop Schizophrenia. You might also place Schizotypal Personality Disorders on a continuum. DSM-5 mentions Schizotypal Personality Disorders as being on the Schizophrenia spectrum, but not Schizoid. Fair enough, they are the experts. However, I've always thoughts of Schizoid Personality Disorders, then Schizotypal Personality Disorders, and next we go onto the psychotic disorders. The continuum doesn't show course of the disorder as much as it is a guide in making a diagnosis. The underlying dimension of this continuum is the severity of the oddness in appearance, speech, behavior, and beliefs."

Delusional Disorders

Delusional Disorders are diagnosed when nonbizarre delusions have been held for at least 1 month, has not exhibited two or more of the characteristic symptoms of Schizophrenia for a significant portion of time during a 1-month period. These symptoms include delusions, hallucinations, disorganized speech, grossly disorganized or catatonic behavior, and negative symptoms (i. e., flat affect, alogia, avolitional behavior). Functioning is reasonably well aside from the impact or ramifications of the delusions. If mood symptoms have been present, their duration has been relatively brief compared to the total duration of the disorder. Finally, symptoms are not due to substance use or a general medical condition. So, what is considered bizarre from a DSM perspective? Hey, some of my relatives can be bizarre! However, DSM defines bizarre as being implausible from ordinary life experiences (e.g., beliefs that organs have been removed without evidence of such procedures, beliefs that thoughts have been inserted or taken). Notwithstanding, DSM's caveat, do you see the difficulty in making a distinction of what delusions are cultural and which are bizarre? Nonbizarre delusions include being stalked, being followed by the FBI, and so on. Remember, not all conspiracy theorists are nuts. The level of socioeconomic impairment depends on how the delusional disorder impacts daily living. If, for example, the delusion makes a person quit his job, flee to a remote wilderness site, subside on whatever is available, then the disorder might be construed as having caused an impairment to their premorbid socioeconomic functioning.

Jealous type is a belief that a spouse or lover is unfaithful without evidence or a reasonable effort to ascertain the facts; confrontations of the spouse/lover and their imagined partner are common. Persecutory type includes the belief that one is being conspired against, cheated, poisoned, maligned, and obstructed in long-term goals. Somatic involves bodily functions or sensations; these beliefs vary and include convictions without evidence that bodily orifices are emitting a foul odor; infestation of insects on the skin; the presence of internal parasites. Mixed is diagnosed when no one delusional theme predominates. Unspecified is diagnosed when a dominant theme cannot be determined or is not described in specific types.

Brief Psychotic Disorder

Brief Psychotic Disorder is diagnosed when your client continuously exhibits one or more of the following symptoms: delusions, hallucinations, disorganized speech, grossly disorganized or catatonic behavior for at least one day but less than a month with full return to premorbid levels of functioning. Exclusionary criteria include ruling out a mood disorder with psychotic features, schizoaffective or schizophrenia that should specify with or without marked stressors and postpartum onset. One final exclusionary criterion is that symptoms should not be due to substance use or a general medical condition. Although DSM doesn't suggest it in this section, it does so earlier that there is an implicit continuum in which Brief Psychotic Disorders are followed by Schizophreniform Disorders are followed by Schizophrenia and its subtypes. The duration variable of the continuum of the episode: Brief Psychotic (1 day to 1 month); Schizophreniform (1 month to 6 months); and Schizophrenia (more than 6 months). Within this continuum, clients all demonstrate some symptoms from Criterion A of Schizophrenia (i.e., delusions, hallucinations, disorganized speech, grossly disorganized or catatonic behavior), but differ primarily in the duration of the disturbance and the return to premorbid levels of functioning. Once again, careful monitoring of functioning is needed to make accurate diagnoses among the three disorders on the continuum.

Schizophreniform Disorder

Schizophreniform Disorder is diagnosed when two or more of the characteristic symptoms are present for a significant portion of time during a 1 month period. These symptoms include delusions, hallucinations, disorganized speech, grossly disorganized or catatonic behavior, and negative symptoms (i. e., flat affect, alogia, avolitional behavior). Second, Schizoaffective Disorder and Mood Disorder with Psychotic Features have been ruled out because no relatively brief depressive, manic, or mixed episodes occurred concurrently with the active phase symptoms (or were relatively brief by comparison to the duration of the symptoms). Although DSM does not explicitly state that you should rule out other non-psychotic disorders, it's implicit in the above criteria. Third, symptoms are not due to substance use or a general medical condition. A key criterion of Schizophreniform is that the entire episode include prodromal, active and residual phases should be last one month but less than six months. Think of it as "Schizophrenia Lite." The two major differences is the duration of the observed symptoms and the lack of significantly impaired socioeconomic functioning (although hallucinations and delusions probably have made others consider him odd). A question: when does schizophrenia go from being provisional to schizophreniform to schizophrenia subtype? What determines when you make the call? How does socioeconomic status fit into making a diagnosis? With Schizophreniform Disorders, specify provisional if diagnosed before recovery (and how will you know that?). Second, specify good prognostic features if 2 or more of prominent psychotic features appeared within 4 weeks of first noticeable change in usual behavior or functioning, there was confusion or perplexity at the height of the episode, there was good premorbid social and occupational functioning, and there was an absence of blunted or flat affect.

Schizophrenia

Schizophrenia is without doubt at the heart of psychopathology. If you want to learn anything in psychopathology, you've got to learn depression and schizophrenia. Those are the heavyweights poised for the psychopathology crown for relevance. Within Schizophrenia, there are normally three phases: prodromal, active, and residual. As you might guess, prodromal is the phase before the symptoms of schizophrenia become florid (i.e., overtly present), active is the phase when the symptoms are florid, and residual are when the symptoms are no longer present and are in remission.

The Schizophrenia subtypes have a common criteria set. They include characteristic symptoms, impairment in socioeconomic functioning, duration, and no or relatively brief mood disturbances, not due to substance use or a general medical condition, if comorbid with developmental disorders, there must be prominent hallucinations and/or delusions for at least a month.

First, two or more of the characteristic symptoms should be present for a significant portion of time during a 1-month period. These symptoms include delusions, hallucinations, disorganized speech, grossly disorganized or catatonic behavior, and negative symptoms (i. e., flat affect, **alogia**, avolitional behavior). Second, impairment in socioeconomic functioning is defined as a decrease in observed capabilities since the onset of symptomology or a failure to achieve expected level of functioning (i.e., used in conjunction when onset occurs in childhood or adolescence). Third, continuous signs of the disturbance persist for at least 6 months; during these six months, there must be at least one month during which the client exhibits active-phase symptoms (e.g., delusions, hallucinations, disorganized speech, grossly disorganized behavior) and occasional periods of prodromal or residual symptoms; during the prodromal or residual phases, clients may only show negative symptoms or less severe versions of the active-phase symptoms. Fourth, Schizoaffective Disorder and Mood Disorder with Psychotic Features have been ruled out because no relatively brief depressive, manic, or mixed episodes occurred concurrently with the active phase symptoms (or were relatively brief by comparison to the duration of the symptoms). Although DSM does not explicitly state that you should rule out other non-psychotic disorders, it's implicit in the above criteria. Fifth, symptoms are not due to substance use or a general medical condition. Sixth, if there a history of developmental disorders exists; Schizophrenia can only be diagnosed if prominent delusions or hallucinations are also present for at least a month.

The course of Schizophrenia is somewhat insidious, with some symptoms manifesting themselves during the prodromal phase. Early adulthood is the typical age during which the symptoms begin to be observed. In general, clients with an early onset of symptoms are more likely to have a poorer prognosis, to be males, have poorer premorbid adjustment (i.e., had poorer socioeconomic functioning), more evidence of neurological abnormalities, more evidence of cognitive impairment, and negative symptomology. Clients with a later onset are more likely to be males, had better premorbid adjustment, fewer neurological abnormalities, less evidence of cognitive impairment, and fewer negative signs. Although cases of complete remission of symptoms have been noted, this is not common. Generally speaking, negative symptoms are present first at the prodromal phase, followed by positive symptomology. Although positive signs generally respond to medication and psychotherapy, the negative symptoms will remain.

In general, the more prominent the negative symptomology, the worse the prognosis for the client.

Course specifiers include Episodic with Interepisode Residual Symptoms in which episodes occur when criterion A is met and clinically significant residual symptoms are apparent between episodes; Episodic with no Interepisode Residual Symptoms are diagnosed when criterion A is met during episodes and no residual symptoms between episodes; Continuous is diagnosed when symptoms of criterion A are met throughout the course (specify if prominent negative symptoms are present); Single Episode in Partial Remission is diagnosed when only one episode of exists when criterion A were met and clinically significant residual symptoms remain (specify if negative symptoms remain); Single Episode, in Full Remission is diagnosed when only one episode of exists when criterion A were met and clinically significant residual symptoms are not present; Other or unspecified pattern (yup, you guessed it, the NOS specifier for schizophrenic subtypes).

The DSM-5 makes the following observations:

There are deficits around types of memory, language, and slower processing speed. Sensory processing and inhibitory capacity, attention difficulties, impaired social cognition, and explanatory delusions were other significant problems.

Some individuals with psychosis may lack insight or awareness of their disorder (i.e., anosognosia). This lack of "insight" includes unawareness of symptoms of schizophrenia and may be present throughout the entire course of the illness. Unawareness of illness is typically a symptom of schizophrenia itself rather than a coping strategy. It is comparable to the lack of awareness of neurological deficits following brain damage, termed *anosognosia*. This symptom is the most common predictor of non-adherence to treatment, and it predicts higher relapse rates, increased number of involuntary treatments, poorer psychosocial functioning, aggression, and a poorer course of illness.

Speaking of aggression: schizophrenics are NOT violent and instead can be victims. That said, Aggression is more frequent for younger males and for individuals with a past history of violence, non-adherence with treatment, substance abuse, and impulsivity. The course for men is in their mid-twenties and late twenties for women. Onset is insidious and course is variable. Most schizophrenics will need help in daily living activities. Schizophrenics can have exaggeration and remission of their active symptoms but others it is progressively worse over time. Here are the formal criteria (APA, 2013) for Schizophrenia.

Diagnostic Criteria

A. Two (or more) of the following, each present for a significant portion of time during a 1-month period (or less if successfully treated). At least one of these must be (1), (2), or (3):
   1. Delusions.
   2. Hallucinations.
   3. Disorganized speech (e.g., frequent derailment or incoherence).

4. Grossly disorganized or catatonic behavior.
5. Negative symptoms (i.e., diminished emotional expression or avolition).
B. For a significant portion of the time since the onset of the disturbance, level of functioning in one or more major areas, such as work, interpersonal relations, or self-care, is markedly below the level achieved prior to the onset (or when the onset is in childhood or adolescence, there is failure to achieve expected level of interpersonal, academic, or occupational functioning).
C. Continuous signs of the disturbance persist for at least 6 months. This 6-month period must include at least 1 month of symptoms (or less if successfully treated) that meet Criterion A (i.e., active-phase symptoms) and may include periods of prodromal or residual symptoms. During these prodromal or residual periods, the signs of the disturbance may be manifested by only negative symptoms or by two or more symptoms listed in Criterion A present in an attenuated form (e.g., odd beliefs, unusual perceptual experiences).
D. Schizoaffective disorder and depressive or bipolar disorder with psychotic features have been ruled out because either 1) no major depressive or manic episodes have occurred concurrently with the active-phase symptoms, or 2) if mood episodes have occurred during active-phase symptoms, they have been present for a minority of the total duration of the active and residual periods of the illness.
E. The disturbance is not attributable to the physiological effects of a substance (e.g., a drug of abuse, a medication) or another medical condition.
F. If there is a history of autism spectrum disorder or a communication disorder of childhood onset, the additional diagnosis of schizophrenia is made only if prominent delusions or hallucinations, in addition to the other required symptoms of schizophrenia, are also present for at least 1 month (or less if successfully treated).

Specify if:

The following course specifiers are only to be used after a 1-year duration of the disorder and if they are not in contradiction to the diagnostic course criteria.

- **First episode, currently in acute episode:** First manifestation of the disorder meeting the defining diagnostic symptom and time criteria. An *acute episode* is a time period in which the symptom criteria are fulfilled.
- **First episode, currently in partial remission:** *Partial remission* is a period of time during which an improvement after a previous episode is maintained and in which the defining criteria of the disorder are only partially fulfilled.
- **First episode, currently in full remission:** *Full remission* is a period of time after a previous episode during which no disorder-specific symptoms are present.
- **Multiple episodes, currently in acute episode:** Multiple episodes may be determined after a minimum of two episodes (i.e., after a first episode, a remission and a minimum of one relapse).
- **Multiple episodes, currently in partial remission**
- **Multiple episodes, currently in full remission**
- **Continuous:** Symptoms fulfilling the diagnostic symptom criteria of the disorder are remaining for the majority of the illness course, with subthreshold symptom periods being very brief relative to the overall course.
- **Unspecified**

Specify if:
- With catatonia (refer to the criteria for catatonia associated with another mental disorder for definition).

Specify current severity:
- Severity is rated by a quantitative assessment of the primary symptoms of psychosis, including delusions, hallucinations, disorganized speech, abnormal psychomotor behavior, and negative symptoms. Each of these symptoms may be rated for its current severity (most severe in the last 7 days) on a 5-point scale ranging from 0 (not present) to 4 (present and severe). (See Clinician-Rated Dimensions of Psychosis Symptom Severity in the chapter "Assessment Measures.")
- Note: Diagnosis of schizophrenia can be made without using this severity specifier.

Diagnostic Features

The characteristic symptoms of schizophrenia involve a range of cognitive, behavioral, and emotional dysfunctions, but no single symptom is pathognomonic of the disorder. The diagnosis involves the recognition of a constellation of signs and symptoms associated with impaired occupational or social functioning. Individuals with the disorder will vary substantially on most features, as schizophrenia is a heterogeneous clinical syndrome.

At least two Criterion A symptoms must be present for a significant portion of time during a 1-month period or longer. At least one of these symptoms must be the clear presence of delusions (Criterion A1), hallucinations (Criterion A2), or disorganized speech (Criterion A3). Grossly disorganized or catatonic behavior (Criterion A4) and negative symptoms (Criterion A5) may also be present. In those situations, in which the active-phase symptoms remit within a month in response to treatment, Criterion A is still met if the clinician estimates that they would have persisted in the absence of treatment.

Schizophrenia involves impairment in one or more major areas of functioning (Criterion B). If the disturbance begins in childhood or adolescence, the expected level of function is not attained. Comparing the individual with unaffected siblings may be helpful. The dysfunction persists for a substantial period during the course of the disorder and does not appear to be a direct result of any single feature. Avolition (i.e., reduced drive to pursue goal-directed behavior; Criterion A5) is linked to the social dysfunction described under Criterion B. There is also strong evidence for a relationship between cognitive impairment (see the section "*Associated Features Supporting Diagnosis*" for this disorder) and functional impairment in individuals with schizophrenia.

Some signs of the disturbance must persist for a continuous period of at least 6 months (Criterion C). Prodromal symptoms often precede the active phase, and residual symptoms may follow it, characterized by mild or subthreshold forms of hallucinations or delusions.

Individuals may express a variety of unusual or odd beliefs that are not of delusional proportions (e.g., ideas of reference or magical thinking); they may have unusual perceptual experiences (e.g., sensing the presence of an unseen person); their speech may be generally understandable but vague; and their behavior may be unusual but not grossly disorganized (e.g., mumbling in public). Negative symptoms are common in the prodromal and residual phases and can be severe. Individuals who had been socially active may become withdrawn from previous routines. Such behaviors are often the first sign of a disorder.

Mood symptoms and full mood episodes are common in schizophrenia and may be concurrent with active-phase symptomatology. However, as distinct from a psychotic mood disorder, a schizophrenia diagnosis requires the presence of delusions or hallucinations in the absence of mood episodes. In addition, mood episodes, taken in total, should be present for only a minority of the total duration of the active and residual periods of the illness.

In addition to the five symptom domain areas identified in the *Diagnostic Criteria*, the assessment of cognition, depression, and mania symptom domains is vital for making critically important distinctions between the various schizophrenia spectrum and other psychotic disorders.

Associated Features Supporting Diagnosis
Individuals with schizophrenia may display inappropriate affect (e.g., laughing in the absence of an appropriate stimulus); a dysphoric mood that can take the form of depression, anxiety, or anger; a disturbed sleep pattern (e.g., daytime sleeping and nighttime activity); and a lack of interest in eating or food refusal. Depersonalization, derealization, and somatic concerns may occur and sometimes reach delusional proportions.

Schizoaffective Disorder

Diagnostic Criteria (APA, 2013)
   A. An uninterrupted period of illness during which there is a major mood episode (major depressive or manic) concurrent with Criterion A of schizophrenia.
      o Note: The major depressive episode must include Criterion A1: Depressed mood.
   B. Delusions or hallucinations for 2 or more weeks in the absence of a major mood episode (depressive or manic) during the lifetime duration of the illness.
   C. Symptoms that meet criteria for a major mood episode are present for the majority of the total duration of the active and residual portions of the illness.
   D. The disturbance is not attributable to the effects of a substance (e.g., a drug of abuse, a medication) or another medical condition.

Specify whether:
- Bipolar type: This subtype applies if a manic episode is part of the presentation. Major depressive episodes may also occur.
- Depressive type: This subtype applies if only major depressive episodes are part of the presentation.

Specify if:

- With catatonia (refer to the criteria for catatonia associated with another mental disorder for definition).
    - Catatonia associated with schizoaffective disorder to indicate the presence of the comorbid catatonia.

Specify if:

The following course specifiers are only to be used after a 1-year duration of the disorder and if they are not in contradiction to the diagnostic course criteria.

- First episode, currently in acute episode: First manifestation of the disorder meeting the defining diagnostic symptom and time criteria. An *acute episode* is a time period in which the symptom criteria are fulfilled.
- First episode, currently in partial remission: *Partial remission* is a time period during which an improvement after a previous episode is maintained and in which the defining criteria of the disorder are only partially fulfilled.
- First episode, currently in full remission: *Full remission* is a period of time after a previous episode during which no disorder-specific symptoms are present.
- Multiple episodes, currently in acute episode: Multiple episodes may be determined after a minimum of two episodes (i.e., after a first episode, a remission and a minimum of one relapse).
- Multiple episodes, currently in partial remission
- Multiple episodes, currently in full remission
- Continuous: Symptoms fulfilling the diagnostic symptom criteria of the disorder are remaining for the majority of the illness course, with subthreshold symptom periods being very brief relative to the overall course.
- Unspecified

Specify current severity:

- Severity is rated by a quantitative assessment of the primary symptoms of psychosis, including delusions, hallucinations, disorganized speech, abnormal psychomotor behavior, and negative symptoms. Each of these symptoms may be rated for its current severity (most severe in the last 7 days) on a 5-point scale ranging from 0 (not present) to 4 (present and severe). (See Clinician-Rated Dimensions of Psychosis Symptom Severity in the chapter "Assessment Measures.")
- Note: Diagnosis of schizoaffective disorder can be made without using this severity specifier.

Note: For additional information on Development and Course (age-related factors), Risk and Prognostic Factors (environmental risk factors), Culture-Related Diagnostic Issues, and Gender-Related Diagnostic Issues, see the corresponding sections in schizophrenia, bipolar I and II disorders, and major depressive disorder in their respective chapters.

Diagnostic Features

The diagnosis of schizoaffective disorder is based on the assessment of an uninterrupted period of illness during which the individual continues to display active or residual symptoms of psychotic illness. The diagnosis is usually, but not necessarily, made during the period of psychotic illness. At some time during the period, Criterion A for schizophrenia has to be met.

Criteria B (social dysfunction) and F (exclusion of autism spectrum disorder or other communication disorder of childhood onset) for schizophrenia do not have to be met. In addition to meeting Criterion A for schizophrenia, there is a major mood episode (major depressive or manic) (Criterion A for schizoaffective disorder). Because loss of interest or pleasure is common in schizophrenia, to meet Criterion A for schizoaffective disorder, the major depressive episode must include pervasive depressed mood (i.e., the presence of markedly diminished interest or pleasure is not sufficient). Episodes of depression or mania are present for the majority of the total duration of the illness (i.e., after Criterion A has been met) (Criterion C for schizoaffective disorder). To separate schizoaffective disorder from a depressive or bipolar disorder with psychotic features, delusions or hallucinations must be present for at least 2 weeks in the absence of a major mood episode (depressive or manic) at some point during the lifetime duration of the illness (Criterion B for schizoaffective disorder). The symptoms must not be attributable to the effects of a substance or another medical condition (Criterion D for schizoaffective disorder).

Criterion C for schizoaffective disorder specifies that mood symptoms meeting criteria for a major mood episode must be present for the majority of the total duration of the active and residual portion of the illness. Criterion C requires the assessment of mood symptoms for the entire course of a psychotic illness, which differs from the criterion in DSM-IV, which required only an assessment of the current period of illness. If the mood symptoms are present for only a relatively brief period, the diagnosis is schizophrenia, not schizoaffective disorder. When deciding whether an individual's presentation meets Criterion C, the clinician should review the total duration of psychotic illness (i.e., both active and residual symptoms) and determine when significant mood symptoms (untreated or in need of treatment with antidepressant and/or mood-stabilizing medication) accompanied the psychotic symptoms. This determination requires sufficient historical information and clinical judgment. For example, an individual with a 4-year history of active and residual symptoms of schizophrenia develops depressive and manic episodes that, taken together, do not occupy more than 1 year during the 4-year history of psychotic illness. This presentation would not meet Criterion C.
In addition to the five symptom domain areas identified in the *Diagnostic Criteria*, the assessment of cognition, depression, and mania symptom domains is vital for making critically important distinctions between the various schizophrenia spectrum and other psychotic disorders.

Associated Features Supporting Diagnosis
Occupational functioning is frequently impaired, but this is not a defining criterion (in contrast to schizophrenia). Restricted social contact and difficulties with self-care are associated with schizoaffective disorder, but negative symptoms may be less severe and less persistent than those seen in schizophrenia. Anosognosia (i.e., poor insight) is also common in schizoaffective disorder, but the deficits in insight may be less severe and pervasive than those in schizophrenia. Individuals with schizoaffective disorder may be at increased risk for later developing episodes of major depressive disorder or bipolar disorder if mood symptoms continue following the remission of symptoms meeting Criterion A for schizophrenia. There may be associated alcohol and other substance-related disorders.

Schizoaffective disorder is diagnosed when your client continuously exhibits two or more of the characteristic symptoms of Schizophrenia for a significant portion of time during a 1-month period. These symptoms include delusions, hallucinations, disorganized speech, grossly disorganized or catatonic behavior, and negative symptoms (i. e., flat affect, alogia, avolitional behavior). During this period of time, your client must also experience a Major Depressive Episode for at least 2 weeks, or a Manic or Mixed Episode for at least 1 week for a substantial portion of the time. Next, your client must have had delusions or hallucinations for at least 2 weeks in absence of the mood symptoms. In addition, your client must have had symptoms that meet the criteria for mood episodes during the prodromal and residual phases of the Schizoaffective Disorder. Although DSM does not explicitly state that you should rule out other non-psychotic disorders, it's implicit in the above criteria. Finally, symptoms are not due to substance use or a general medical condition. DSM asserts that the prognosis for Schizoaffective Disorders is better than that of Schizophrenia. It suggests that the Mood Disorders have a better prognosis than Schizoaffective Disorders and Schizophrenia has the worst prognosis of all. Note however that not all Schizophrenic subtypes have equally dismal prognoses. The difficulty in diagnosing Schizoaffective Disorders is distinguishing it from either Schizophrenia or Mood Disorders with Psychotic Features. Mood disturbances can occur in Schizophrenia in the active phase of Schizophrenia but should be relatively brief. What defines "relatively brief?" It suggests that you'd have to observe your client for a lengthy period of time to correctly make the differential diagnosis. It's even worse with Mood Disorders with Psychotic Features. If the psychotic symptoms occur exclusively during a mood disturbance, then it's a Mood Disorder with Psychotic Features. What happens if the history isn't perfect? Or if the collaterals aren't with the identified patient a lot to report to you? To say that the diagnosis is difficult is an underestimate that just won't go away.

Substance Induced Psychotic Disorder is diagnosed when delusions or hallucinations exist; evidence exists, usually from a history, physical examination, or laboratory findings that your client exhibits two or more of the characteristic symptoms of Schizophrenia for a significant portion of time during a 1 month period. These symptoms include delusions, hallucinations, disorganized speech, grossly disorganized or catatonic behavior, and negative symptoms (i. e., flat affect, alogia, avolitional behavior) that were caused by substance intoxication or withdrawal. An additional criterion is that the above symptomology does not occur exclusively during the course of a delirium. Aside from the first three criteria, some usual criteria are also present: symptoms are not better accounted for by a Psychotic Disorder that is not substance-induced. The difficult part of this diagnosis is that you can make the diagnosis only if the psychotic symptomology was in excess of what was expected from the substance intoxication or withdrawal. and onset during intoxication or withdrawal.

Other Specified Schizophrenic Spectrum and Other Psychotic Disorder and *Unspecified Schizophrenic Spectrum and Other Psychotic* are diagnosed when there are inadequate or contradictory information or symptoms do not meet criteria for any specific disorder.
To make a differential diagnosis within the psychotic disorders, you need to collect lots of history. They include a history of documented psychiatric illness, a history of socially unusual, odd or isolative behavior history of substance abuse, history of medical illnesses, current experience of hallucinations or odd perceptual experiences, evidence of disorganized thought of

speech, evidence of delusions, evidence of negative symptoms, evidence of depression, evidence of mania and the duration of symptoms. Collectively, these items can help inform clinicians in weaving together a diagnosis. These items help in answering some eight key questions involved in choosing a diagnosis from among the psychotic disorders. First, could symptoms be produced by drugs or a nonpsychiatric medical illness? This is always a primary exclusionary question and must be considered before any other concern. Second, does the individual currently meet Criterion A symptoms for Schizophrenia that include delusions, hallucinations, disorganized speech, grossly disorganized or catatonic behavior, and negative symptoms (i. e., flat affect, alogia, avolitional behavior)? If yes, schizophrenia residual type, delusional disorder and psychotic disorder NOS are all excluded. Third, have the symptoms lasted less than 6 months? If yes, all schizophrenia subtype diagnoses are excluded. Fourth, is there a concurrent major depressive or manic episode concurrent with Criterion A symptoms for Schizophrenia? If no, schizoaffective disorder is excluded. Fifth, is there significant disorganized speech and behavior? If speech or behaviors are disorganized, schizophrenia, paranoid type is excluded. If there is flat or inappropriate affect in addition to disorganization, likely diagnosis is schizophrenia, disorganized type. If disorganization is present without flat affect, schizophrenia, undifferentiated type is likely. Sixth, is there unusual or peculiar motor activity? If yes, likely schizophrenia, catatonic type. Seventh, are there prominent hallucinations that the individual realizes are not real? If yes, generally will be due to general medical condition or substance induced. Eighth, are there bizarre delusions? If yes, exclude Delusional Disorder and tend toward schizophrenia, paranoid type.

SESSION #15
Theme: Paraphilias; sexual dysfunctions; gender dysphoria; sexual assault; power dynamics

Although it's not as common as Bipolar Disorder or PTSD, clinicians should have a working knowledge of sexual disorders and their manifestation. Especially with the current focus on pedophilia and the Catholic Church, the Supreme Court's decision to allow virtual child pornography, and legal challenges to sexual predators' directories, it's increasingly important that clinicians be familiar with who these individuals are. No, not the Supreme Court justices, pedophiles and others with sexual disorders.

Just a note before we get started. DSM-5 divides up the paraphilias into two groups: anomalous activity preferences and anomalous target preferences I really can't say it better than what is written in the DSM-5. These paraphilic disorders are subdivided into courtship disorders, which resemble distorted components of human courtship behavior (voyeuristic disorder, exhibitionistic disorder, and frotteuristic disorder), and algolagnic disorders, which involve pain and suffering (sexual masochism disorder and sexual sadism disorder). The second group of disorders is based on anomalous target preferences. These disorders include one directed at other humans (pedophilic disorder) and two directed elsewhere (fetishistic disorder and transvetic disorder).

Paraphilia

First, let's talk about changes from DSM-IV. There are new course specifiers *"in a controlled environment"* and *"in remission"* to the Diagnostic Criteria sets for all the paraphilic disorders. There is a distinction between paraphilias and paraphilic disorders. Not important, you say? Well, yeah, it does seem like a fine point. Basically, a *paraphilic disorder is* paraphilia that is currently causing distress or impairment to the individual or a paraphilia whose satisfaction has entailed personal harm, or risk of harm, to others. A paraphilia is a *necessary but not a sufficient* condition for having a paraphilic disorder, and a paraphilia by itself does not automatically justify or require clinical intervention. The distinction between paraphilias and paraphilic disorders was implemented without making any changes to the basic structure of the *Diagnostic Criteria* as they had existed since DSM-III-R. "The change proposed for DSM-5 is that individuals who meet both Criterion A and Criterion B would now be diagnosed as having a paraphilic disorder. A diagnosis would not be given to individuals whose symptoms meet Criterion A but not Criterion B — that is, to individuals who have a paraphilia but not a paraphilic disorder". Basically, you can have a paraphilia but its okay as long as no one gets hurt. Wow! Quite a change.First, let's define paraphilic disorders. They are recurrent, intense sexually arousing fantasies, urges, and behaviors involving nonhuman objects (i.e., animate or inanimate), suffering and humiliation of self and/or partner, and children or other nonconsenting persons that occur for at least 6 months. Generally speaking, the paraphilias are not diagnoses unless there has been impairment in the identified patient's socioeconomic functioning. That usually translates to getting caught by legal authorities for pedophilia, having interpersonal difficulties with one's spouse after discovery of fetishism, and so on. Most paraphilias have a specific stimulus and will seek contact with them. Some pedophiles will seek refuge in child pornography and others will perpetrate crimes by victimizing children. In a nutshell, the latter is the crisis afflicting the Catholic Church today. Although the vast majority of priests are not pedophiles, the concern about celibate priests who counsel, coach, and teach children has grown exponentially. Although one can have many views about the Catholic Church, it is apparent even to the casual observer that it did not know how to make informed decisions about priests who were pedophiles. Paraphilias generally begin childhood or early adolescence and have a chronic course. DSM-5 also discusses the intensity of the fantasies or urges. Basically, their point was that the intensity should be seen in the context of what would be normal for that group of people. Hmmm, I'm not sure how to measure what might be considered normal. Seems like a slippery slope there.

In general, exhibitionism, fetishism, transvestite fetishism, and voyeurism are relatively benign disorders in that there is seldom harm done to self or others except as a result of the shock of seeing a person display his genitalia and so on. First, there frotteurism, pedophilia, sexual masochism, and sexual sadism can have a much darker side. Although frotteurism generally involves activity that might be construed as the normal type of contact in a crowded bus, it still constitutes an assault on another person's body and should be regarded as such. Pedophilia is undoubtedly the most serious because it preys on the most innocent and should be regarded as the most severe of the paraphilias for that reason. Some people enjoy sexual masochism and sexual sadism; although it's probably difficult for most individuals to understand the thrill of S & M, they should be considered a disorder primarily when they involve nonconsenting adults and/or cause harm to premorbid functioning. The following paraphilias listed below have much the same criteria except for the foci of interest.

Exhibitionism is diagnosed when over a period of 6 months, clients have recurrent, sexually intense and arousing fantasies, urges or behaviors that involve exposing genitalia to an unsuspecting stranger; clients experience marked distress or interpersonal difficulty from the fantasies or urges, or have engaged in the behavior. The extent of activities with this disorder involves exhibiting genitalia or more vividly, masturbating in front of the unsuspecting person.

Fetishism is diagnosed when over a period of 6 months; clients have recurrent, sexually intense and arousing fantasies, urges or behaviors that involve the use of nonliving things (e.g., shoes, female undergarments); clients experience impairment in their socioeconomic functioning as a result of their fantasies, urges, and behavior. The items are not limited to those used in cross-dressing or those used in tactile genital stimulation.

Frotteurism is diagnosed when over a period of 6 months, clients have recurrent, sexually intense and arousing fantasies, urges or behaviors that involve touching and rubbing against a nonconsenting person; clients experience marked distress or interpersonal difficulty from the fantasies or urges, or have engaged in the behavior. Frotteurism typically occurs in crowded places where escape is easy. Most acts of frottage occur in adolescence or early adulthood with a decline in frequency with age.

Pedophilia is diagnosed when over a period of 6 months, clients have recurrent, sexually intense and arousing fantasies, urges or behaviors that involve sexual activity with a prepubescent child or children (i.e., generally, ages 13 or younger); clients experience marked distress or interpersonal difficulty from the fantasies or urges, or have engaged in the behavior; pedophiles must be at least 16 years old and 5 years older than their victims. Some more thoughts on pedophilia. The issue really is the age of consent and whether the power differential of the two parties was similar. For example, can someone in a position of high authority take advantage of someone who is 15 years old? Is that pedophilia? Many would argue that a legal distinction of the mere age of consent has no place in determining whether an individual should be diagnosed as a pedophile or a sexual predator. Some developmentally delayed individuals can have a chronological age of 30 and still easily be a victim for a pedophile. So, although DSM sets some age limits, I'd urge you to go carefully and make a clinical judgment on whether the victim could give consent given the power differential of the perpetrator. DSM does ask for specifiers that help provide a profile of the prognosis of and treatment planning for pedophilia. For example, pedophilia that is limited to incest will probably have a different treatment plan that a sexual predator who preys on children. Onset is around puberty that corresponds to normal arousal in same age teens. Pedophilia appears to be a lifelong condition but may increase or decrease as a person ages. DSM-5 also states that antisocial traits correlate to pedophilia. Thus, antisocial personality disorder is a risk factor for pedophilia.

Sexual Masochism is diagnosed when over a period of 6 months, clients have recurrent, sexually intense and arousing fantasies, urges or behaviors that involve the act (real, not simulated) of being humiliated, beaten, bound, or otherwise made to suffer; clients experience an impairment in their socioeconomic functioning as a result of their fantasies, urges, and behavior.

Sexual Sadism is diagnosed when over a period of 6 months, clients have recurrent, sexually intense and arousing fantasies, urges or behaviors that involve acts (real, not simulated) in which the psychological or physical humiliation of others is sexually exciting; clients experience marked distress or interpersonal difficulty from the fantasies or urges, or have engaged in the behavior with a nonconsenting adult. This brings us to the topic of rape, sexual assault, sexual offense, sociopathy and all the other words used to describe it. Rape is variously defined as promiscuity, college adventures with too much alcohol, anger, domination, control, and narcissism. It is a controversial topic that spans ethics, morals, law and even science. What does it mean for you? That's the ethics part. How does it fit into your personal code of conduct, professional code of ethics, or other defining aspects? Ethics are just rules that inform and guide what you do. Men and women have different ethics . . . I mean, really?

On the other hand, there is also morality and that has to do with a Judeo-Christian set of rules and beliefs. I know a 37-year-old attractive woman who is a virgin! The exclamation point is because people react in incredulity when they learn that she is a virgin. Why is she a virgin? She believes in God, reads the Bible, obeys lots of commandments, and is faithful in much of what she does. On the other hand, there are terms like "hooking up" which can be anything from dating to casual intercourse (but more like the latter than the former). The difference between ethics and morality? Ethics are derived from morality.

Law is the third leg of the stool. It is derived from local and federal law. Local law is built on city and county ordinances and statutes. Basically, it's criminal law. You know, "You do the crime, you do the time." Well, there are other types of non-federal law, but this is a course on badass crazy guys and not legal niceties. Federal law is all about the constitutionality of an event or events. In terms of sexual sadism, there is a real dilemma. It's easy to see why coercive sexual interactions should be discouraged. The discouragement comes in the form of legal consequences for people who engage in sexual crimes. But there is a problem in defining sexual crimes. In fact, remember that crime is defined in local terms. Good part is that it allows flexibility to match local sensibilities. Bad part is that local sensibilities aren't always sensible.

Provincial attitudes toward women and ethnic minorities have littered the legal landscape with blatantly unfair and illegal penalties. Crimes are generally decided by popular vote . . . but they are in many cases. The people who hire and maintain police and sheriff departments are elected by the constituents of their locale. So, law enforcements can go counter to their constituents at their own risk. In short, sexual sadism and rape isn't the same thing. In fact, sexual crimes vary a lot across locales. To better understand the dilemma, watch the movie, "Rashoman," that showed how rape was viewed from the perspective of all the parties involved. Great movie, scary implications.

Tranvestic Fetishism is diagnosed when over a period of 6 months, heterosexual male clients have recurrent, sexually intense and arousing fantasies, urges or behaviors that crossdressing; clients experience impairment in their socioeconomic functioning as a result of their fantasies, urges, and behavior.

Voyeurism is diagnosed when over a period of 6 months, clients have recurrent, sexually intense and arousing fantasies, urges or behaviors that involve observing unsuspecting person who is disrobing, naked, or engaged in sexual activity; clients experience marked distress or interpersonal difficulty from the fantasies or urges, or have engaged in the behavior.

Some last thoughts about sexual assault and power. Technically speaking, sexual assault is more of legal terms about which clinicians are asked to make predictions. Unfortunately, sexual assault is culture specific and in some ways, community specific. It all has to do with the mores of the dominant community. After all, laws are a statement of the Judeo-Christian ethical standards. Therefore, the law helps us set boundaries on what we like and don't like. The distinction between permissible sexual behavior and forbidden behavior sometimes can change from one era to another era, from one region to another and so on. It all depends on what year, what place, and what people are involved because the mores of a community proscribe sexual behaviors in different places with people of different ages and so on.

Sexual assault can be complicated because it can be a statement of the power balance among gender, age, ethnicity, and/or class. It's another way of saying that you may not agree at all on what is sexual assault with someone else. It doesn't make anyone good or bad. It does make a statement about a personal understanding of power. My advice: follow the law above all else. The law provides us with our sociopolitical boundaries of what we can as professional caregivers. Go beyond that and you're pushing an "interpretation" of statute to the place where you may be negligent. Fundamentally, sexual assault says a lot about the need to dominate; what we can do about it is constrained by the mores of a community.

Gender Dysphoria

Gulp. Well, this topic is loaded with controversy. No matter what a person says, he or she will receive flak from someone. Hard to keep everything straight. That said, let's start with definitions. Sex and sexual refer to biological indicators; gender is the public lived role as boy or girl, man or woman. Basically, biology is seen as interacting with social and psychological influences in gender development. Gender assignment refers to the initial (i.e., at birth) assignment as male or female. Gender identity is a person's identification as male or female. Gender dysphoria refers to discontent with gender assignment. Transsexual refers to a person who has made a cross gender transition.
Below are the DSM-5 criteria (APA, 2013)

Gender Dysphoria in Children
   A. A marked incongruence between one's experienced/expressed gender and assigned gender, of at least 6 months' duration, as manifested by at least six of the following (one of which must be Criterion A1):
      1. A strong desire to be of the other gender or an insistence that one is the other gender (or some alternative gender different from one's assigned gender).
      2. In boys (assigned gender), a strong preference for cross-dressing or simulating female attire; or in girls (assigned gender), a strong preference for wearing only typical masculine clothing and a strong resistance to the wearing of typical feminine clothing.
      3. A strong preference for cross-gender roles in make-believe play or fantasy play.
      4. A strong preference for the toys, games, or activities stereotypically used or engaged in by the other gender.
      5. A strong preference for playmates of the other gender.
      6. In boys (assigned gender), a strong rejection of typically masculine toys, games, and activities and a strong avoidance of rough-and-tumble play; or in girls (assigned gender), a strong rejection of typically feminine toys, games, and activities.

7. A strong dislike of one's sexual anatomy.
8. A strong desire for the primary and/or secondary sex characteristics that match one's experienced gender.

B. The condition is associated with clinically significant distress or impairment in social, school, or other important areas of functioning.

Specify if:
- With a disorder of sex development (e.g., a congenital adrenogenital disorder such as 255.2 [E25.0] congenital adrenal hyperplasia or 259.50 [E34.50] androgen insensitivity syndrome).
- Coding note: Code the disorder of sex development as well as gender dysphoria.

Gender Dysphoria in Adolescents and Adults

A. A marked incongruence between one's experienced/expressed gender and assigned gender, of at least 6 months' duration, as manifested by at least two of the following:
1. A marked incongruence between one's experienced/expressed gender and primary and/or secondary sex characteristics (or in young adolescents, the anticipated secondary sex characteristics).
2. A strong desire to be rid of one's primary and/or secondary sex characteristics because of a marked incongruence with one's experienced/expressed gender (or in young adolescents, a desire to prevent the development of the anticipated secondary sex characteristics).
3. A strong desire for the primary and/or secondary sex characteristics of the other gender.
4. A strong desire to be of the other gender (or some alternative gender different from one's assigned gender).
5. A strong desire to be treated as the other gender (or some alternative gender different from one's assigned gender).
6. A strong conviction that one has the typical feelings and reactions of the other gender (or some alternative gender different from one's assigned gender).

B. The condition is associated with clinically significant distress or impairment in social, occupational, or other important areas of functioning.

Coding note: Code the disorder of sex development as well as gender dysphoria.

Specify if:
- Posttransition: The individual has transitioned to full-time living in the desired gender (with or without legalization of gender change) and has undergone (or is preparing to have) at least one cross-sex medical procedure or treatment regimen—namely, regular cross-sex hormone treatment or gender reassignment surgery confirming the desired gender (e.g., penectomy, vaginoplasty in a natal male; mastectomy or phalloplasty in a natal female).

A couple observations are in order. Over time, there is an increasing intrusiveness of the cross-gender transition. Whereas a young child can cross dress without much comment, the same behavior in adolescents or adults are considered a paraphilia. Further, when surgical options are considered, the level of transition is a complete rejection of their gender assignment. Not surprisingly, early onset gender dysphoria starts in childhood and frequently results in same sex sexual partners. By contrast, late onset gender dysphoria may simply result in transvestic behaviors. In fact, late onset may result in traditional cross gender marriages. Their early onset cohort members may result in hormone treatment and surgical interventions. However, DSM-5 does conclude that early gender atypical behavior does not result in gender dysphoria. What I conclude is that it's nearly impossible to make too many generalizations on what causes what and what should be done to whom. There is so much biological, sociology, and psychology involved in gender dysphoria that it makes little sense to think about psychopathology.

Comments on Types of Sexual Dysfunction

What can I say about sex that hasn't been said by thousands of others? It has continued to fascinate everyone from kids to elderly adults. Politicians always seem to have an interest in it, professional or otherwise. Within religious circles, sex is exalted (or at least tolerated) within marriage and disparaged outside of it. Within social work, sex is considered important but doesn't usually have a whole lot of coursework devoted to it. As a result, it's difficult to know exactly how to respond when clients present with sexual dysfunctions. I suppose that it's important to talk about sexual dysfunction. I started with the paraphilias as a way of saying that although paraphilias are sexual, DSM really doesn't place them in the Sexual Dysfunctions. This is surprising because most of the paraphilias could easily be viewed as a problem of the human sexual response cycle: Desire-Arousal-Orgasm-Resolution. More about this cycle later. Because the paraphilias generally involve a forensic component to them, it's probably more convenient to keep them separated from the sexual dysfunctions. However, as we discuss the sexual dysfunctions, think to yourself how the paraphilias might also be sexual dysfunction and where they fit on the sexual response cycle.

The first phase of the cycle is *sexual desire* (i.e., fantasies about sexual activity and desire to have it). The second phase, *sexual arousal or excitement* that consists of a sense of subjective pleasure and physiological changes. For males, the changes consist of an erection; for females, they consist mostly of lubrication of the vagina with accompanying expansion and swelling of external genitalia (e.g., clitoris). The third phase, *orgasm*, consists of the peaking of sexual pleasure, a release of sexual tension, and rhythmic contraction of perineal muscles and reproductive organs. Males ejaculate semen while females experience a contraction of the outer third of vaginal wall during orgasm. The fourth phase, *Resolution*, consists of a sense of muscular relaxation and well-being. Although females may be ready to engage in further sexual intercourse, males may need a period of time (i.e., refractory period of time) to achieve an erection.

The specifiers are important for the dysfunction (alright, alright, I suppose that they are important for most of the disorders). Lifelong type versus acquired type is two considerations. Acquired type suggests that something happened that resulted in a disruption of the sexual response cycle. Generalized type versus situational type refers to a consideration of the context in which there is a disruption. Finally, psychological type versus combined type. The combined type refers to a combination of psychological and medical conditions contributing to a disruption of the sexual response cycle.

Sexual Desire Disorders include Hypoactive Sexual Desire Disorder and Sexual Aversion Disorder. *Hypoactive sexual desire disorder* is characterized by a lack of sexual desire and a lack of sexual fantasies that causes distress or interpersonal difficulties. Symptoms should not be due to substance use or a general medical condition; symptoms should not be better accounted for by another Axis I disorder. The lack of sexual desire may be global or specific to an individual or activity. As the specifiers above indicated, the lack of sexual desire may be indicative of a lot of things including excessive demands by a sexual partner. That's why it's so important to ascertain whether the lack of desire is global or specific to a person. I don't know if you remember, but at one time, it was believed that a lack of sexual desire was primarily a matter of poor technique. In short, desire was a mechanistic issue that had more to do with biology than psychology. To some extent, this view has been replaced with the idea that with sexual desire disorders, relational dynamics play a key role. What this suggests is that technique is not important in and of them as it is as an indicator of relationship. Although it's always essential to rule out a general medical condition, don't neglect the relationship aspect either.

The second desire disorder is the *Sexual Aversion Disorder*. It is diagnosed when there is persistent or recurrent extreme aversion to and avoidance of all genital sexual contact with a partner that causes marked distress and/or interpersonal difficulty. Sexual dysfunction not better accounted for by another Axis I disorder. Lots of reasons for sexual aversion. It might well be that a person has experienced really bad sexual relationships in the past. It could be that a person's religious upbringing has unfortunately led him or her to have an aversion to sexual desire and intercourse. And of course it might be PTSD from a sexual assault. Go carefully when you suspect that your client has a sexual aversion disorder. There's lot of pain here.

Sexual Arousal is the second phase of the sexual cycle and their disorders have both female and male varieties. The female variety (Female Sexual Arousal Disorder) of a sexual arousal disorder consists of a persistent inability to attain or maintain an adequate lubrication/swelling response of sexual excitement that causes marked distress and/or interpersonal difficulty. The inability must not be better explained by another Axis I disorder. The male variety (Male Erectile Disorder) consists of a persistent inability to attain or maintain an erection until completion of the sexual activity that causes marked distress and/or interpersonal difficulty. It also must not be better explained by other psychiatric disorders. Remember all my comments about the relational factors that surround sexual arousal? Well, ditto. It's easy for either a male or female to "lose interest" in the other when any number of things occur. It might be due to hurtful statements about any aspect of each other's body, mind, or soul, use of substances, lack of privacy, and so on. It doesn't take much to destroy sexual arousal. Many young males have no problems with sexual arousal and in fact their preoccupation with their sexual arousal becomes their problem! Perhaps, time will assist them to dance better with their female partners. I suppose that's one reason that sex within marriages is exalted; there is more commitment by each person to work through problems in communication and to ensure mutual arousal. After saying all this, please be sure that you've ruled out a general medical condition that could be causing the problem.

Orgasm is the third phase of the sexual response cycle and their disorders also have female and male varieties. The female variety (Female Orgasmic Disorder) consists of a persistent or recurrent delay in or absence of, orgasm following a normal sexual excitement phase. Women exhibit a wide variability in the type or intensity of stimulation that triggers an orgasm. Prudence and clinical judgment should be used in making this diagnosis. The inability must cause marked distress and/or interpersonal difficulty and it must not be better explained by another Axis I disorder. The male varieties (either Male Orgasmic Disorder or Premature Ejaculation) consist of a persistent or recurrent delay in or absence of, orgasm following a normal sexual excitement phase or conversely orgasm and ejaculation shortly after penetration. Men with Male Orgasmic Disorder can reach an orgasm only after very prolonged and intense non-coital (i.e., manual) stimulation. Care should be taken to assess the focus, intensity, and duration of stimulation. At times, men with this disorder also are experiencing some type of paraphilia that is resulting in the lack of orgasm. By contrast, other men experience premature ejaculation. In this disorder, there is persistent or recurrent ejaculation with minimal sexual stimulation before, on or shortly after penetration and well before your client wishes it. Care should be taken to assess the focus, intensity, and duration of stimulation. The premature ejaculation should not be due exclusively to the direct effects of a substance. The inability must cause marked distress and/or interpersonal difficulty and it must not be better explained by another Axis I disorder. Perhaps, it's hard to know what a disorder is and what's normal in orgasmic disorders. Women frequently learn how to have orgasms with age. Men might learn better control. I don't believe that it is a disorder to not experience orgasm. It's when your clients never experience orgasms or always have premature ejaculations that you should investigate the specifics of how and when their sexual intercourse occurs. It could be that a woman previously "faked" having orgasms and now is seeking assistance with aspect of her life and her sexuality. It could be that a couple is dissatisfied with a husband's ability to sustain an erection long enough for both of them to enjoy their intimacy. Probably, males with Male Orgasmic Disorder will require careful attention to their history to ensure that some type of paraphilia is not interfering with a normal orgasmic response.

Sexual Pain Disorders consists of two disorders: Vaginismus (Not Due to a General Medical Condition) and Dyspareunia. Vaginismus is diagnosed when there is a recurrent or persistent involuntary muscular spasm of the outer third of the vagina that interferes with sexual intercourse that causes clients to experience marked distress or interpersonal difficulty. It also must not be better explained by another Axis I disorder or due to the direct effects of a general medical condition. The muscle contractions can occur even when a woman contemplates penetration of her vagina. As you might guess, this is a painful and sensitive topic for your client so be gentle! Dyspareunia is diagnosed when either men or women experience genital pain associated with intercourse, should not be due exclusively to the direct effects of a substance, must cause marked distress and/or interpersonal difficulty and must not be better explained by another Axis I disorder. Specifiers with Dyspareunia can range from mild to severe.

Sexual Dysfunction Due to General Medical Condition is diagnosed when clinically significant sexual dysfunction exist that results in marked distress or interpersonal difficulty; evidence exists, usually from a history, physical examination, or laboratory findings that your clients' symptoms were caused by the direct physiological effects of a general medical condition. Finally, you should follow the normal caveat that you rule out other mental disorders that would better account for your clients' symptoms.

Substance Induced Psychotic Disorder is diagnosed when clinically significant sexual dysfunction exists that result in marked distress or interpersonal difficulty; evidence exists, usually from a history, physical examination, or laboratory findings that your client exhibits the sexual dysfunction within a month of or during substance intoxication. Aside from the first two criteria, some usual criteria are also present: symptoms are not better accounted for by another mental disorder that is not substance-induced. The difficult part of this diagnosis is that you can make the diagnosis only if the psychotic symptomology was in excess of what was expected from the substance intoxication or withdrawal and onset during intoxication or withdrawal. Sexual Dysfunction NOS is probably one of those potpourris of symptoms. Of course, the actual diagnosis may be something that the client doesn't want to admit! But wait, we're not done because we have. . . .

A Lecture on Porn Galore

Alright, what is porn? There's the dictionary definition:

1. the depiction of erotic behavior (as in pictures or writing) intended to cause sexual excitement
2. material (as books or a photograph) that depicts erotic behavior and is intended to cause sexual excitement
3. the depiction of acts in a sensational manner so as to arouse a quick intense emotional reaction<the *pornography* of violence>

But the Supreme Court a long time ago refused to make some distinctions. It was more akin to "y'all know it when you see (or hear) it, but we can't define it." But why would it be so difficult to understand? First Amendment or Freedom of Speech generally covers a lot of sins. And porn falls in the gray area. Ever go into an "Adult Toy Store?" or leer at "Adult Literature?" Probably not. . ... but it's all covered by some very gray lines. What was obvious porn 30 years ago doesn't cause many people to raise their eyebrows. In many, many ways, we've become desensitized to porn.

Perhaps, the problem is that porn, sex, gender, and power have become completely intertwined. It's hard to separate one's habits from another's moral failings. But what does seem to be related are things like human trafficking with pornography. And of course this is another male thing. Since I'm ignorant about porn (doesn't that make you feel better?), I googled "porn" and got depressed. At Pornhub, 78.9 billion porn videos were viewed in 2014. It's probably not surprising that porn is strongly related with marital discord. It can also cause a lot of family problems. But in the end, it has devastating effects on children. Statutes are pretty tough on child porn. Not much leeway there. It's fascinating to read on how many prominent people are heavily invested in child porn. I guess that adult porn just wasn't enough.

So, porn is not a paraphilia even though it can have a lot of similarities.

"Sex addiction is typically defined as repetitive patterns of compulsive or impulsive sexual activity with self or others that is shameful, oftentimes secretive, and causes negative consequences to the individual and his/her spouse and family. Sex addicts typically engage in impulsive or planned patterns of emotionally arousing sexual rituals and behaviors to escape or tolerate uncomfortable feelings and emotions. For these individuals, sexual acting out is used to emotionally self-regulate. Addictive sexual behavior can create relationship, career, legal, emotional, and physical problems both short- and long-term. Sex addicts often continue to engage in their compulsive sexual behaviors despite repeated attempts to limit or eliminate those behaviors, and despite their inevitable negative consequences."

"In 1952, the *DSM I* officially categorized homosexuality as a mental disorder. As the gay rights movement gathered momentum in the 1960s, however, the psychiatric community introduced a diagnostic compromise by saying that people who were comfortable with their sexual orientation did not have a mental disorder. The APA triumphantly removed general homosexuality from the *DSM* in 1973. But for people who were "in conflict with" their homosexuality, they introduced a new condition instead: "sexual orientation disturbance" (SOD). The 1980 *DSM III* replaced SOD with "ego-dystonic homosexuality," but the basic principle remained the same: Happy homosexuals did not have a mental disorder, while unhappy ones did."

But it's still tough to parse the distinction between non-criminal and criminal paraphilias. Quick, name one non-criminal paraphilia. Should it be considered a crime? Did it really start when intercourse became a sport versus an act to reproduce humans? From this perspective, contraception is the pathway to pornography. It does seem clear that young kids can't handle porn; adolescents may secretly use it; adults can become seriously affected by it; society has a lot of problems because of it.

So, let's summarize:

Criminal paraphilia
Non-criminal paraphilia
Adult Pornography (tacky, but not criminal)
Criminal pornography (as in child porn)
Sexual Addiction (weird ego thing)
Regular sex
Sex Therapy (legal, but difficult to learn)
Prostitution
Human Trafficking

You're stuck in the middle of all these nuances. Sex is a royal mess; don't you agree?

LAST SESSION
Theme: Psychopharmacology; Big Pharma; Bioethics

Talk about a depressing topic. Legal psychotropic drugs. I'm not a MD so I won't get too much into prescription psychotropic drugs. But it's important to know some basics. Brand names are fancy names given to generic psychotropic drugs. Yup, the same drug only with different names. Did I say that the big pharmaceutical companies make generic psychotropic drugs? Well, yes and no. Brand name psychotropic drugs are patented and they go into public domain after about seven to twelve years. Brand name psychotropic drugs usually cost a whole lot more than their generic cousins. So, big pharmaceutical companies don't have much incentive to allow people to make and sell generic psychotropic drugs. So, there are always a lot of fights around generic psychotropic drugs. Big pharmaceutical companies are otherwise known as "Big Pharm." The first part of the lecture is pretty much a condemnation of Big Pharm. But don't let that keep you from understanding psychotropic drugs are a necessary evil of modern psychiatry. Both words are important for you to remember.

Big Pharm:

1) Lots of people usually non-medical people have a lot of strong feelings about the bad effects of prescribed psychotropic drugs.
2) Big Pharm makes a lot of money and jacks up the price of psychotropic drugs (as in mindless and soul deprived profiteers)
3) Doctors prescribe at levels and potency not intended by Big Pharm.
4) Prescription psychotropic drugs are primarily used to control symptoms and sometimes used with kids to control their aggressive behavior
5) Types of psychotropic drugs

Strong feelings.
Wow, this one is a biggie. I mean, we're talking about frothing at the mouth angry at Big Pharm. I mean some people think that Big Pharm both steals milk from babies AND sells rotten milk to them as well. How low can you go? Some people even advocate that no prescription psychotropic drugs ever be used at all. Obviously, not the parents of a kid with ADHD or worse yet, a schizophrenic offspring who has delusions and hallucinations. Opposition to the use of drugs stems from several reasons. The key problem is that strong psychotropic drugs have serious side effects. Sometimes, it seems that the side effects are worse than the disorders that they are designed to control. One poster child for a medication with strong effects and side-effects is the category of anti-psychotic drugs. A reasonable question is why anyone would want their child to received anti-psychotic medication. It's all about predictability and control. Unpredictable behavior drives people wild. They don't like it at all. There are only so many times that a person can be startled awake or be pulled from their job to be told that their child or spouse has engaged in yet again another bizarre episode. Well, just be careful because some people will tell you that medication is a "medical necessity" while others will try to convince you that psychotropic drugs are terrible. The truth is somewhere in between.

Big Pharm
Well, this one is easy or is it? There is no question that pharmaceutical companies are ruled by the iron fist of capitalistic greed. Shareholders want larger and larger dividends and profit margins. So, Big Pharm is all bad, right? Well, yes and no. For better or worse, it's not easy or cheap to create psychotropic drugs that help people. They have to be safe and effective. So, the companies will tell you that the prices are necessary to help do research to create more and better psychotropic drugs. But the reality is that Big Pharm wants to make a lot of money and they do. It's not always clear whether they really don't care whether people die or not. I mean they care as people but not as a company. Their job is make money and that's about it. However, remember that all companies in the US have profitability as a goal; it's just that some companies go hog-wild in trying to become rich. The last twenty years in the dot-com bubble, the real estate bubble, and the commercial banks fiasco and so on have shown that one weakness of capitalism is that it doesn't mandate ethical behavior. Greed is part of the US culture. Now, here's the rub. Social workers take a vow of poverty so they don't understand corporate greed. From the perspective of a company, it is their ethical responsibility to do their best to make as much money for their shareholders. Big Pharm has taken of vow of greed. Beware.

But next, let's go to the real purpose of this lecture: use of psychotropic drugs. Without these drugs, it would be impossible to cope with the myriad of symptoms that present themselves. They help keep the symptoms under control. Only medical doctors can prescribe psychotropic medications. However, social workers can keep track of the effects of the medications. By keeping track of the effects of the medication, doctors know whether a change is necessary. Doctors prescribe; social workers document the effects and help ensure that patients keep using the drugs correctly.

Best Guess
Medication is not easy to understand. There's something called a "mechanism" in how psychotropic drugs interact with the brain. The mechanism explains why the psychotropic drugs work. The relevance for us is that sometimes Big Pharm does research with a certain medication and finds it effective for certain people with a certain dose for certain potency over some certain period of time. Although I'm sure that the research is okay as far as it goes, but remember that your client may not be like the folks who were in the research study. That's another way of saying "It should work for a lot of people" but it doesn't guarantee that it'll work for your clients.

Pharmaceutical research is always a little flawed. Many times, the research ends by saying that one drug is statistically better than another drug. But "statistically" doesn't mean "clinically." It means that the drug is effective . . . kinda. Chances are that medical doctors do their best to prescribe the right drug at the right dosage at the right potency and so on. The research tells doctors what the normal dose is and should be used. But the research doesn't necessary mean that the drug for one kid will be effective with all kids. It's just too complex and misleading to say that a certain drug is definitely always going to work. So, what is a poor soul to do? Well, medical doctors try their best to use the right dosage of psychotropic drugs. Remember, they start with the recommended dose and work from there. If the type and dosage of psychotropic drugs are not effective, then they have to adjust what they prescribe to their patients.

Control the Symptoms
Psychotropic drugs are about treating symptoms and not curing the disorder. That's because it's not always clear what is causing a disorder. The symptoms are what cause patients to wander into your office. The cause of the disorder without any symptoms may go undetected for a long while. Sometimes, it's clear what is causing the symptoms; however, there is just no way to cure the disorder without causing more harm than good. So, let's talk about schizophrenia. Realistically, no one knows the cause of schizophrenia. However, symptoms like delusions and hallucinations are pretty clear cut. From a doctor's perspective, it's all about "managing" the symptoms to make the patients comfortable. Now, that sounds like a doctor is giving up on a patient and thinks that nothing can be done. Nope. What the doctor is trying to do is to make the symptoms not as irritating or devastating. Does he or she want to cure the disorder? Sure, but short of that goal, managing the symptoms isn't a bad start.

5) *Types of psychotropic drugs*

Here is a list of psychotropic drugs (Generic names are in italics) Before I get into the good stuff, let's go through what these drugs are supposed to do. It's all about neurotransmitters. You know, neurotransmitters like glutamate, serotonin, dopamine, GABA, norepinephrine reuptake inhibitor and many more. If you know all the neurotransmitters, what are you doing taking this class?

Antidepressants
As you might guess, this category of psychotropic drugs is designed to manage the symptoms of mood disorders. (When I first read about reuptake inhibitor, I thought that they were talking about reupchuck; that's what happens when I try to cook). Let's talk about what each of these subcategories of psychotropic drugs attempt to do. SSRIs work on the *serotonin receptors*. Each person needs a certain level of serotonin in their brain to be able to be "normal." When there is an insufficient level of serotonin, a person shows symptoms of depression. SSRI prevent the absorption (reuptake) of serotonin into the brain. By so doing, they help maintain a proper level of serotonin. However, there is a kicker to SSRIs: too high a level of serotonin and a person will develop what is called a "serotonin syndrome." This is a potentially life-threatening condition and when spotted usually means a trip to the ER.

- Selective Serotonin Reuptake Inhibitors (SSRI)
    - Celexa (*citalopram**)
    - Luvox (*fluvoxamine*)
    - Paxil (*paroxetine*)
    - Prozac (*fluoxetine*)
    - Zoloft (*sertraline*)

- Tricyclics (another kind of anti-depressives but it is an older drug and not used as much anymore).

- - Anafranil (*clomipramine*)
  - Elavil (*amitriptyline*)
  - Norpramin (*desipramine*)
  - Pamelor (*nortriptyline*)
  - Aventyl Sinequan (*doxepin*)
  - Surmontil (*trimipramine*)
  - Tofranil (*imipramine*)
  - Vivactil (*protriptyline*)
- Others (that's why MDs get paid a lot of money to know all these drugs and what they do)
  - Effexor (*venlafaxine*)
  - Desyrel (*trazodone*)
  - Ludiomil (*maprotiline*)
  - Parnate (*tranylcypromine*)
  - Wellbutrin (*bupropion*), Zyban

Antianxiety Psychotropic drugs

This category is commonly populated by benzodiazepines. These drugs can be addictive and so is only prescribed with care. But you might ask, how do anti-anxiety drugs work? I know that you really have not much interest in the answer but are fearful of questions on the exam. It's all about GABA and glutamate. "Cortical excitability reflects a balance between excitation and inhibition. Glutamate is the main excitatory and GABA the main inhibitory neurotransmitter in the mammalian cortex. Changes in glutamate and GABA metabolism may play important roles in the control of cortical excitability." The last couple sentences I got from PubMed. Basically, you've got to find a balance between being too excited and too laid back. Yes, I got excited in just reading this stuff. So, it comes down to trying to find a balance in the cortical excitability using medications. Now, aren't you glad that you asked the question about how the medication works?

- Ativan (*lorazepam*)
- BuSpar (*buspirone*)
- Klonopin (*clonazepam*)
- Valium (*diazepam*)
- Xanax (*alprazolam*)

Mood Stabilizers (Anti-manic) psychotropic medications

Yup, you got it: these are the medications for Bipolar disorders. The title says it all. The mechanism is interesting. By and large, the medication lowers the manic phase of the disorder. It might seem puzzling that it only describes lowering the manic phase but nothing about the depressive phase. That's because the depressive cycle is a "rebound" from the manic phase. What goes up must come down . . . into a depressive cycle. So, if there is no manic phase, then the depressive phase is not pronounced. But having said that, all sorts of medications are prescribed for Bipolar disorders because it's never clear whether a patient coming in for treatment is just a normal depression or is in the depressive phase of the Bipolar disorder.

- Depakene (*valproic acid, sodium divalproex*)
- Lamictal (*lamatrogine*)
- Lithium, (*lithium carbonate*)
- Tegretol (*carbamazepine*)

Antipsychotics (both typical and atypical)
Generally speaking, antipsychotic medications work by blocking a specific subtype of the dopamine receptor, referred to as the *D2 receptor*. Older antipsychotics, known as typical antipsychotics, *block the D2 receptor (i.e., dopamine receptor)* and decrease positive symptoms (e.g., hallucinations and delusions). Unfortunately, these typical antipsychotics also block D2 receptors outside the mesolimbic pathway. This can result in a worsening of the negative symptoms associated with the illness. Typical antipsychotic medications include

- Clozaril (*clozapine*)
- Haldol (*haloperidol*)
- Mellaril (*thioridazine*)
- Stelazine (*trifluoperazine*)
- Thorazine (*chlorpromazine*)
- Prolixin (*fluphenazine*)

Atypical antipsychotics are a second generation of antipsychotics and block D2 receptors as well as a specific subtype of serotonin receptor, the 5HT2A receptor. It is believed that this combined action at D2 and 5HT2A receptors treats both the *positive and the negative symptoms*. One unfortunate side effect is weight gain which some people develop. Weight gain may increase the risk of developing diabetes and heart problems in the longer term. This is a particular problem with the atypical antipsychotics - notably, clozapine and olanzapine.

- Risperdal (*risperidone*)
- Seroquel (*quetiapine*)
- Zyprexa (*olanzapine*)

Here are the typical side-effects of anti-psychotic medications.
- Dry mouth, blurred vision, flushing and constipation. These may ease off over time.
- Drowsiness (sedation), which is common and may be an indication that the dose is too high.
- Movement disorders which develop in some cases. These include:
  - Parkinsonism - this can cause symptoms similar to those that occur in people with Parkinson's disease - for example, tremor and muscle stiffness.
  - Akathisia - this is like a restlessness of the legs.
  - Dystonia - this means abnormal movements of the face and body.
  - Tardive dyskinesia (TD) - this is a movement disorder that can occur if you take antipsychotics for several years. It causes rhythmical, involuntary movements. These are usually lip-smacking and tongue-rotating movements, although it can

affect the arms and legs too. About 1 in 5 people treated with typical (older) antipsychotics eventually develop TD.

Stimulants

Candy for misbehaving kids? Hmm, giving stimulants to a hyper kid... sounds like the ingredients for disaster. But weary parents, frustrated teachers and premed students swear by them. Whoops, what's this about premed students? Definitely not an academic slacker. With ADHD, the neurons are firing every which way; with just a little bit of stimulants, the neurons are firing in one direction. The stimulants help the kid and premed student be more focused. The kid has plenty of energy; it just has to be focused.

- Adderall (*amphetamine, mixed salts*)
- Concerta (*methylphenidate, long acting*)
- Dexedrine (*dextroamphetamine*), Dextrostat
- Ritalin (*methylphenidate*)

OK, now what? Well, go to the APA Patient's Guide to get more information about each drug about which you're interested. It gives information about normal dosages and potency. The list above is not comprehensive. It does give a sense of which psychotropic drugs are used with which category of disorders. Only a medical doctor can give an educated answer on which drug is best with which disorder with which person. Although medical doctors make mistakes, the same can be said of every health-care professional. That said, a lot of medical doctors prescribe psychotropic drugs as a fact of life since insurance companies only pays in 15 minute intervals.

Some Parting Thoughts about Psychopathology

Psychopathology is a necessary evil in doing any kind of therapy in this day and age. I've known people who refuse to accept insurance; for them, it's a cash-only setup. The reason that they gave was that they didn't want to use any kind of DSM. They believed that it was an infringement on privacy rights. It's a good point. But there are a couple considerations. First, a lot of people have insurance and won't be willing to go with a cash-only approach. But there's another concern as well. Say that your client got mad at you and tried to sue you. Then, his or her attorney would state that you didn't use a diagnosis because you didn't know how to do so and so on. That would constitute negligence if it were true. It would be a lie because you do know the DSM-5, but in a court of law, it's all about winning. So, even if you don't want to use insurance, it's important to know enough about psychopathology to protect your practice. Second, a lot of clinical sites will require a working knowledge of the DSM. It doesn't matter whether you like it or not. No DSM, no job. At that point, it doesn't matter whether it's good or bad. Good is having a job; bad is being bankrupt. Finally, anything can be misused including psychopathology. An informed use will help clients feel better about themselves because of the misdiagnoses that they have already been given. Get it right so that clients can defend themselves. In the end, you've got to protect you and your clients: so learn your DSM and use it correctly. If you don't, I'll probably come and haunt you. Worse yet, you'll have to repeat the course! Stay well and never stop learning.

References

American Psychiatric Association. (2013). *Diagnostic and Statistical Manual of Mental Disorders, Fifth Edition (DSM-5)*. New York: American Psychiatric Association.

Made in the USA
Columbia, SC
27 August 2018